Paul for Today

Paul for Today

New Perspectives on a Controversial Apostle

Neil Richardson

✴ EPWORTH

Copyright © Neil Richardson 2008

The Author has asserted his right under the Copyright, Designs
and Patents Act, 1988, to be identified as the Author of this Work

Scripture quotations are from the New Revised Standard
Version of the Bible, copyright 1989 by the Division of Christian
Education of the National Council of the Churches of Christ in
the USA. Used by permission. All rights reserved.

British Library Cataloguing in Publication data

A catalogue record for this book is available
from the British Library

978 0 7162 0646 0

First published in 2008
by Epworth
Methodist Church House
25 Marylebone Road
London NW1 5JR

Typeset by Regent Typesetting, London
Printed in the UK by
CPI William Clowes Beccles NR34 7TL

Contents

Acknowledgements

Thanks are due to many people. First of all, I wish to thank Canon David Hewlett, Principal of The Queen's Foundation, and the staff of Queen's, for the Senior Research Scholarship which alone made possible the writing of this book. Thanks are due, too, to the whole community at Queen's for the stimulating environment and the hospitality they afforded me during the academic year 2007–08. I'm grateful, too, to my own Church, the British Methodist Church, for allowing me to take up that post. I should also like to thank the members of Lidgett Park Methodist Church and the Leeds North East Methodist Circuit for their stimulus and help in the shaping of the book during the six years I served as their Superintendent Minister. And I want to thank members of my family for readily reading first and second drafts: my sons Mark, James and Simon, my daughter-in-law Jane, and my sister Jean. Most of all, I owe most, as always, to my wife Rhiannon, who has had to put up with St Paul more than any wife should.

Introduction

Paul is a problem. His writings always have been. The New Testament itself carries a warning that reading the letters of Paul can damage your spiritual health (2 Peter 3.15–16). Paul continues to get a bad press, and people both in the Church and outside it find his letters difficult – an obstacle, rather than an aid to Christian faith. Yet Paul is indispensable to the Church and its faith, and has been thought to be so since at least the third century. That is why his problematic letters are part of our New Testament.

This book is written in the conviction that recovering the message of Paul for today is crucial if the contemporary Church is to find renewal, and if the world is to be saved from self-destruction. The Church is easily compromised; it is also easily demoralized. It can distort, or even forget, the gospel. Not least, it can become, or at least appear to be, irrelevant to a needy world. As for that wider world, though there are strident voices asserting that Christianity has had its day, and that God is a delusion, the case for both has yet to be made.

So rediscovering the apostle Paul is an urgent matter. Paul was an extraordinarily adaptable preacher of the gospel; he provides a penetrating analysis of the human predicament, and yet, at the same time, has a searching, yet profoundly hopeful, message for both the Church and the whole world. I expand a little on these three themes in the next section.

i An apostle whose time has come?

The Church needs the teaching of Paul if its life is to be revitalized, and its mission renewed. His message is relevant to the wider world also, not least in an age of globalization. Paul is the first person we know of to grasp the idea that Christianity mutates. As T. S. Eliot put it: 'Christianity is always changing itself into something that can be believed.'[1] Or to make the same point less provocatively: if you want to preach the same gospel in a different context, you have to say it differently. Every preacher knows it: a different congregation and a different Sunday mean, if not a new sermon, at least the editing of an old one.

Paul's adaptability finds expression in a phrase which has become famous. 'I became all things to all people' (1 Corinthians 9.22). That did not mean Paul was a charlatan: a preacher without principle, like the young interviewee for a teaching post in a school in the USA who, when asked whether he would teach creationism or evolution, replied, 'I can teach it either way.' On the contrary, Paul's adaptability was both dangerous and costly. No one could seek to be a Jew to Jews and a Greek to Greeks without being misunderstood and punished for it.

This is one reason why Paul's letters present such a challenge. The way he expressed the faith when he wrote to the Christians at Thessalonika was different from the way he expressed it when he wrote to the church at Corinth, and different again when he wrote to the Galatians. There are some close similarities between his letters to the Galatians and the Romans, but even here the situations were not the same, and Paul had to express himself and his arguments in new ways. Paul seldom repeats himself, but that does not mean his gospel is totally shapeless. Christian faith could not then, and cannot now, simply adapt to contemporary market or cultural forces. Paul believed that God is the only God there is, that Jesus Christ is vital for the world's salvation, and that the Spirit of God and of Christ (the Holy Spirit) transforms human lives. These core convictions are present almost everywhere in his writings, and he never says anything contrary to them. But his extraordinary adaptability in expressing the gospel makes him the apostle *par excellence* for a multi-cultural world.

There is a second reason why Paul is particularly relevant to the twenty-first century: he offers a penetrating analysis of the human condition. This perhaps is why he is often accused of gloom and doom, and it is true he has much to say about sin and human sinfulness, especially in Romans. At a first reading, his language in Romans 1.18–32, with its reference to God's wrath, sounds repellent and strange. But we need to grapple with this difficult, deeply unfashionable language; just because it is unfashionable does not necessarily mean it is wrong. What he has to say about homosexuality in this same passage is also difficult, though not, it has to be said, difficult for everyone. But in view of the importance of this issue in the churches today, we shall need to return to this subject. Paul has more to say about this than first meets the eye.

Despite his bleak language about sin and wrath – this is the paradox – Paul was a man of hope. This is a third reason why he is so important for a time when the world's future, threatened by violence and climate change, is as uncertain as it has ever been. It does not mean that we can speak glibly of a divine sovereignty or divine rescue-acts, like the preacher who confidently announced, 'I'm not afraid of global warming because God is in control.' Rather, hope flourishes in Paul in the context of suffering, and always the origin of hope is God, whom Paul describes in Romans as 'the God of hope' (15.13).

So there are good reasons why the contemporary Church and world need to hear Paul. But we shall do greater justice to Paul if we look at his words in their original contexts. Fortunately, New Testament scholars have shed a flood of light on those contexts, and we shall be looking at those particularly in Chapter 2. First, though, we need to recognize honestly that the man whose time (I argue) has come, is also someone who, for many people, has become more problematic than ever.

ii A man for no seasons?

If even the second century found Paul's writings obscure and difficult,[2] the last 100 years or so have compounded the difficulties. I recall a colleague reading the passage from Colossians containing the command 'Wives obey your husbands' (Colossians 3.18). She ended the lesson by announcing, 'This is *not* the word of the Lord!' She did so with a twinkle in her eye, but there is a serious issue here for many women today. Nor is this verse the only problematical one. We shall need to ask whether Paul wrote the verses containing the opinion that 'women should be silent in the churches' (1 Corinthians 14.34–35), even though these words are printed in every modern version I know of.

Other teaching in Paul's letters is enormously difficult, and has been the cause of much suffering. From the same 'household code' in Colossians comes the command, 'Slaves, obey your earthly masters in everything ...' (3.22), a section of Scripture which an emancipated slave of the nineteenth century told her grandchildren studiously to avoid. Another passage – in Paul's letter to the Romans – has also caused hardship and suffering: 'Let every person be subject to the governing authorities' (13.1). Did Paul mean in all circumstances?

Fortunately, recent scholarship has shed some light on this, as on other difficult passages in Paul's writings. But this is to anticipate, and here we are simply trying to gauge the extent of the problem.

So far I have mentioned only some of the most difficult aspects of Paul's ethical teaching, but many have found his theology equally hard. It seems a far cry from what we often like to think of as the simple gospel of Jesus. Paul's language about the atoning sacrifice of Christ for sin (for example, Romans 3.21–26) seems less accessible than Jesus' parable about a 'prodigal' son (Luke 15.11–32). Paul himself comes across to many modern readers as forbiddingly authoritarian, unlike the compassionate Jesus who healed the sick.

A further difficulty has arisen since World War Two. We have become painfully aware of how the anti-Semitism which found horrific expression in the Holocaust was fuelled in part by Christendom and the Christian Scriptures. In the last half century, scholars have struggled to understand Paul's negative and positive statements about his fellow-Jews, asking whether, ever since the Reformation, we have got some things badly wrong. Subsequently, many have read what Paul has to say about Jews and the Jewish law more critically than before.

These sometimes passionate debates – a lot is at stake – remain a storm-centre in the contemporary study of Paul.[3]

So it would not be surprising if Paul's writings are heard less frequently in church today. Indeed, they probably are. Most ordained ministers and lay preachers often choose two out of the three lectionary readings for each Sunday; the Gospel, understandably, is always, or nearly always, read – and so either the Old Testament reading or the epistle is not read. Even if a passage from Paul is read, it is likely to present a formidable challenge to the preacher, who may well feel that she (or he) has neither the time nor the knowledge to offer a thoughtful sermon based on it. It is a bold preacher who ventures to expound the mysteries of the atonement, according to Romans 3.21–26, or of predestination according to Romans 8 and 9, not to mention the contemporary relevance (if any) of Paul's teaching about the law.

Some years ago an Old Testament scholar wrote a challenging book entitled *The Strange Silence of the Bible in the Church.*[4] Should we now speak more specifically of 'The Strange Silence of Paul in the Churches'? Or perhaps – in the light of the argument here – it is not so strange and not so surprising that our 'Pauline canon' (that is, the 'Paul' section of the Bible that we really take notice of) has been reduced to a handful of passages. Few if any of us have a problem with 1 Corinthians 13, Paul's famous 'hymn' to love, read often at church weddings and, most famously, at the funeral of Princess Diana. Two other passages are usually read at funerals, and perhaps at other times, including Easter: Romans 8.31–39, with its ringing declaration that nothing can separate us from the love of God in Christ, and short sections of Paul's long chapter on the resurrection (1 Corinthians 15). Apart from these, there is only one other passage from Paul's letters which, in my experience, is read regularly today, and that is another 'hymn': 'Let the same mind be in you that was in Christ Jesus ...' (Philippians 2.5–11).

So, I submit that we have a problem! The writings of Paul are found by many to be more difficult or less well-known than ever, and yet I am suggesting that these very writings are vital if our churches are to find renewal. In the next section we shall try to get our bearings by attempting to answer some preliminary questions.

iii What did Paul write and when?

The first question might seem a strange one to ask: surely we know which are Paul's letters, because he tells us. However, scholars have come to realize that authorship in the ancient world was not always quite so straightforward. (There is a partial parallel today in the way that a journalist may 'ghost-write' an 'autobiography' of a famous footballer or cricketer. The dustjacket bears the celebrity's name, even though he may not have written a single word.) In a similar manner, it is clear that in both Jewish and Greek literature we have examples of pseudonymous writings – that is, writings which bear the name of a famous person of the remote or recent past, but which clearly cannot have been written by them.

A few scholars still argue that the Christians did not go in for such literary deceptions, but it is unlikely that most pseudonymous writings were intended to deceive (though some may have been), and it seems undeniable that at least one (2 Peter, mentioned earlier), and probably more, of the New Testament writings are pseudonymous. So what is 'the state of play' with regard to Paul's letters? I put it like that because few historical and literary questions of this kind can ever be conclusively settled. But scholars can help us identify which letters were definitely written by Paul, which probably were, and which were almost certainly *not* written by him.

The first category can be quickly dealt with. Romans, 1 and 2 Corinthians, Galatians, Philippians, 1 Thessalonians and Philemon are universally regarded as Paul's work (give or take a few verses here and there), but scholars are divided about whether Colossians and 2 Thessalonians come from Paul's hand. Some think that some details in Colossians, such as the description of Christ as 'the head of the body, the Church' (Colossians 1.18), is a development of what the 'real' Paul wrote in 1 Corinthians 12. Some also wonder how the man who wrote

'In Christ there is neither male nor female ...' (Galatians 3.28) could also have written 'Wives obey your husbands' (Colossians 3.18). But some of those alleged contradictions are there in the letters which are definitely written by Paul. So, in my view, there are no compelling reasons for saying Colossians was not written by him.

As for 2 Thessalonians, it is almost too like 1 Thessalonians! If that seems a strange thing to say, this letter could be read as an imitation, by a later Christian writer, of the earlier letter. On the other hand, 2 Thessalonians 3.17, 'I, Paul, write this greeting with my own hand. This is the mark in every letter of mine; it is the way I write', sounds a bit 'barefaced', even by ancient standards of pseudonymous writing – particularly after the earlier warning in this same letter about documents purporting to come from Paul (2.2). So, the jury is still out on 2 Thessalonians and, for many, on Colossians. In fact, it is difficult to imagine scholars ever reaching unanimity about the authorship of these two letters. That doesn't mean we pretend the question doesn't exist, or that we lose any sleep over it. We simply have to live with it.

That is true also of Ephesians, although fewer scholars would argue that this letter was written by Paul. Again, it is too like another letter – this time, Colossians. In view of the identical references to 'postman' Tychicus at Colossians 4.7 and Ephesians 6.21, I think we have to say *either* that Paul sent off these two letters by the same post(man), *or* that a later writer has edited or re-written Colossians and created the letter we know as Paul's letter to the Ephesians.

Finally, there are the letters to Timothy and Titus, the so-called Pastoral Letters. (Hebrews should not even need to be considered here, in spite of the assumption by Richard Dawkins in *The God Delusion* that it is Paul's work; it *was* so regarded for many centuries, but according to a widely influential New Testament Introduction of the last century, conclusive proof that Hebrews is not Pauline was produced as long ago as 1828.) As for the Pastorals, they are so different in vocabulary, style, theology and – as far as we can tell – historical setting from the letters by the real Paul that few scholars now believe they are his work. But it *is* possible that 2 Timothy may contain genuine fragments of his writings.

All this may seem boringly technical and irrelevant. It is tempting, when faced with these still recent questionings of long-established beliefs about authorship, to respond as someone is alleged to have done when hearing about Darwin's theory of evolution: 'Lord, may it not be true; or, at least let it be hushed up!' But to anaesthetize painful questions with unthinking faith – if that is not a contradiction in terms – is neither healthy nor honest. Even so, some may wonder whether these conclusions – or probable conclusions – mean that the letters not by Paul are less authoritative than those which are. But all these letters are part of the Christian Scriptures, and so uniquely authoritative. The early Church judged them to be 'apostolic' and, even though they may not all be from an apostolic hand, they come from the apostolic age; and, more important still, they stand within the tradition of the apostles.

There is one more writing in the New Testament we need to include here, and that is the Acts of the Apostles, since so much of Acts is devoted to Paul's travels, preaching, miracles and sufferings. Indeed, for an earlier generation brought up on 'the three missionary journeys' of Paul, Acts would seem the obvious place to start. But Acts was probably written after Paul's death.[5] Scholars continue to debate whether it was really written by Luke, supposedly a companion of Paul,[6] and how accurate it is as a source for Paul's life. Suffice to say here that, in my judgement, the alleged differences between Acts and Paul's letters have sometimes been exaggerated, even though they are there. For example, Acts presents Paul as a consistently observant Jew. His own mission strategy ('all things to all people') suggests otherwise; he may not have scrupulously observed Jewish food-laws when staying in the home of a Gentile.

In the chapters which follow, however, our major concern will be the letters universally regarded as Paul's own. Even if he dictated them,[7] or co-wrote them with, for example, Sosthenes (1 Corinthians 1.1) or Timothy (2 Corinthians 1.1), these letters will provide us with more than enough to be going on with in the course of this book! We cannot be entirely certain in what order Paul wrote them, though everyone agrees 1 (and 2, if Paul's) Thessalonians were his first letters. Galatians may have come next, as parts of chapters 3 and 4 read like an early version of Romans 4. Next, Paul's references to his 'collection' in 1 Corinthians 16.1–4, 2 Corinthians 8 and 9, and Romans 15.24–28 seem to show that he wrote these three letters in that order – in the early and mid-50s. Philippians, with its reference to imprisonment (1.12–13), Colossians and Philemon probably came a little later.

The order of Paul's letters, however, unlike succeeding episodes of a TV series, is not essential to understanding the 'plot'. There *are* questions of whether Paul's thought developed during his letter-writing period, but one scholar has suggested that the best way to picture the letters is like the spokes of a wheel, with all coming, obviously, from the same 'hub'. So exact dates are not vital.

But before we begin our main task, it will be useful to return to some of the urgent questions we face today, and to remind ourselves that the study of Paul is not just an intellectual pastime.

iv Paul, Jesus and the Church

Would we do better, in view of the difficulties of understanding Paul, and in spite of the arguments presented so far, simply to concentrate on God and on Jesus, and quietly to forget about this hornets' nest called the 'letters of Paul'? Can the Church get along perfectly well without the good apostle? Can we have a gospel minus Paul?

Many people believe Paul obscured or complicated or distorted the gospel of Jesus. Jesus told simple stories; Paul presents convoluted arguments. Jesus talked about shepherds, the birds of the air, a Good Samaritan (among, it must be said, other things); Paul wrote about being crucified with Christ, of God's righteousness and wrath. Jesus showed compassion; Paul sometimes sounds a little short on compassion, not to mention patience.

Of course, this last paragraph is highly selective, but it reflects widely held views about both Jesus and Paul. Where does the truth lie? I shall try to show, in the course of this book, that Paul, so far from being the man who distorted the gospel of Jesus, was Jesus' most faithful interpreter. Paul did more than anyone else we know to secure the lasting legacy of Jesus (to put the point rather oddly). Suffice it to say for now that Jesus preached the kingdom of God. (We have no reason to doubt that Mark 1.14–15 represents a historically accurate summary of his message.) Paul, however, preached 'Christ crucified' (1 Corinthians 1.23), and 'Christ Jesus as Lord' (2 Corinthians 4.5). But what if Jesus, in his life, death and resurrection, came to epitomize and to realize the kingdom? After the resurrection, the early Christians *identified* Jesus with the kingdom; when they said 'Jesus is Lord', they meant 'God's kingdom has dawned'. So might this not suggest that Paul was continuing where Jesus, so to speak, left off?

Or, to take another major theme of the Gospels and of the epistles, one of the best-documented characteristics of the life of Jesus is his mission to the marginalized and the ostracized. He ministered to outsiders, and died as an outsider. Paul saw his own mission as one to 'outsiders' – that is, to Gentiles. Paul may have been one of the first to see that the life, death and resurrection of Jesus had inaugurated the time of the Gentiles. So, again, the apostle to outsiders carried on where Jesus left off – now beyond the boundaries of Judaism.

And what of the contemporary Church? It is possible that we find Paul difficult because we do not follow in his footsteps. A church in which outsiders do not find a home may be a church which hasn't really heard the gospel according to Paul. Perhaps whole tracts of his writings will only really come alive when our churches are overwhelmed by 'Gentiles', when familiar ecclesiastical 'goalposts' begin to move, and we have to face all over again what being a Christian is all about. Paul has much else to say. He has some extraordinarily searching and helpful words for Christian communities in danger of being torn apart because committed Christians hold diametrically opposite views.

But, first, we need to hear St Paul in his context. If we can understand more fully and accurately what he said then and why, we shall be a little nearer appropriating his words for ourselves, and being renewed and transformed by them. In the last half-century (not to mention earlier decades of work), scholars have engaged in a remarkable amount of research. We have learned more about Paul's background, and the contexts in which he worked. We have gained new insights into the language he used, and the style in which he wrote. It is worth remembering, too, that scholars have engaged in passionate arguments about Paul – and still do. We can eavesdrop on some of their conversations: they are more relevant to the churches than is often supposed! We owe it to Paul at least to try to understand him better. We also owe it to ourselves, the Church and, not least, a needy world.

Notes

1 Quoted in D. E. Nineham, *The Use and Abuse of the Bible*, Macmillan Press, London, 1976, p. 281.

2 Many scholars regard 2 Peter as a second-century letter, and probably the latest of all the New Testament documents to be written. If so, 2 Peter is a 'pseudonymous' writing. That does not mean it is a 'fake', but that a later writer assumed the 'mantle' of Peter in addressing the churches of his day. (On this, see also section iii of this chapter.)

3 Subsequent chapters outline what have been some of the main uses, and Suggestions for Further Reading (page 204) indicates avenues for further exploration.

4 J. D. Smart, *The Strange Silence of the Bible in the Church*, SCM, London, 1970.

5 Luke 21.20, with its reference to Jerusalem surrounded by armies, is thought to have been written down in the knowledge that this prophecy of Jesus (even if not originally in these words) had come true. Similarly, Acts 20.29, in Paul's so-called farewell speech, with its reference to 'after I am gone', may have been penned after the apostle's death – probably in the early 60s.

6 See Chapter 1, section v, for a further discussion of this.

7 At Romans 16.22, the scribe Tertius speaks for himself, while Galatians 6.11 seems to be Paul's personal autograph.

The Same Old Paul? Or Have Things Changed?

Three good reasons, at least, have been alleged for not reading Paul: what he appears to say about sin and sex, his apparent misogyny, and the absence from his letters of any criticism of the institution of slavery. So we shall devote the first three sections of this chapter to looking at these issues, and asking whether Paul is as bad as he has been made out to be. At the same time, we need to ask whether some of the traditional views of Paul, both the man and his message, are well-founded or not. That will be the task of the second half of the chapter.

i Was Paul obsessed with sin and sex?

Many people today think of Paul as a repressed individual who appears to have had a problem with sex and human sexuality. And even if he hadn't a problem himself, what he has to say on the subject has not endeared him to most of his readers. We look first at what Paul says about homosexuality.

Did Paul regard sexual relations between people of the same sex as sinful? If we put the question in that way, there is no doubt that he did. The only two explicit references to homosexuality in the letters which he certainly wrote are unquestionably negative (Romans 1.26–27, 1 Corinthians 6.9). But there may be more to be said than that. In saying this, I am not advocating a 'liberal' view, but instead suggesting that the fundamental issue is not simply what the Bible says, but how we interpret it. On a host of other subjects, such as war and peace, marriage and divorce, we have learned to see that the Bible doesn't supply ready-made answers to modern questions. This doesn't mean the Bible is out-of-date; it remains a uniquely authoritative book for all Christians. *But that does not necessarily mean taking it literally.*

Paul, in the two passages to which I have just referred, was writing as any Jew of his time would about Gentile homosexual practices – that is, promiscuous practices. It is possible, though less certain, that he was referring mainly to paederasty (men–boy relationships), which were prevalent in the Greek and Roman world of his day. If that was what he had in mind, it wouldn't necessarily follow that he would condemn a lifelong same-sex partnership of love and faithfulness today. But it doesn't mean that he would not, either! This is one of the areas for disagreement.

People may also disagree about how much of Paul's argument depends upon a particular understanding of what, for him, was 'natural' and 'unnatural'. Today we have our own ideas about that, but they are not necessarily the same as Paul's. (Paul believed that men wearing their hair long in church was unnatural (1 Corinthians 11.14).) Again, Paul's strictures on homosexual relationships may have derived from his understanding of maleness and femaleness. In Paul's world, the male was regarded as the active partner in sexual intercourse, the female as the passive partner. In fact, a woman was regarded, physically, as a lesser version of a man. So a key issue here is how far different understandings of women and men and of human sexuality should affect our interpretation of Paul.

I repeat, I am not advocating a particular moral view here, but suggesting that there is *an interpretative question* to be answered: should we take Paul's two condemnations of the homosexual practices of his day as applicable to the homosexual practices and relationships of our day? It would be healthier for the Church worldwide if Christians acknowledged that this is the question to be answered, instead of hurling biblical texts at each other. But Paul has more to say on this subject than first meets the eye, and I come back to this in Chapter 4, section iv.

We turn now to what has become a problem word. 'Sin'

is often regarded now as an old-fashioned, unhelpful notion. Memories of a strict upbringing or of a strict church school give the word, for many people, unpleasantly negative connotations. ('In the beginning was the word, and the word was "No".') This has coloured their impressions of Christian faith, leading some to reject it altogether, and others, still in the churches, to be allergic to sermons which dare to mention the subject. So 'sin' is a word more likely to be jested about than taken seriously, and many preachers avoid it altogether. What does Paul teach?

Paul doesn't mean by 'sin' what we normally mean by it. We tend to talk of 'sins' in the plural, as, 'Be sure your sins will find you out.' Or we speak of a particular sin ('my besetting sin ...') such as greed, or pride. Paul hardly ever uses the plural 'sins', and doesn't very often refer to the act of sinning. Most often he uses the noun 'sin' in the singular, mainly in Romans chapters 4—7. There he means a power which dominates and destroys human life – for example, 'sin exercised dominion in death' (Romans 5.21a). In individuals, too, sin takes up residence as a kind of occupying power: 'Now if I do what I do not want, it is no longer I that do it, but sin that dwells within me' (Romans 7.20).

So 'sin' is a power almost with a life of its own. It is more than immorality, even though immorality stems from sin. So sin can't be dealt with just by new year resolutions and the like. Legislation may sometimes help, but it is not enough. Sin is alienation not only from life and God, but also from other people and from our own deepest selves. Therefore sin, according to Paul, denotes our religious *and human* failure; when Paul says 'everyone falls short of the glory of God' (Romans 3.23), he is referring to the universal human failure to be what God meant us to be.

Paul traced sin back to Adam (Romans 5.12–14). Understood literally, that is problematic for us today. In the light of our understanding of how the world has evolved over countless millennia, the Adam story cannot be historical. Even if Paul understood it in that way, it does not mean we have to. But it would be a mistake to conclude that the story, because it's not historical, has nothing to say to us. The inspiration of Scripture has to be understood differently.

So where, in Paul's view, does human sin come from? Admittedly, the passage in Romans seems to suggest that the Garden of Eden was where it all started to go wrong. Whether Paul understood the Genesis story as historically true we have no way of knowing. But he has another, deeper answer to the question of where human sin originates. Its root cause is our idolatry, another difficult but important idea. Paul believed that the Gentile world was an idolatrous one. What humankind has done is to *'exchange'* God's glory for physical images (of humans, birds, quadrupeds and reptiles), to exchange God's truth for a lie, and to exchange natural sexual intercourse for unnatural (Romans 1.23, 25, and 26–27). To today's readers, this is neither obvious nor convincing – idolatry being less apparent now than in Paul's day. In Corinth, and the other cities Paul frequented, there would be idols in or near every marketplace, and in every home.

But idolatry can be identified, according to the Bible, by the effect it has on its worshippers. The worship of God is life-giving, whereas the worship of idols drains the human life out of their devotees. In the startling words of Psalm 115, those who make idols, or trust them, grow like them: they lose the power of sight, smell, hearing and feeling. Again, understood literally, this is far-fetched; but if we interpret 'losing our sight', for example, as a diminishing ability to distinguish truth from falsehood, like a government starting to believe its own propaganda, or a newspaper accepting its own skewed version of the facts, then the Bible's teaching may strike some resonant chords. The greatest 'blindness', however, is a heart so 'darkened' (Romans 1.21) that we can no longer see God.

So in Paul's view there is what one commentator has called a 'downward spiral' at work in the world: these 'exchanges' – and, above all, our exchange of the Creator for created things – *dehumanize* us: if we worship what is less than God, we become less than human, and society itself begins to dissolve, and creation to unravel. That is the downward slope described in this passage in Romans.

4

In the downward spiral in which humans exchange truth for falsehood, what has God done? According to Paul, God has matched all these ill-starred human 'exchanges' with an action of his own: God 'handed people over' (Romans 1.24, 26, 28) to experience the consequences of their wrongdoing. This may confirm some people's worst fears about Paul's God. Yet Paul doesn't mean that God has given up, or that God is being vindictive. But God doesn't suddenly abolish human freewill when humankind goes off the rails. Instead, he holds fast to his creation; in spite of everything, God will not abandon his world to its self-imposed self-destruction. There is divine love at work in the darkness, as Paul has already made clear: 'For I am not ashamed of the gospel; it is the power of God for salvation to everyone who has faith, to the Jew first and also to the Greek. For in it the righteousness of God is revealed through faith for faith ...' (Romans 1.16–17a). He immediately goes on to say, 'the wrath of God is revealed from heaven' (v. 18). Unfortunately, the wrath of God has become another much misunderstood idea, and the newspaper headline about 'wrath' the day after lightning struck a cathedral where a controversial bishop was about to be consecrated was wide of the mark. God's wrath is not God flying off the handle; it is not the opposite of his love. In Romans 1.18–32, the revelation of God's wrath are the effects of humankind's closing of minds and hearts to God's light, truth and love. If God made the world, and endowed it with a particular 'constitution', then consequences follow: the downward slope to dehumanization, immorality and social fragmentation begins.

But still, perhaps, the suspicion remains that Paul was a repressed, life-denying individual, and this suspicion may owe its origins to one particular word in his letters which, for centuries, was misleadingly translated as 'flesh'. It is to that word we now turn.

Unfortunately, the Greek word translated as 'flesh', *sarx*, is very difficult to translate. It has a neutral and a negative meaning in Paul's letters. Translations do better with the neutral occurrences; the word *sarx* can often be detected behind the English translation by expressions such as 'according to human standards' (for example, 2 Corinthians 1.17, 5.16, and 10.2–3), or 'our mortal flesh' (2 Corinthians 4.11). Sometimes, that's just what the word means: 'in the flesh' means 'in the body' (e.g. Galatians 2.20). So far, so good! *Sarx* in its neutral meaning simply refers to the human, the natural, the physical.

Sarx in its negative meaning is more difficult to translate. Most versions are, frankly, misleading. The Authorized Version, influential for so long in English-speaking countries, translated *sarx* as 'flesh'. Unfortunately, the New Revised Standard Version has done the same. But this has created the abiding impression that the body is either sinful or, at best, a danger to the spiritual life. (Hence the expression 'the world, the flesh and the devil'.) So the idea has spread that Paul makes an unhealthy, life-denying distinction between the soul and the body; basically, in this view, he is in favour of the soul, and against the body. But this interpretation of Paul's teaching, still widely current, is quite mistaken.

It helps to realize that in the Greek Old Testament the word *sarx* tends to mean 'human beings in their mortality' (as in the Authorized Version rendering of Isaiah 40.3, 'All flesh is as grass'), or even 'human beings apart from God'. So *sarx* often has the connotation of weakness – as in the well-known saying of Jesus to his disciples in Gethsemane, 'the spirit is willing, but the flesh is weak' (Mark 14.38).

Most modern translations avoid 'flesh' as a translation for *sarx*, but are still misleading. The Contemporary English Version replaces 'living according to the flesh' with 'being ruled by their desires' (Romans 8.5), while the New International Version has 'our sinful nature', and the Revised English Bible our 'old nature'. But 'nature', whether 'lower', 'carnal' or 'old', tends to suggest only a part of us, whereas Paul is talking about human life *as a whole*. That is what makes his diagnosis of the human situation both more searching, and also more holistic, than most translations give him credit for.

So what does Paul mean by this problematical word *sarx* in its negative sense? The two most important passages are Romans 8.1–13 and Galatians 5.13–24, where it is clear that by 'life in the flesh' (to use the Authorized Version and New

Revised Standard Version translations for the moment) Paul means the opposite of life in the Spirit, and so, also, the opposite of life in Christ. It means allowing the merely human, material or physical to determine and control your life *as if that were all there is, or all that matters.* When a church lives in this way, it breaks up into squabbling factions (1 Corinthians 3.1–4); when a whole society, or an individual, lives in this way, their best-intentioned efforts can be self-defeating, or even achieve the opposite of what they hoped for and intended: 'For I know that nothing good dwells within me, that is, in my flesh. I can will what is right, but I cannot do it. For I do not do the good I want, but the evil I do not want is what I do' (Romans 7.18–19).

Is this too negative? Or is it an indelible part of human experience? It is not the whole picture, since there are traces of God – and, therefore, of goodness – everywhere. In the face of huge global challenges, such as poverty and climate change, most people recognize what is good and desirable: justice for all, bread for the hungry, healing for a stressed planet. But at the time of writing there is precious little evidence that radical, remedial action on any of these fronts is likely. The most frequent explanation for this is 'There is little political will'. But what lies behind the lack of political will? The electorates in liberal democracies may blame their leaders; the leaders will probably blame the voters. It would be profoundly tragic if Paul's words in Romans turned out to be an epitaph for the human race: 'I can will what is right; but I cannot do it'.

In spite of Paul's searching analysis of the human predicament, he preached a gospel. In spite of all he believed about human sinfulness and idolatry, derived from his life-transforming experience on the Damascus Road, Paul's life was characterized by hope. That is not the same as optimism, which is more rooted in a person's temperament, or in future prospects, rather than belief in God, the fundamental root of Christian hope. But before we come to Paul's life-changing experience, there are other serious objections to Paul – two more reasons for not reading him today.

ii Did Paul hate women?

There can be little doubt that what Paul says, or has been thought to say, about women, sex and marriage has contributed much to the apostle's dubious reputation today. We shall look at the most difficult passages, beginning with 1 Corinthians 7. But, first, it is important to look briefly at the patriarchal culture of Paul's world. It was even reflected in the language in which he wrote his letters. Paul often appeals to his addressees as *adelphoi*, the Greek word for brothers. The New Revised Standard Version translates this one word as 'brothers and sisters', and rightly so, because we can be certain that Paul intended to include women as well as men. But the language in which he wrote clearly did not help to make the females of the early communities more visible. Life for nearly all women in Paul's world was extremely difficult. In the Gentile world female infants were often left to die (that is, exposed); malnutrition was common among poorer girls; all would be forced into early marriage, and if they were widowed – which often happened at an early age – they came under pressure to marry again, especially if they were still of child-bearing age. Yet bearing children was fraught with risks, given the widespread gynaecological ignorance of the time. This did not stop the Roman authorities seeking to make marriage obligatory for all women between the ages of 20 and 50, and requiring women who had been divorced or widowed to re-marry.

With these preliminary remarks, we come to 1 Corinthians 7. For a long time we used to think that Paul, in verse 1, roundly declares that it's a good thing for a man not to marry. Some modern versions, such as the Good News Bible, still give that impression. But the Greek manuscripts from which our New Testament has been translated into English did not have quotation marks or, in fact, any punctuation marks at all. So it is much more likely that Paul was quoting the view of some of the Corinthian Christians back at them. The New Revised Standard Version has probably got it right: 'Now concerning the matters about which you wrote: "It is well for a man not to touch a woman".' The Contemporary English Version represents the Corinthians as asking Paul a question: 'Is it best for people not to marry?' Either way, the idea that Christians shouldn't marry was theirs, not Paul's.

Why should they think that? The reason was probably their unrealistic, otherworldly idea of what a truly spiritual life was like. There were Greek teachers of the time who believed that sexual intercourse undermined a person's spirituality, and it seems, in the light of verse 1, some of the Christians at Corinth were putting what they considered to be a spiritual life before the physical intimacy of marriage.

How did Paul respond? His immediate response sounds like a grudging acceptance of marriage (v. 2), rather like his later statement that 'it is better to marry than burn' (v. 9). That's the old translation, which led many to think that Paul was referring here to the flames of hell, but what Paul almost certainly meant was 'better to marry than be aflame with passion' (so the New Revised Standard Version). It sounds negative to us, but against the otherworldly attitude of some of the Corinthian Christians, it was much more realistic. It is true that he does go on to say that there was something to be said for people remaining, like him, unmarried, especially if they have been widowed (vv. 8, 38–40). Yet, given the terrible pressures on women in that society, especially to bear children, it would not be surprising if 'being single and free from sexuality in a protective community would be attractive to women'.[1]

But Paul has other things to say about marriage, not least the importance of sexual intercourse (vv. 3 and 4). These verses come as a surprise, if we think Paul has a grudging, negative view of marriage. This physical intimacy, he tells wives and husbands, is what they owe each other. Again, the mutuality of the language in such a patriarchal culture is surprising. Paul, in fact, is more positive than many contemporary teachers; one Stoic philosopher, Musonius, argued that sexual intercourse within marriage was only justified if it was for the purpose of having children.

There was another factor in the situation which seems to have influenced Paul's thinking. He was writing at a time when famines and wars were frequent, and life expectancy for most

people was about 30. Women who were widowed, as we have
noted, were expected to re-marry, not least to bear more children. So it is not so surprising that, in those circumstances, Paul
thought that married Christians would experience anxiety
(v. 32). But he is quite clear that being married did not make
them second-class Christians: '... if you marry, you do not sin'
(v. 28). A little later, when addressing (probably) couples who
were engaged to each other, he says 'he who marries his fiancée
does well; and he who refrains from marriage will do better' (v.
38). So Paul does go a little way towards the view of the 'super-
spiritual' Christians of Corinth, but several times throughout
this long discussion he affirms the rightness of marriage. Compared with the Corinthians, and later interpreters who thought
celibacy was the best course for all Christians, Paul offers a
rather more balanced view.

Unfortunately, 1 Corinthians 7 isn't the only problem passage in this long letter. In chapter 11 Paul insists that women
should cover their heads in church. For centuries, women did
precisely that – and many still do. I remember my own mother
holding consistently to the custom of wearing a hat to go to
church. On the face of it, this seems another example of the
subordination of women. But, again, it is helpful to look at
both the customs of the time and what was going on in the
church at Corinth. But first we need to take a closer look at the
'problem passage' (11.2–16).

Although the verse which everyone knows best is the one
about women covering their heads, the passage as a whole
deals with men every bit as much as women. Paul tells the
men of Corinth that it's shameful for them to wear their hair
long (v. 14), or to cover their heads with a veil when they pray
or prophesy in church (vv. 4 and 7). So there is no question of
Paul 'picking on' the women here.

The social conventions which would have been prevalent at
Corinth are important in helping us to understand this passage. The Romans had re-founded Corinth about a century
before Paul wrote, and Roman influence was still strong in
Paul's day. So it was simply 'good practice' for a respectable
woman to wear a headcovering; it was a way of protecting her

dignity and status. To do otherwise was to risk implying that she was sexually available.

So why shouldn't the Christian women of Corinth have complied with this convention? Almost certainly they had taken on board the gospel message: 'in Christ there is neither male nor female' (Paul's message to at least one other church – Galatians 3.28). In other words, they knew that the gospel conferred on them a fundamental equality with men. So why, in Paul's view, did they have to go back to wearing headcoverings?

We might say it was a compromise. But, again, it's important to imagine the circumstances of the time. The Christians, small in number as they were, were a vulnerable enough minority without inviting the additional scandal and controversy of women literally 'letting their hair down' in worship. And, to be realistic: would the men in the same service of worship really concentrate on their prayers if all the women were letting their hair down? It's different now, though it isn't difficult to think of how, even today, we could still distract one another in church if we really wanted to!

But what about the men at Corinth? Here the situation was rather more complex. Roman men covered their heads when praying, but not so the Greeks. As for Jewish men, we know that in later centuries they covered their heads, and still do. We can't be sure whether they did so in Paul's day. Whatever the background, Paul clearly frowns upon both headcoverings and long hair for men (vv. 4 and 14), and thinks it healthy, especially given the emotion and enthusiasm in Corinthian worship, for gender distinctions to remain. And it seems that, given the social conventions of the time, women – literally – letting their hair down were more likely to give the Christians a bad name than men complying with Greek, rather than Roman custom, and praying bareheaded.

So did Paul go back on his ringing declaration of male–female equality in his (probably) earlier letter to Galatia? It's interesting that in emphasizing the unity of Jew and Greek, slave and free when writing to Corinth, he omits a reference to male and female equality (1 Corinthians 12.13). The reason, probably, is that the Christians of Corinth didn't need to be told; the problem there was to rein in their exuberant enthusiasm with a little social realism.

All of this will seem very difficult to women readers of Paul today. Many might wonder why Paul did not champion female equality, not to mention the emancipation of slaves. But Paul, and most of the early Christians, lived their lives on the understanding that, though the new world of Jesus Christ had been inaugurated, the old world was still very much with them. The early Christian communities, small as they were, were a sort of 'advance-guard' (Paul calls them the 'firstfruits') of this new creation. So they could not live as if the kingdom had already come in all its fullness.

So Paul is struggling with three 'maps' or 'templates' in front of him. First, he has the gospel 'map', on which there is equality between male and female (Galatians 3.28); second, he has a creation 'map', which despite the difficult language about 'headship' here, especially in verse 3, is more about men and women complementing one another than about superiority and inferiority. Paul's third 'map' is the cultural one, with its conventions about dress and hairstyle.

In this long discussion Paul clearly does not find it easy to reconcile his three 'maps': the gospel one, the creation one, and the cultural one. I think he knew he was struggling, because he ends his involved discussion with what sounds very much like a last-ditch argument: 'But if anyone is disposed to be contentious – we have no such custom, nor do the churches of God' (1 Corinthians 11.16). This sounds almost like: 'So there! No other churches let their women come to the assembly bareheaded. So why should Corinth?' We may feel that this is not Paul at his best, but perhaps he deserves some credit for wrestling as best he could with a tricky problem, occasioned by the heady enthusiasm at one of his churches. And even if we don't like his solution, his 'three-map' method may still have something to teach us.

There are just two more problem passages to look at under this heading. Paul is, notoriously, thought to have forbidden women to speak in church (that is, in the Christian meetings of his day). That has been the normal understanding of verses later in this same letter: 'women should be silent in the churches' (1 Corinthians 14.34). But is that what Paul meant to say, especially since, as 1 Corinthians 11 clearly shows, the women of Corinth prophesied?

The problem Paul addresses here was a specifically Corinthian problem. Their meetings were inclined to be riotous and noisy – as much of chapter 14 shows – and Paul is arguing for some semblance of order. Well then, we might ask, why pick on the women? A fair question! The answer is probably that, given the social conventions of the day, they were speaking more than the men thought they should! Or, they were interrupting others who were prophesying – perhaps asking their own husbands questions when their husbands were in full flow. It is difficult to be sure. But, whatever was going on at Corinth – and that is the key to what Paul really meant here – it cannot, in view of chapter 11, be a blanket ban on women speaking. A recent commentator, stressing how difficult it is to translate these verses, let alone understand them, suggests the following version:

> As in all the churches of God's holy people, when congregations meet in public the women should allow for silence. For there exists no permission for them to speak [in the way they do?]. Let them keep to their ordered place, as the law indicates. If they want to learn anything, let them interrogate their own husbands at home. For a woman to speak thus in public worship brings disgrace (1 Corinthians 14.33b–35).[2]

This rendering does not entirely remove the difficulties for women concerning this passage. But it ought to be clear that, if Paul was addressing a problem specific to Corinth – and a problem in which a new religious movement came up against a deeply patriarchal society – there can be no question of applying Paul's teaching unchanged to vastly different situations and cultures today. So is it a waste of our time reading passages like these? My answer is no – illumination is still possible, even from such difficult verses, by asking a question like this: 'If that is how Christians *then* tackled *their* problems, how should we tackle *ours now*?'

This is probably the way to make some modern sense of the command 'Wives obey your husbands' (for example, Colossians 3.18). And if, as many scholars think, Paul did not write Colossians, we cannot blame him for this one! But the command is there in the New Testament, not just once, but three times (also at Ephesians 5.22 and 1 Peter 3.1).

Once again, the social background of the time is the key. Wives were expected to obey their husbands, although it may be worth pointing out that the Greek word for wives obeying their husbands is, with one exception, a different word from the Greek word for slaves obeying their masters, or Christians obeying their Lord. This second word means absolute obedience; the word used of wives obeying their husbands is connected more with the idea of order: let wives remember their proper place!

This still seems bleak and unhelpful by twenty-first century standards, but it is worth remembering that many of the Christian wives would have been the only Christians in their household. So being a 'dutiful' wife, however unpleasant that may sound to many women today, would have been a realistic way of trying to win her (pagan) husband for the faith (as the writer of 1 Peter realized). So, to make use of the question I suggested earlier ('If that's how *they* tackled *their* problems ...'), this command of Paul's might give some help to those, whether female or male, who find themselves the only Christian in their family, their neighbourhood, or place of work.

So what practical conclusions are we to draw from all this? I suggest two. First, it would be a travesty to continue to take Paul's teaching literally (though some still do). To do that, insisting that women must be silent in church, cover their heads, obey their husbands, is to fail to see that when Paul said what he did, he was addressing a very different world from ours. (At the time of writing, a group of Moslem scholars in Turkey are adopting a similar approach to one of the sacred texts of Islam.) Paul was seeking to help Christians to work out how to live in the world of their time. If we reject a literalist approach to these difficult texts, we may find he can still help us in ours.

The second point is related to the first. Paul's words and arguments always make better sense if we can put them in their first-century context. Fortunately, the research of scholars in recent years has shed a flood of light on Paul's letters, and we shall come to this in our next chapter.

As for the place of women in the New Testament, the dawning of God's kingdom meant that something new had undoubtedly happened, as Paul told the Galatians: 'in Christ there is neither male nor female'. (There is nothing grudging or compromising about his language here.) And even if there had to be adjustments or compromises, especially when Christians met in households which were still patriarchal, there were plenty of signs in the churches that a new world was dawning. Women were prophesying in Christian assemblies, and they held positions of leadership and responsibility in the church, as the number of women referred to in Romans 16 shows. Out of 26 Christians mentioned in this chapter, 9 are women, 17 are men. On the other hand, as a recent study points out,[3] more women than men are praised for being especially active in the church.

One woman mentioned in Romans 16 deserves a special mention. And woman she is, because we now know that one of the two 'apostles' referred to in verse 7 was 'Junia', a woman. Until recently, it was thought that it must be a man called 'Junias' (the Greek is in the accusative case *Iounian*). But there is no evidence at all for there being a man's name 'Junias' in those days. On the other hand, 'Junia' was a common enough name for a woman. Not all modern translations, however, have caught up with this recent research. It's also been pointed out that, out of six references to Priscilla and Aquila in the New Testament, Priscilla's name, more often than not, comes first – an unusual thing by the standards of the time.

I suggest, by way of conclusion, that Paul's controversial statements about women should be read against their background: the patriarchal culture of the day, and the particular problems of Paul's churches, including the questions they put to their founding apostle. It doesn't solve all our difficulties with these texts, and some may disagree with some of Paul's conclusions. But I suggest that he deserves some credit for two things: recognizing that something new and subversive had come into the world in the gospel of Christ, and trying to relate it to the harsh realities of that world.

iii Paul, politics and slavery

Paul has a bad reputation here, too. A quick glance at what he wrote suggests there is good reason for it. He told Christian slaves simply to obey their masters (Colossians 3.22). (Even if Paul didn't write Colossians, someone wrote these words in his name.) In another letter, he asks his hearers, 'Were you a slave when God called you [that is, to be a Christian]?' Paul astonishingly replies, 'Well, never mind' or 'Don't let that bother you'. At least, that is how the Good News Bible and the Contemporary English Version translate Paul's reply, though it is possible that the original would not have sounded quite so bland. Even so, Paul nowhere appears to condemn, or even to question, the ghastly practice of slavery.

Ghastly it certainly was. Although we don't have a lot of evidence, we can be quite certain from what we do have that most slaves would not have been well-treated. A few probably were; most were not. A slave-owner possessed his slaves as if they were just another piece of property; he had absolute power over them. So to become a slave was to become a non-person; slavery meant social death. Punishments could be, and usually were, terrible. For a slave, capital punishment was likely to be death by crucifixion.

How many slaves were there in the Roman Empire? Again, we don't know for sure, but estimates range from just over one in every six people to one in every three. It is not surprising that the Roman Senate, faced with the proposal that slaves should wear distinctive clothing to distinguish them from 'freedmen' and 'freedwomen', rejected the proposal. As the Roman patrician and philosopher Seneca said: if the slaves did that, they would know how numerous they were!

The emancipation of slaves lay far in the future. The 'manumission' practised in Paul's day was a much more limited form of enfranchisement. Manumission was the name for a legal procedure by which a slave became, legally, a freedman (or freedwoman). However, they might be worse off than before. They would still be under the thumb of their former owner; they would owe him a specified number of working days because, technically freed though they were, they were now the 'clients' of their former owner, and he their 'patron'. In any case, manumission didn't happen automatically, however long a person had been a slave. A slave-owner only manumitted a slave if it was in his own interests to do so; sometimes a freed slave could be more use to him as a freedman than as a slave, because he could assume new responsibilities.

To return to Paul, what else did he tell Christian slaves apart from 'Obey your masters'? After telling them, in effect, to accept their lot (1 Corinthians 7.21, the verse quoted earlier), Paul goes on at once to imagine another scenario: 'Suppose you have a chance of freedom' (that is, manumission, not emancipation). What does Paul say to that? For a long time we did not know for sure what advice he gave to Christian slaves faced with the opportunity of freedom, however limited it might have been. That was because the two crucial Greek words which follow in this verse (v. 21), *mallon chresai*, seemed so ambiguous that they might mean either 'make use of your present condition [that is, of slavery] now more than ever' or 'avail yourself of the opportunity'. The New Revised Standard Version has both these translations, the second in a footnote. Now, after painstaking research by scholars, we can be confident that Paul meant the second, as the Contemporary English Version recognizes: '... if you can win your freedom, you should'.

But what difference did being a Christian slave make *in the community of the church*? This is where it must have been complicated. As one commentator remarks, Paul avoids saying 'Everything has changed', even though 'in Christ there is neither slave nor free' (Galatians 3.28). But he also avoids saying 'Nothing has changed'. We know this because of an extraordinary remark he goes on to make after telling slaves who have the chance of freedom to take it. He says: 'When the

Lord chooses slaves, they become his free people. And when he chooses free people, they become slaves of Christ. God paid a great price for you. So don't become slaves of anyone else' (1 Corinthians 7.22–23, Contemporary English Version).

So here is a remarkable reversal in the language used of two groups of Christians. Paul doesn't simply say 'We are all equal in the fellowship of the Church', though it seems he did believe that. Instead, he uses more specific, and so more socially radical language: the slave now has the higher order of a freed person in Christ, and the free person has the equal honour of being a slave of Christ.

It will seem surprising to many that Paul still did not question the institution of slavery. A major reason may lie in a combination of two things: his expectation of Christ's imminent return, against the background of an over-mighty empire, with all its deeply entrenched power structures. Apart from his Christian hope for the future, the modern concepts of progress, political freedom and political change simply would not have shown up on Paul's 'radar screen', nor, probably, on anyone else's at that time.

Before we leave the subject of slavery, there is another story to be told: the story of Philemon. Or, rather, we can try to reconstruct the story from what is by far the shortest of Paul's surviving letters, his letter to the Christian slave-owner of that name. In the popular view of this letter, Onesimus was a slave who had run away from his owner, Philemon, and Paul writes to Philemon, asking him to forgive Onesimus and take him back. But this is to read into the text quite a lot which isn't there! This runaway slave theory is far from certain. There is no clear reference in the letter to Onesimus having run away at all, and Paul makes no request to Philemon to forgive him. Admittedly, Paul says, 'If he [that is, Onesimus] has wronged you in any way, or owes you anything, charge that to my account' (Philemon 18). That hardly suggests a runaway slave ('*If* he has wronged you ...'), and, anyway, how could Paul reimburse Philemon for that? But even if Onesimus hadn't run away from Philemon, it seems he had upset him in some way. In a pun on Onesimus' name (meaning 'useful'), Paul seems to concede that Onesimus had been pretty 'useless' (v. 11). Presumably, there was something behind this blunt remark!

So what had happened? Onesimus had sought out Paul. (Others think Philemon had sent him, but this doesn't really explain the 'useless' remark.) Perhaps Onesimus felt that Paul was one of the few people who might have had some influence on his master, Philemon. Paul, after all, had been responsible for bringing Philemon to faith (v. 19), and now he had brought Onesimus to Christian faith, too (v. 10). In fact, seeking Paul's help may just have kept Onesimus on the right side of the law because, even if he had run away, a slave who deliberately sought an advocate to intercede for him was not technically guilty of being a runaway.

What the sequel was to this letter we do not know. The theory that Philemon gave Onesimus his freedom, and that Onesimus later became a bishop in the Church, is rather far-fetched. It may be that Paul was hoping Philemon would free his slave: 'confident of your obedience, I am writing to you, knowing that you will do even more than I say' (v. 21). Was this a veiled way of saying 'Give Onesimus his freedom'? We don't know, but the mere fact that this letter has survived suggests its outcome was positive in some way. Philemon appears not to have done the first-century equivalent of binning or shredding it.

To sum up this brief survey of Paul and slavery, the apostle may well appear to twenty-first-century readers disappointingly conservative. To be fair to him, it is not easy to see what other practical advice he could have given to Christian slaves. On the other hand, there are in his letters the seeds of a revolution: 'In Christ there is neither slave nor free'. It was to take a long time – it *is* taking a long time – for this 'leaven' to transform the massive injustice of the world's slaveries. Yet in the request to a Christian slave-owner to welcome back a slave, now also a Christian, we see the dawn of a new situation: 'Perhaps this is the reason he was separated from you for a while, so that you might have him back for ever, no longer as a slave but as more than a slave, a beloved brother – especially to me but how much more to you ...' (Philemon 16).

Conclusion to sections i to iii

Readers will probably differ on whether these three sections exonerate Paul 'from all charges'. Personally, I do not think that they do, but I hope I have demonstrated that our difficulties with Paul are not so great when we abandon a wooden, literalist approach to his writings, and read him in context. But even if certain charges against Paul still stand in the eyes of some, I hope that those readers will be prepared to see that, for all his cultural limitations, he still might have much to say to us. Recent research has lit up his life and letters in new ways, and to this we now turn.

iv What happened to Paul on the road to Damascus?

Most people have heard the phrase 'a Damascus Road' experience, and that experience – whatever it was – is by far the best-known fact about Paul's life. Yet in the last half-century or so, scholars have had fresh things to say about it, and about Paul's life as a whole. So, do we need to revise our views of the man, as well as of some aspects of his teaching? In answering that question, we need to look first at the picture of Paul which has come down to us, in various ways, from the Reformation.

According to this picture, Saul of Tarsus was a zealous Pharisee whose zeal for the Jewish law provoked him to persecute the early 'Christians' (though at this early stage they may not have been called 'Christians'). But Saul increasingly realized that his own efforts to keep the law were doomed to failure. He could not win salvation that way. As he was later to say, 'I do not do the good I want, but the evil I do not want is what I do' (Romans 7.19). Saul was oppressed not only by his own sense of failure; he became increasingly conscience-stricken about what he was doing to the disciples of Jesus.

What actually did Saul do to the Christians? Some scholars think that Luke in Acts has exaggerated the violence of the persecutions; Acts 26.10 refers to death penalties. Whatever the actual facts concerning this, it is quite likely that Christians, at Saul's instigation, received the 'thirty-nine lashes', as he himself did later, as an apostle (2 Corinthians 11.24). And if Acts is correct in saying that Saul approved of and witnessed the lynching of Stephen, his misgivings about the rightness of what he was doing may well have increased.

Then came his encounter with the risen Christ on the Damascus Road. So important was it to the author of Acts that he tells the story not once, but three times, the second and third times as told by Paul himself (Acts 9.1–22; 22.6–16; 26.12–18). In the third version, some words spoken by Jesus to Saul seem to support the traditional picture of a conscience-stricken Pharisee: 'Saul, Saul, why persecutest thou me? It is hard for thee to kick against the pricks' (Acts 26.14). That is how the Authorized Version puts it, and it was perhaps natural to assume that the 'pricks' mentioned here were the pricks of conscience. But the phrase 'kick against the pricks' does not occur in the two earlier versions in Acts of Paul's conversion. (Luke clearly felt able to engage in some artistic licence as he re-told the story.) In fact, 'to kick against the pricks' is a Greek proverb, taken from the world of horse-riding, and refers to the horse's inability to withstand the prick of the rider's spur (as all modern translations recognize). So these words don't refer to Saul's supposedly guilty conscience at all, but to the difficulty of holding out against God's will.

But, to continue our summary of the traditional Protestant view of Paul, this Damascus Road encounter led to Saul's conversion. According to Acts, the revelation blinded him; he was led by the hand to Damascus where he was baptized, after a disciple called Ananias prayed for him and he was healed (Acts 9.8–19). It is curious that Paul himself nowhere mentions Ananias (or Stephen for that matter). What Paul *does* say is that he went to 'Arabia' before returning to Damascus (Galatians 1.17). Did this mean that he went on a kind of 'retreat', withdrawing to 'a desert place' to reflect on what had happened to him? This, too, has been part of the picture. After this 're-treat', he began to preach the message which was eventually to transform Martin Luther, and trigger the Reformation: a person is not justified by 'the works of the law', but by 'faith'.

Judaism, Paul now saw (in this traditional view of him), was wrong to insist on 'salvation by works', for the law, which he himself had failed to live up to, was now abolished through the death and resurrection of Christ. This was why he preached to all who would hear – but especially to Gentiles – that God's grace and forgiveness are free; they cannot be earned.

Such is the picture of Paul and his message which has been handed down in the Christian, and particularly the Protestant, tradition. Almost all of it, though, has been challenged by recent scholarship. Some scholars in recent years have argued that we need to liberate Paul from his 'Lutheran captivity'. By that they mean that we have read Paul too much through Luther's eyes. For example, *was* Paul, like Luther, preoccupied with his shortcomings and sins, and desperate to find the forgiveness of God? We have tended to assume that he was.

This isn't just an 'academic' question. The traditional picture of Paul which I have just sketched has had important practical consequences. Christian evangelists have often proceeded on the basis that, in order to convert people, they must first convince them that they are sinners (if, unlike Paul, Luther, Wesley etc., they are not already convinced). But what if this is simply wrong? What if Paul's conversion was not preceded by a growing sense of failure and sin? So, how much of this traditional view still stands?

We can be quite sure about two things: 1) Saul the Pharisee persecuted the early Church, and 2) he had a life-changing experience – which he and his 'biographer' Luke believed was an encounter with the risen Christ. But we don't know for certain *why* Saul persecuted the disciples, for nowhere does the New Testament tell us. Saul, as a 'zealot' (his own self-description, Galatians 1.14), may have objected to the message of a crucified Messiah; to a devout Jew, it would have seemed a contradiction in terms, if not outright blasphemy. If the cross wasn't Saul's main objection to this new movement, perhaps he thought disciples like Stephen were the problem. Stephen, according to Acts (6.13–14), was falsely accused of speaking against the Temple, and the law of Moses; to Saul, to speak in that way was to undermine the cause of God to which he was so passionately committed.

There are other gaps in our knowledge. We don't know, for

example, the date of Paul's Damascus Road experience. It could have been a matter of weeks or months after the resurrection – and so some time in the years from AD 30 to AD 34 inclusive – or two or three years after the resurrection. A more interesting and important gap in our knowledge is Paul's state of mind at the time. We don't know for sure that Paul's conversion was preceded by the inner struggles which people like Martin Luther and John Wesley experienced. The spiritual anguish they experienced probably reinforced this picture of Paul, particularly in the Protestant tradition of the Christian Church. Although Paul's words in Romans 7 may have been shaped retrospectively by his memories of his earlier years ('The good I want to do I do not do ...'), most scholars now take the view that Romans 7 does not describe his pre-conversion struggles. For one thing, Paul uses the present tense. For another, Paul appears to describe himself elsewhere as a successful, not a failed, Pharisee: '... circumcised on the eighth day, a member of the people of Israel, of the tribe of Benjamin, a Hebrew born of Hebrews; as to the law, a Pharisee; as to zeal, a persecutor of the Church; as to righteousness under the law, *blameless*' [my italics] (Philippians 3.5–6).[4]

This is no doubt how Paul appeared both to other people and to himself. It doesn't mean he was complacent, legalistic or self-righteous – just zealous and passionately committed. It was only *in retrospect*, in the light of his Christian experience, that he learnt to distinguish 'my righteousness' (Philippians 3.9) from God's righteousness. ('Righteousness' is one of Paul's most important words, but not a word we use in modern English; Chapters 3 and 4 return to this subject.)

So Paul's conversion may not have been preceded by a growing sense of failure and sin. The New Testament certainly doesn't say so. If this is so, then our revised picture of Paul raises an interesting question: should we regard a conviction of moral failure and sin as the normal prelude to the Christian life? Or should we now think of the experience of people like Luther and Wesley as exceptional? Of course, it would be natural for a person who had led an evil life before coming to Christian faith to be convicted of sin, but there is evidence in the Bible – and from saints down the ages – that we become more conscious of our shortcomings after we come to faith, and the nearer we come to God.

Krister Stendahl is an American scholar who was one of the first to ask whether we have seen Paul too much through the eyes of Luther. He also questioned whether it is accurate to speak of Paul's 'conversion'.[5] This sounds a startling – even shocking – idea, but Stendahl was making two important points. If by Paul's 'conversion' we mean he was converted from one religion (that is, Judaism) to another (that is, Christianity), that is clearly wrong. The fledgling 'Christian' movement had not yet separated from Judaism. Even 'Judaism' may be a misleading way to describe the faith and way of life of the Jewish people; it makes them sound more systematic and monochrome than they were.

Whether Paul continued to be a practising Jew is an interesting question. The Acts of the Apostles gives the impression that he was, but Paul himself gives a different picture. He was 'all things to all people': he lived as a Jew when he was among Jews, but when he was among those outside the Jewish law, he did not (1 Corinthians 9.19–23). A policy like that sounds like a recipe for disaster, and it probably was in some ways. But for Paul it was a much more costly and principled policy than it might first appear. And it would certainly have made it difficult to put a label of any kind on him!

But there is another reason for questioning the word 'conversion', and that is Paul's own descriptions of what happened to him. He reserves the standard Old Testament term for conversion – to *turn*, that is, from idols to the living God – for Gentiles (1 Thessalonians 1.9, Galatians 4.9), but he describes his own experience in other ways: he 'saw' the risen Christ, and so became an apostle (1 Corinthians 9.1 and 15.8). In another letter he says God 'called' him in the way God called some of the Old Testament prophets (Galatians 1.15). So, Stendahl argued – and, again, this has been a very influential view – it is more appropriate to speak of Paul's *commission* from God rather than his 'conversion'. In the end, it depends on what we mean by 'conversion': if we mean a 'U turn', a life transformed, then the word is clearly appropriate. But it is important to notice the words Paul himself uses about what happened to him.

What else has been questioned? Jesus, of course, did not give 'Saul' a new name on the Damascus Road. 'Saul' remained 'Saul' until Acts 13.9, where Luke substitutes his Roman name Paul, for what was almost certainly his Hebrew one. But what of the traditional view that Paul, immediately after his conversion, went 'on retreat' in the desert? The New Testament says nothing explicit about this; the apostle himself says he went to 'Arabia', which may not have been a desert place at all. Luther, in one of his rather caustic jibes against St Jerome, in his Commentary on Galatians, observes that Jerome wondered what Paul did in Arabia: 'What else should he do', says Luther, 'but preach Christ?' That, certainly, is the impression Luke gives us in Acts (Acts 9.20–30).

To summarize: it is clear that a man who called himself a 'zealot' and a 'Pharisee' persecuted the Church, and then, through a life-changing experience, became a passionate Christian apostle. But why he persecuted the Church, what religious experience preceded his 'conversion', and whether that word is the best one to describe what happened to Paul, are parts of the traditional picture which, for good reason, have been questioned. In the next section, we look at other aspects of Paul's life, asking whether widespread perceptions of him are well-founded or not.

v Paul's 'three missionary journeys'

Many of us, especially if we were taught about St Paul in Sunday School or Junior Church, will probably have a picture of Paul which owes more to the Acts of the Apostles than to Paul's own letters. This is not surprising. Luke – or whoever wrote Acts – tells a good story! On the whole, the second half of Acts, which is almost entirely about Paul, is more action-packed than the letters. So, if we 'cherry-pick' the most memorable stories from Acts, we get a lively picture: the apostle Paul embarked on three adventure-filled 'missionary journeys', journeys punctuated by 'sermons' in colourful places like the

Acropolis in Athens, and culminating in a dramatic shipwreck off the coast of Malta as Paul made his final journey to Rome. Is this all wrong?

Scholars have long debated how accurate Acts is. If that sounds a rather negative activity in which to engage, it should be said that they had noticed how different is the picture of Paul which Acts gives from the picture Paul himself gives in his letters. At one extreme, some scholars have exaggerated the differences; at the other extreme, others have said there aren't any! The truth probably lies somewhere in between. In any case, Acts was written at least 20 years after Paul wrote his letters, and it was written by a 'fan' of Paul who, like every historian, had his own agenda.

Tradition has it that Acts was written by Luke, a companion of Paul. It may well have been. There are four sections of Acts where the narrative suddenly slips into the first person plural: the so-called 'we' passages. Doesn't that prove that the picture of Paul in Acts comes from an eye-witness who knew him well? That is one view. Another approach asks: how is it that, if a friend and colleague of Paul wrote Acts, it is so different from the letters? Some scholars think that 'we' comes from a travel-diary which the author of Acts has included in his work. Others think it's stylistic in the tradition of Homer's *Odyssey*; on this view, people narrated sea-voyages in the first person plural. That may sound far-fetched, but it is a curious fact that the 'we' which appears and disappears so mysteriously in Acts usually appears when Paul sets out to sea, and disappears soon after he lands. Is this why Acts 27, with its account of the shipwreck, is the longest 'we' passage of all?

Be that as it may, before we ask what kind of picture Paul's letters give of the man, it's worth taking a closer look at Acts. 'Three missionary journeys' give an impression of a man constantly on the move. But it wasn't quite like that. It is more likely he established bases for his work; he spent a year and a half at Corinth (18.11), and two years at Ephesus (19.10). What did he do most of the time? Presumably, as Paul himself tells us (for example, 1 Corinthians 4.12), he worked for his living, which, according to Acts was making tents (Acts

18.3). So Paul's 'set-piece' speech at Athens, if such it was (Acts 17.22–31), was the exception, not the rule. Most of the time he was engaged in discussions, whether in the shop, in a local synagogue or, later on, at Ephesus, in a 'school', rather than 'preaching' as we understand it.

But there is one particular impression which Acts gives of Paul which we probably ought to correct. Luke, if indeed he was the author, in his enthusiasm for Paul, portrays a sort of apostolic 'James Bond', a hero who gets into all sorts of scrapes, but always emerges victorious. But was it really like that? One 'adventure' is mentioned both in Acts, and by Paul himself in one of his own letters. It is the apostle's escape from Damascus in a basket lowered over the city wall (2 Corinthians 11.33–34, Acts 9.25). Luke thinks of it as a providential escape: Paul lives to 'fight' another day! For Paul, it's the crowning humiliation in the long list he recounts in 2 Corinthians. We shouldn't be misled by the word 'boast' here; Paul is doing something unheard of in the ancient world, boasting of 'the things that show my weakness' (2 Corinthians 11.30). After all, a soldier is supposed to scale city walls and win battles, not go the other way and escape ignominiously in a basket!

So the Acts of the Apostles gives us a lively, colourful picture of Paul. A generation on, the author could see more clearly than Paul the fruits of his labours. In fact, the controversy about Paul may still have been raging, and that may be why Luke devotes so much space on his papyrus roll to the apostle. Perhaps he was setting the record straight. But now we need to hear how it was 'straight from the horse's mouth'; so what kind of picture of Paul's life and character do we get from his own writings?

The short answer is this: a life strewn with both successes and failures, dogged by controversy and conflict, some of them perhaps of Paul's own making. As a Methodist, I find some similarity with John Wesley! Looked at in retrospect, Wesley might seem a 'success': the founder of the movement which became the Methodist Church. But the closer we look at Wesley the man – the controversies he was engaged in, the number of members he expelled for misconduct and, not least, his own personal foibles and the disastrous marriage he contracted – the more messy and complicated the picture looks. That is how it was with Paul.

Was he ever fully accepted by those who were disciples of Jesus before him? According to Acts, Barnabas was a disciple who not once, but twice, introduced Paul to the two leading Christian communities of the time; he spoke for him to a wary church in Jerusalem (Acts 9.26–27) and, many years later, perhaps, brought him back from Paul's home city in Tarsus to help with the growing evangelistic work at Antioch (Acts 11.25–26). What Paul spent this time doing in Tarsus during those years we don't know; Paul himself says he spent 14 years there (Galatians 1.21). As with Jesus, these are 'hidden years', and we can only guess at what Paul did.

Was Barnabas, in accepting Paul as a fellow-disciple, typical of others? Again, we can't be sure. But, to judge from the opposition Paul was to encounter, it seems likely that there were Jews who carried over into their new Christian faith something of their 'zeal' and passion for their inherited Jewish faith. Although I have expressed it like that, it's important to stress that there were not two faiths. At this stage, 'Christians' were more like a movement, or a sect, within the various kinds of Jewish faith practised then. Even so, Jewish, and Jewish-Christian, opposition seems to have been a problem for Paul for most of the period during which he wrote those letters now in the New Testament.

With the encouragement and support of Barnabas, Paul returned first to Antioch (Acts 11.26), which by now was the main Christian centre outside Jerusalem. (Antioch was a large city in what is now north-west Syria.) It was from Antioch that the momentous step was taken to preach the gospel to Gentiles as well as to Jews (Acts 11.20; 13.1–3). This is why Luke, from this point on, drops Paul's Jewish name 'Saul'; after this (Acts 13.9), he is never called Saul again, only 'Paul'.

The last paragraph was dependent on Acts. But if we reverse the usual procedure, putting Luke's 'three missionary journeys' in the background, and concentrate mainly on Paul's letters for evidence, what kind of picture of Paul's travels and work emerges? We start with what Paul saw to be his life's work: to preach the gospel of Christ to the Gentiles (Galatians 1.16). The Church made this 'official' when, some years later, a summit-meeting in Jerusalem recognized that Peter would head up the mission to the Jews, and Paul the mission to the Gentiles (Galatians 2.7). But it was one thing to agree that in theory, quite another to put it into practice. Jews and Gentiles lived together not only in Judaea itself, but also in many of the major cities of the Roman Empire. So it would not be surprising at all if Peter, or representatives of him, encroached on Paul's 'territory'. Paul seems to be complaining about that in one of his letters (2 Corinthians 10.13–14).

Imagine this 'Hebrew of Hebrews', this erstwhile Pharisee, living and working in Gentile lands. He had done so before in Tarsus, both as a boy and, later, as a young Christian. But this time it was different. If his advice to his churches is anything to go by, he would have been more relaxed about incurring 'impurities'. He still would not set foot in a pagan temple, but now, when he shared a meal in a Gentile's house, he ate what was put in front of him, provided it gave no offence to anyone else who was there (1 Corinthians 10.23–30). He had reached the conclusion that no foods were unclean in themselves (Romans 14.14), and so, by most people's standards, he was no longer a practising Jew.

To begin with, though, Paul would have stayed with a Jewish family. The local Jewish community offered him an obvious entrée, even if the local synagogue was simply a meeting-point rather than a building. (Most often, it was probably the fairly large house of one of the better-off Jewish families.) But word would eventually have got around that this 'Jew' was something of a renegade. In any case, as time went by, Paul's hosts, especially on his return visits, would have been Christian, even if Jewish-Christian.

At Corinth he stayed with Priscilla and Aquila. They shared his trade of tent-making (Acts 18.2–3), but as they were already established (it seems), and probably well-to-do, Paul would have been their 'employee'. He may have stayed with them again in Ephesus, and perhaps it was there, in the riot recounted by Luke in Acts 19, that they risked their lives for him, as he gratefully acknowledges (Romans 16.3–4). One other person we know Paul stayed with was Gaius, because Paul tells us so (Romans 16.23). But here there seems to be a puzzle. Paul was anxious to keep his independence, unlike most teachers and philosophers of the period. They relied on a 'patron' for hospitality and support; in return, their patron might well have expected, at the very least, complementary references in what they said and, certainly, nothing socially subversive. But Paul also describes (Romans 16.23 again) Gaius as 'host to the whole church' – and so, presumably, the owner of a larger-than-average house.

So did Paul end up staying with one of the 'big men' of Corinth after all? Whatever Paul's personal hospitality arrangements were, it is very clear that Corinth and Ephesus were important bases for him. So it is not surprising that he 'covered' a large part of what we now call Turkey and Greece: in southern, or southern central, Turkey he formed the churches of Galatia, while in northern Greece (Paul's 'Macedonia') he established the churches of Thessalonika and Philippi, and in central and southern Greece (Paul's 'Achaea') the churches of Corinth, Cenchreae and others (1 Corinthians 1.1, Romans 16.1–2).

How easy would travelling have been for Paul? An earlier generation took a rather rosy-eyed view of the Roman Empire. Travel was no doubt better in places than it was when Octavian (later the Emperor Augustus) and Mark Antony, aided or hindered by Cleopatra, were fighting for political supremacy, but Paul's own catalogue of deprivations makes a modern traffic jam seem a mere hiccup:

> Three times I was shipwrecked; for a night and a day I was adrift at sea; on frequent journeys, in danger from rivers, dangers from bandits, danger from my own people, danger from Gentiles, danger in the city, danger in the wilderness, danger at sea, danger from false brothers and sisters ... (2 Corinthians 11.25b–26).

Where else did Paul go? He reached 'Illyricum' (modern Serbia, Romans 15.19), before eventually returning to Jerusalem. He had been back there more than once since his Damascus Road experience – once to stay with Peter for a fortnight (Galatians 1.18), and again, many years later, for a sort of summit-meeting (Galatians 2.1–11). But Jerusalem and Judaea were becoming increasingly dangerous, especially for someone with Paul's reputation. Not only were social and economic conditions deteriorating, the political scene was becoming explosive as Jewish resentment at oppressive Roman rule reached boiling-point.

In such difficult and volatile conditions, the Jerusalem church members, led by James, the brother of Jesus, found themselves in a difficult position. Should they disassociate from the nationalist fervour of the day? Probably yes, in view of what Jesus had said. Should they, as disciples of Jesus, continue to be devout, practising Jews? Again, the answer was 'yes'. But how would they receive the 'Jew' who had stirred up controversy wherever he had gone?

It is no wonder Paul journeyed apprehensively to Jerusalem, as he told the Christians at Rome (Romans 15.25, 30–31). He travelled, accompanied by a number of Gentile Christians, with 'the collection' raised by him from his Gentile churches (1 Corinthians 16.1–4) for famine relief among the Christians in Jerusalem and Judaea. What happened to that collection we do not know. It is one of the mysteries of the New Testament. Paul experienced a 'hot' reception in Jerusalem according to Luke in Acts. The sequel to the jittery words of James and the church's elders to Paul ('people will know you're here', Acts 21.20–22) was a riot in the Temple, culminating in Paul's rescue and arrest at the hands of the Roman military (Acts 21.27–36). Eventually, Paul was taken to Rome, and there Luke's story ends. Was he eventually released? Did he ever reach Spain, as he hoped and prayed he would (Romans 1.9–10, 15.28)? Half a century later, Clement, bishop of Rome, thought so, but he may not have been certain. We simply do not know.

In all these travels, was Paul an effective evangelist? Our answer depends partly on our definition. But the very existence of the churches to which he wrote, and other churches which he helped to form, shows that he cannot have been *in*effective. His style – apart from occasional homilies given, presumably by invitation at local synagogues – was discussion and dialogue, not least while making tents in his workshop. The southern Mediterranean climate for much of the year, together with a more public culture and narrow, crowded streets, meant Paul would never have been short of passers-by.

As for his letter-writing, we know little about the details. We know he dictated Romans because Tertius, the scribe, 'pipes up' at the end (Romans 16.22), and we know Paul put his autograph on at least one letter because he tells us so (Galatians 6.11). But did he really co-write some of his letters – for example, 1 and 2 Thessalonians with Silvanus and Timothy? It's difficult for us to imagine the others getting a word in edgeways, and they probably didn't. On the other hand, some scholars wonder whether the reason why 2 Thessalonians is so similar and yet different from 1 Thessalonians is because it was mainly Silvanus' work. Writing the letters cannot have been easy, given the scarcity and cost of writing materials, not to mention the scarcity of people able to write. As for delivering them, it could only be done by personal envoy, Timothy or Titus, or, in the case of both Colossians and Ephesians, Tychicus.[6] (Titus may have drawn the short straw, entrusted as he probably was with 'the letter of tears' (2 Corinthians 2.4, 13; 7.6–8).)

How were the letters received? Well, they have survived – even the short letter to Philemon – so no one 'binned' them. On the other hand, we know Paul wrote at least two more letters to Corinth, the so-called 'previous letter' and 'the letter of tears' (1 Corinthians 5.9 and 2 Corinthians 2.4 and 9). They would have been read aloud at one sitting, and almost certainly much more dramatically than we read them in church. So, even if someone once fell asleep during one of Paul's sermons (Acts 20.9), it is unlikely anyone would do so during a public reading of one of his letters. On the contrary, is it possible that more than one person stalked out while 1 Corinthians was being read out to the Christians of Corinth assembled at the house of Gaius? As for the letters to Thessalonika and Philippi, they were political dynamite – so were they read in a conspiratorial whisper behind closed doors?

In the next section we shall ask what kind of a pastor Paul was to his churches, but we end this section by noting that controversy dogged Paul's steps almost to the end. Other Christian teachers turned up at Galatia, provoking a crisis there. Criticisms about Paul may have filtered through to him from the Thessalonians, under intense pressure as they were from the moment of their conversion. Philippi seems to have been the most trouble-free zone, although even here Paul inserts a sharp warning (Philippians 3.2). The church at Corinth seems to have been in a class by itself. How many sleepless nights did they give Paul? They supported apostles as if they were rival football teams (1 Corinthians 1.12). Had Peter ('Cephas') passed that way? Probably he had or, if not, his supporters certainly had, otherwise there would have been no 'Peter' supporters' club. Apollos, with his rhetorical skills and learning (Acts 18.24), had clearly gone down well. Even Jesus seemed to have his own fan club, so what kind of a misunderstanding was that?

All the while, as Paul wrestled with the headaches he called churches ('I am under pressure every day, with anxiety for all the churches' (2 Corinthians 11.28)), rumours, accurate and inaccurate, about him were spreading. Some people may already have been sending letters in his name, but without his authority or permission (2 Thessalonians 2.2); in those days it was very difficult to distinguish the genuine from the counterfeit. It would be two or three generations before the dust began to settle, and Paul's letters were received by the Church as a whole as part of its Scriptures. Subsequent chapters of this book will fill out this picture of Paul a little more. But in this chapter, as part of our initial ground-clearing exercise, we ought to look briefly at the man himself.

vi But still a disagreeable man?

What sort of man was Paul, and how should we read his letters today? Everyone will have their own picture of Paul; that is inevitable. The distance in time, the fragmentary evidence, and our own life-experiences are just three things which will affect how we see him. Yet, given his importance, we should at least ask ourselves whether our picture of Paul does justice to all the evidence, or whether it owes more to our preconceived ideas about him.

Paul does not always come across well in his letters. At times, he sounds intolerant, angry, authoritarian and arrogant. We look at the evidence for each of these accusations in turn.

Paul sounds at his most intolerant in his letter to the Galatians, and his second to the Corinthians. In both, he complains about other Christian teachers who had come to Galatia and to Corinth preaching a different gospel from the one he had preached (Galatians 1.6–9, 2 Corinthians 11.4). That does not fit comfortably with our pluralist cultures, nor the ethos of post-modernism: 'This is how I see things, that is how you see things'. Can this apparent intolerance of Paul in any way be justified?

Rightly or wrongly, Paul shows a parental attitude to these churches at Galatia and Corinth (Galatians 4.19, 1 Corinthians 4.15). Whether they appreciated it we have no way of knowing. But since Paul had founded these churches, his attitude was understandable. In the two crises which he is addressing in these letters, he clearly believed that his churches' very identity, if not existence, was at stake. To appreciate his attitude, we might compare modern-day parents challenging their offspring about conduct or habits which threatened their education, their health, or their freedom from legal action and prison. In such situations, a relaxed tolerance is not what we look for in a good parent. But we only have Paul's side of the story.

Does Paul's paternal (and 'maternal', in view of the 'child-birth' image of Galatians 4.19) concern for his churches explain his anger? Again, Galatians and 2 Corinthians 10—13 provide most of the examples. In fact, the last four chapters of 2 Corinthians, which many scholars think was originally a separate letter, show Paul at his most passionate. It is difficult to piece together all that happened, but his relationship with the church at Corinth was in a state of crisis, if not meltdown. Was Paul justified in thinking he was the only one who could be their 'minister'? That may be a misleading analogy. In any case, he had said in an earlier letter that he had no problem about working with Apollos (1 Corinthians 4.6). Whether Apollos felt the same about Paul we don't know. But the issue in 2 Corinthians 10–13 was the other Christian or 'Christian' teachers who had come to Corinth. Paul felt that they were not only undermining him by their criticisms, but also undermining his work by leading 'his' church astray.

Again, we have only Paul's side of the story, but preaching 'another gospel', 'another Jesus' and 'another spirit' (2 Corinthians 11.4) sounds seriously different from Paul's gospel. We can only guess at what they were saying, though their Jewish credentials (2 Corinthians 11.22) seem to have played a significant role. But if their message was one in which the cross played no part, that would have changed drastically both the self-understanding and the lifestyle of both the Corinthian and the Galatian churches. In these controversies Paul was not averse to using strong language. Perhaps he did not know of the teaching of Jesus according to Matthew (Matthew 5.33–37) that prohibited disciples from swearing oaths. At any rate, when he has his back to the wall, Paul resorts to oaths to reinforce his credibility (for example, Galatians 1.20, 2 Corinthians 11.31). Nor is he above using the equivalent of a crude four-letter word to make a point as sharply as he can: 'For his sake I have suffered the loss of all things, and I regard them as rubbish [word could be translated as sh*t in today's slang], in order that I may gain Christ and be found in him' (Philippians 3.8–9). Most crudely of all, Paul goes 'off the deep end' in what he says about the Christian teachers seeking to persuade the Gentile male converts to be circumcised; the New Revised Standard Version doesn't mince words: 'I wish those who unsettle you would castrate themselves!' (Galatians 5.12).

In this survey of Paul's angry-sounding language, I do not want to give the impression that it is always wrong to be angry. Much of church life proceeds on the basis that it is. (All the angry things are sometimes said after a meeting, not during it.) Yet Mark's Gospel has several references to Jesus being angry (even if Luke omits them all!). So we look now at one final group of angry expressions in Paul's letters.

These consist of his solemn pronouncement of curses on those who are bringing another gospel to Galatia (1.8–9), and on those at Corinth who 'do not love the Lord' (1 Corinthians 16.22). This sounds distinctly unpleasant – by modern 'Western' standards, outrageous. Yet, as one commentator points out, the implication of another gospel might well have been to make Jesus himself accursed. Jesus, if he was not God's Messiah by virtue of his resurrection (Romans 1.3–4), must have died under God's curse. That is what the Scriptures implied about people who died by crucifixion (Galatians 3.13, Deuteronomy 21.23). So this may be another example of Paul's reaction *in extremis*: if it is a choice between allowing Jesus to become the accursed one, or cursing his opponents, Paul does not hesitate.

Finally, was Paul arrogant or authoritarian? At times he sounds both: 'What would you prefer? Am I to come to you with a stick, or with love in a spirit of gentleness?' (1 Corinthians 4.21), and, perhaps two years later, '... if I come again, I will not be lenient' (2 Corinthians 13.2). How did the good Christians of Corinth react to this kind of language? They cannot have 'broken off diplomatic relations' with Paul after the first outburst, because he made a second visit to them. Admittedly, Paul's relations with this church went up and down like a yo-yo. This second visit resulted in a personal humiliation for Paul (2 Corinthians 2.1–5). Paul followed it up with his 'letter of tears', which Titus probably took to Corinth. That seems to have worked (2 Corinthians 7.5–8) before the final crisis which precipitated letter number five (at least) – namely, our 2 Corinthians 10–13. After that we hear no more. But Clement, bishop of Rome, wrote to the church at Corinth nearly half a century later, so they were still there – and, according to Clement's letter, still arguing.

Today, most of us would be horrified and repelled by the style of leadership we seem to see here – especially in the letters to Corinth. But is it fair to judge Paul by our standards – especially if, in his view, the stakes could not have been higher? In any case, we should not overlook other passages in his letters where we see a different Paul. He does not always command;

sometimes he 'exhorts' or expresses a view (for example, 1 Corinthians 7.40, 2 Corinthians 2.8). And leader though he was, he clearly worked with, and was heavily dependent on, colleagues, as the many personal references show, particularly at the beginnings and ends of his letters.

Last but not least, how accurate an impression of the man do his letters give us? If what the Christians at Corinth said about him is anything to go by, his bark (that is, his letters) may have been worse than his bite (that is, Paul in person): 'For they say "His letters are weighty and strong, but his bodily presence is weak, and his speech contemptible"' (2 Corinthians 10.10).

In a later chapter, we continue our search for the person behind the letters, when we ask whether Paul practised what he preached (Chapter 3, section iv). But first we look at the remarkable new light shed on Paul's letters by recent scholarship.

Notes

1 S. Hack Polaski, *A Feminist Introduction to Paul*, Chalic Press, St Louis, Missouri, 2005, p. 51.

2 A. C. Thistleton, *The First Epistle to the Corinthians: A Commentary on the Greek Text*, Eerdmans, Grand Rapids, Michigan/ Cambridge, UK, 2000, p. 1131.

3 P. Lampe, 'The Roman Christians of Romans 16', in W. A. Meeks and J. T. Fitzgerald, eds, *The Writings of St Paul*, W. W. Norton & Co., New York/London, 2007.

4 In accepting this verse in Philippians 3, rather than the passage in Romans 7, as a more accurate picture of Paul's pre-conversion experience, most scholars have followed the lead of K. Stendahl, in *Paul Among Jews and Gentiles*, Fortress Press, Minneapolis, 1976/SCM 1977, pp. 78–96.

5 Stendahl, *Paul Among Jews and Gentiles*, pp. 7–23.

6 See the Introduction, section iii.

2

Fresh Light on Paul's World and Paul's Churches

So far, I have been suggesting that Paul may not have been the man we thought he was, and that his letters may not say what we have always thought they said. If we allow our preconceptions about Paul to be challenged in this way, I believe we shall notice new things in his writings. But it also helps our reading of Paul if we are able to discover more about his background and the situations he was addressing. Fortunately, in the last few decades especially, scholars have shed fresh light on many of the more difficult or obscure passages in Paul's letters.

In this chapter we shall look, first, at the broader context, both Graeco-Roman and Jewish, in which Paul lived and worked, before turning our attention to the various problems and crises which he had to deal with in the churches to which he wrote.

i Was Paul a revolutionary?

A status-ridden society

A man who told slaves to obey their masters, and wives to obey their husbands, does not sound like a revolutionary, although, as we argued in the last chapter, that teaching needs to be put in the social context of his time. Paul's world was very hierarchical. The television sketch in which the taller man said 'I look down on him' and the smaller man standing beside him said 'And I look up to him', illustrates what society was like. It was basically a patriarchal world, although there were new freedoms for wealthier women in the early Roman Empire under Augustus. In this male-dominated society a man's status was based on his 'honour', and that in turn was measured by how much influence and wealth – and, not least, how many 'clients' – he had. In such a world, where almost everyone both looked up to, and down on, someone else, it was a constant battle to keep your honour intact. The goal was to increase your honour if possible, but at all costs to avoid 'shame' (the opposite of honour). So a man needed, unless he was right at the top of the social pyramid, a 'patron' or 'lord'. The patron would provide some kind of protection or employment for the men who looked up to him, and they in turn were his 'clients', making themselves useful to him. At the very top of this pyramid was the emperor. (Claudius, AD 41–54, and Nero, AD 54–68, were the emperors during the period in which Paul wrote his letters.)

In the Greek and Roman world, the distinction between gods and men, such as heroes and rulers, tended to get blurred, and the imperial cult, in which the emperor was revered as a kind of god, was a way of controlling both the world of religion and the world of politics. (In the ancient world, as in some parts of the world today, religion and politics were never sharply separated anyway.) So statues, inscriptions, temples and coins all reinforced the message: Caesar is lord, and he has been enrolled in the ranks of the gods.

Who were the people at the bottom of this social pyramid? Certainly the very poor, of whom there were vast numbers. Many of the countless slaves were also among the lowest members of this structured society, although if a slave had a master of high status, that status might enhance his or her own. Another, more specific, answer to the question 'Who was at the very bottom of the ladder?' is especially important for us: those people who ended their days being crucified. This was a grisly fact of life in the Roman world. But such was the horror and obscenity of death by crucifixion – a penalty usually reserved for the lowest of the low – that men of letters such as Julius Caesar and Cicero avoided using words like 'cross' and 'crucify' in their writings. It was an unpleasant reality airbrushed out of polite society.

So Paul's message of a Messiah crucified like the lowest slave or criminal was bound to be subversive and even revolutionary. As we have seen, his teaching was tempered by realism, but there is no mistaking the revolutionary, political potential of this new faith. Key terms were politically 'loaded': in particular, did calling this crucified man Son of God, and Lord (*Kyrios*), make him a rival, or even a threat to Caesar? Even the word 'gospel' (*euangelion*) would have carried political overtones, being the technical term for news of victory.

A problem passage

So why, if Paul was the preacher of a revolutionary gospel, did he tell the Christians at Rome to obey those in authority (Romans 13.1–7)? Scholars have scratched their heads over this passage, and it is difficult to be sure why Paul said what he did. The likeliest explanation is Emperor Claudius' expulsion of Jews from Rome – probably in AD 49, just five or six years before Paul wrote those words. According to the book of Acts (18.2), Jews like Aquila and Priscilla, who were also Christians, were expelled at this time. The Roman historian Suetonius (who was really a bit of a gossip-monger) says the reason for the emperor's edict was the rioting in the Jewish communities of Rome, 'the instigator being Chrestus' (*impulsore Chresto*). Scholars usually take those words to mean that the arrival of the new Christian faith caused the unrest. If this is so, and all this happened just before Paul wrote Romans, it's not perhaps surprising that he urged the Christians at Rome to obey the authorities and to pay their taxes. Unfortunately, Paul's command to obey those in authority has been taken out of context, as with other teachings of his. People in power have quoted it to justify themselves and it has been used to perpetuate injustice, oppression and inequality. It has also to be remembered that the command to obey governments is not the only teaching on the subject in the New Testament: Jesus' saying 'Render to Caesar what is Caesar, and render to God what is God's' (Mark 12.17) sharply qualifies Christian obedience to the state, and puts it in proportion at the same time.

The parables of Jesus about the mustard seed and the leaven help us to understand Paul's perspective. The new faith which Paul proclaimed was unpromisingly small in its origins and undoubtedly subversive in its message of a crucified 'lord', but its day would eventually come. In the meantime, Christians, wherever they were in the social pyramid, had to live out their faith as best they could in their particular situation.

A riot of religions

That situation was permeated by paganism, a colourless, uninformative term for the varied, often colourful and lively polytheistic religions to be found throughout the Roman Empire. As well as the traditional gods and goddesses of Greek and Roman mythology, such as Zeus (Roman equivalent Jupiter) or Athene (Roman equivalent Diana), there were countless local cults as well. Not only were there temples and cults everywhere, but religious practices associated with them spread into every part of life; each household had its own gods, every social occasion would include an invocation or an offering to a deity, and even business contracts were sealed with religious oaths.

There were two other very prominent features of the religious scene. Given the proliferation of deities, there was a tendency to think of life and the world in terms of the law of the religious jungle: get whatever powers there may be on your side. Therefore magic was widespread, especially among the poor; incantations and the like were used, for example, by people who were sick or who were in love. At the other end of the social scale, the elite had the luxury of philosophy. This was not as academic as it sounds. Philosophies such as Stoicism or Epicureanism – both mentioned at Acts 17.18 – were both a creed and a way of life, and so, to all intents and purposes, religions, or substitutes for religion.

In such a world of extraordinary religious variety, most people's religion was not exclusive of others. (Here Jews and Christians were decidedly the odd ones out.) So many people sought the religious equivalent of a comprehensive life insurance policy. Archaeologists have not found an inscription 'to an unknown god' (Acts 17.23), but they have found an altar to all the gods and goddesses. This looks as though whoever built this altar wanted to be quite sure he didn't miss any gods out.

So Paul was both revolutionary and subversive. A man who spoke of a crucified God (1 Corinthians 1.25), and of 'one God, one Lord Jesus Christ' (1 Corinthians 8.6) lived and preached a creed which was profoundly counter-cultural. But how revolutionary would Paul have seemed against his Jewish background? This is both more complex and more sensitive.

The Dead Sea Scrolls

New discoveries and new research have shed fresh light on Paul's world, changing and even transforming our previous understandings of it. But it is important not to distinguish too sharply between what I am calling 'the Jewish world' and the wider Graeco-Roman world. For one thing, there were more Jews living outside Palestine – as far west as Massilia (Marseilles) – than lived inside Palestine. For another, Greek culture, in the wake of Alexander the Great's conquests, had permeated much of Palestine. So many Jews, possibly Jesus himself, would have been bilingual, speaking Greek as well as Aramaic.

Yet with that important caveat, our understanding of Paul's Jewish background has indeed changed. One day in 1947, some Bedouin shepherd boys happened to throw stones into a cave, and found there some ancient scrolls which turned out to be part of a religious library we now call the Dead Sea Scrolls. These scrolls have shown very clearly that we cannot generalize about Judaism. Jewish faith and practice then, as now, were varied, as Christian faith and practice always have been. Even more important for our understanding of Paul, we have learned that Judaism did not teach that we are saved by our good works. Generations of Christians since the Reformation have thought so, contrasting Paul's message that we are saved (justified) by grace through faith with the 'salvation by works' supposedly taught by Judaism.

This reassessment of the Judaism of Paul's day has been part of the process, referred to in the last chapter, of trying not to read Paul through a Lutheran 'lens'. The Dead Sea Scrolls themselves contain some moving testimonies to the grace and forgiveness of God. They were the product of a devoutly religious community which could be reasonably described as 'zealous for the law' (that is, the law of Moses). This inevitably affects how we understand some key words and ideas in Paul. For now, though, we need to remind ourselves that Paul never calls himself a 'Christian'. That word never occurs in his letters, and only three times altogether in the New Testament. Paul does not call himself a Jew either. That, too, is important. All that mattered to him was Christ, and 'a new creation' (for example, Galatians 6.15).

So Paul's relationship to his Jewish background was very different from his relationship to the wider Graeco-Roman world with its 'many gods and many lords' (1 Corinthians 8.6). As his letters show, there was a vital continuity between the new world into which Paul believed Christ had led him, and the Jewish world which, in part – but only in part – he had left behind.

But for all the continuity, there is no escaping the revolutionary implications of a crucified Messiah. Paul acknowledges that this message was an 'offence' to Jews (1 Corinthians 1.23). 'Offending' and 'offence' are strong words in the New Testament, and in verses such 1 Corinthians 8.13 they usually refer to damaging or destroying someone's faith. In his letter to the Galatians, Paul quotes a verse from Leviticus to mean that a crucified man died outside the law, and therefore under a divine curse (Galatians 3.13). So a crucified Messiah to devout Jews could only have seemed a contradiction in terms.

So the context in which Paul lived and worked was, as we should expect, richly varied and complex. Working out the 'nitty-gritty' of Christian living in such a world was never going to be easy. Paul's crossing of racial, religious and cultural boundaries makes him an especially interesting figure for our multi-cultural age, as I shall seek to show in a later chapter (Chapter 5, section iii). But, for all Paul's adaptability, the revolutionary implications of a message that a crucified man, not Caesar, was 'Lord' were unmistakable.

ii You are invited to a pagan supper party (1 Corinthians)

Dining out in Corinth

Being a Christian in the early Roman Empire was not easy. What should you do, for example, if you received an invitation like this: 'Apollonius requests you to dine at the table of the lord Serapis on the occasion of the coming of age of his brothers in the temple of Thoeris'? It could easily happen. The temple of Asclepius had been rebuilt by the Roman colonists at Corinth, and three dining rooms had been added on at a later stage on the east side of the temple courtyard. So birthday parties, other family events and social occasions were held in dining rooms such as these. Should a Christian go? The meat at such a meal would have been meat used, perhaps earlier in the day, in a sacrifice in the temple. To make matters worse, the party you have been invited to would probably include an invocation or prayer to Asclepius, the god of healing. After all, you are meeting on his premises! It was very difficult indeed for Christians to extricate themselves completely from the all-pervasive presence of the lively, colourful religious cults which we dub 'pagan', but which comprised such a major part of the religious, political and social life of Paul's time. Where should they draw the line?

The Christians at Corinth took different attitudes; as 1 Corinthians shows, these differences were damaging the church. Most Christians came from the lower socio-economic strata of society, but not all (1 Corinthians 1.26–29). We know the church at Corinth also included Erastus, the city treasurer, and Gaius, a man apparently with a house large enough to host the whole church, because Paul refers to them in his letter to the Romans (16.23), which he dictated while at Corinth. The more affluent, socially assured Christians, like Erastus and Gaius, probably took a very relaxed attitude: 'Why shouldn't we go? We know idols aren't real! We couldn't possibly be contaminated by setting foot inside a dining room on pagan premises!'

We have a fairly good idea that this was how Christians such as Erastus thought because Paul devotes three chapters in 1 Corinthians (chapters 8–10) to the question of whether Christians should eat meat associated with pagan sacrifices. As with the earlier chapter in this letter on marriage, we can work out when Paul is quoting the confident Christians at Corinth – the well-to-do ones like Erastus and Gaius. The New Revised Standard Version identifies three of their slogans: 'All of us possess knowledge' (8.1); 'No idol in the world really exists' (8.4); 'There is no God but one' (8.4). And, of course, Erastus and Co. may have said to themselves, 'We have our reputation to think about – not to mention our businesses. How many contracts might we lose if we turn down an invitation like this?'

Paul goes a long way towards agreeing with Erastus and his friends, as we can see from the opening of his argument (8.1–6). Their three slogans were all perfectly true! But they have to think of their fellow-Christians who don't share their confident knowledge: '… not everyone', says Paul, 'has this knowledge' (v. 7). Erastus was probably used to eating meat regularly, and most meat in Corinth would have been used in temple sacrifices before being sold in the meat market. But Erastus, being a confident man-of-the world, and now a *Christian* man of the world, could handle that. However, a poor Christian – let's imagine a slave called Demetrius – would probably, in his pre-Christian days, only ever have eaten meat at pagan religious festivals. He couldn't have afforded to pay for it himself, but at a religious festival he probably wouldn't have had to. So it was much harder for Demetrius to dissociate eating meat from his old pagan beliefs – especially if he was actually eating it on pagan premises! And Demetrius may well have had a less sophisticated view of idols than Erastus anyway.

What does Paul have to say, after agreeing so far with Erastus and friends? Paul's view of pagan idols is interesting: no, he agrees, they are not real, but they can still exercise demonic power. That is not as self-contradictory as it sounds, for even illusions can be destructive. Paul insists that the more self-confident have to think about the Christians whose conscience is not as robust as theirs (v. 7). Several times in these chapters

Paul refers to 'weak' Christians. He did not mean exactly what we mean by 'weak'. Basically, he was referring to the poorer Christians of Corinth, converts like our imaginary Demetrius who could not interact with paganism without damaging or even losing their new faith.

It is into this argument that Paul inserts his own *adaptability* as the model they should follow: 'all things to all people, that by all means I might save some' (1 Corinthians 9.22). Here we need to recognize that 'being all things to all people' (in the proverbial wording of this expression) was anything but the spineless, unprincipled behaviour it has come to denote today. For Paul, being all things to all people in the service of the gospel would have been costly, especially as he seems to have kept 'criss-crossing' between the Jewish and Gentile 'worlds'. If we imagine a Christian pastor seeking to be an effective minister to both sides in the sectarian conflict in Northern Ireland in the twentieth century, we shall be using the right kind of analogy. Paul, however, is free; he is an apostle, but forgoes both his freedom and his apostolic 'rights' in the service of the gospel, and in the interests of others. In all this he imitates Christ (1 Corinthians 11.1) who, in the words of another of Paul's letters, 'did not please himself' (Romans 15.3a).

Far more was at stake in this situation than simply hurting someone else's feelings:

> ... if others see you, who possess knowledge, eating in the temple of an idol, might they not, since their conscience is weak, be encouraged to the point of eating food sacrificed to idols? So by your knowledge those weak believers for whom Christ died are destroyed. (1 Corinthians 8.10–11)

We explore the contemporary relevance of this, and a similar passage (Romans 14—15), in Chapter 4 (section iv).

Holy Communion?

The socially mixed character of the church at Corinth is probably the key to understanding other problems in the church there. Some scholars think that the man guilty of incest (1 Corinthians 5) was a wealthy patron of the church; that was why no one had so far said anything to him. It is even more likely that the Christian who had taken another Christian to court (1 Corinthians 6) was one of the well-to-do ones; usually it was only the wealthy person who took legal action, and a local judge and jury would find it very difficult, with or without bribes, not to be biased in his favour.

The Lord's Supper at Corinth had also become problematic. Such celebrations were held almost certainly in the home of one of the more affluent members, because he had a house large enough to accommodate the whole congregation. But that was the trouble. Imagine a small church today having a special communion service to which special guests, church and civic leaders had been invited and the church was large enough only for them. Everyone else is squashed into a draughty, uncomfortable church hall. Sharing communion in those circumstances would hardly feel like *sharing* communion at all.

Gaius' house would have been big enough, it seems, to accommodate the whole church, not just a 'house-group' (Romans 16.23). It would have had a *triclinium*, a dining room where, at a dinner party, the well-off reclined at a kind of 'high table', while poorer guests sat on benches near the door, or were herded together in the *atrium*, the courtyard just outside. Is that what was happening at the Lord's Supper in Corinth? It seems likely. But that wasn't all.

The communion service at Corinth seems to have been all too like a pagan dinner party: 'each of you goes ahead with your own supper, and one goes hungry and another becomes drunk' complains Paul (1 Corinthians 11.21). Scholars have cited many examples from Graeco-Roman dinner parties of this kind of scenario. The first-century Roman poet Martial complains about a guest called Caecilianus who scoffed all the mushrooms and, on another occasion, complains to his host for serving himself different (and no doubt better) food than he served to his guest. Pliny, the Roman patrician and man of letters, prided himself on being enlightened: drinking the same wine as his poorer guests. But even Pliny made sure he served the cheapest wine on such occasions, and kept the best for himself another time!

In view of all this, it was no wonder that Paul goes on to say the equivalent of 'If it's a dinner party you want, go home!' (1 Corinthians 11.22). And no wonder, either, that Paul then says what he does about the body of Christ (1 Corinthians 12.12–27). We tend to reduce Paul's teaching here to banal platitudes, such as 'Everyone has their part to play' or 'We are all different, but we all belong'. Both points are true, but Paul is saying far more, as the situation in the church at Corinth shows.

The image of the body was a familiar political one. Usually, it was pressed into service by politicians and historians who wished the lower classes to remember their place (a familiar theme of Christian sermons in earlier centuries!). Paul adapted the image, and pressed its application to the church, in the light of the tensions there between 'the weak' and 'the strong'. So it is the voice of the 'weak' (that is, poor) Christian, like my imaginary slave called Demetrius, which we hear when the foot and the ear say words to the effect of 'Because I am not the hand/the eye, I do not belong' (vv. 15–16). And it is the voice of the 'strong', such as Erastus, which we hear when the eye and the head say – to the hand and the feet respectively – 'I don't need you' (v. 21).

Most important of all

The most famous passage Paul ever wrote, his 'hymn' to love in 1 Corinthians 13, acquires new significance against the background which modern scholarship has illuminated for us. Paul begins: 'If I speak in the tongues of mortals and of angels, but do not have love, I am a noisy gong or a clanging cymbal. And if I have prophetic powers, and understand all mysteries and all knowledge ... but do not have love, I am nothing' (vv. 1–2). Throughout this chapter, Paul is 'gunning' for all the things on which at least some Corinthians (we don't know how many) prided themselves – gifts such as speaking in tongues and inspired prophecies. Spiritual gifts though these undoubtedly were, the Christians at Corinth seem to have *over*-valued them. That is why Paul insists, in memorable language, on the primacy of love. To be without love is to be like the bronze jars placed round the edge of a Greek auditorium, and used as sound-amplifiers. It is well known that Paul's word for 'love' here is the Greek word *agape*. It is not true to say, as some have done, that Christians virtually invented this word. But it did come to have a distinctive meaning for them: the *agape* of God is utterly selfless and never-ending. Where did Paul derive this distinctive understanding of 'love' from? There can be little doubt about this: it was the cross of Christ.

I pointed out earlier that crucifixion was a ghastly, humiliatingly public execution reserved for the 'lowest of the low' – that is, most often slaves and subversive revolutionaries. So Paul was not exaggerating when he called the message of Christ crucified 'a stumbling-block to Jews and foolishness to Gentiles' (1 Corinthians 1.23): to religious people, the cross turned their ideas of God and religion upside down; for others, not least the most rational and successful, the cross turned upside down all that they understood by success, wisdom and, not least, status. This was because, above all, Paul says of the message of the cross, 'God's foolishness is wiser than human wisdom, and God's weakness is stronger than human strength' (1 Corinthians 1.25).

Placed alongside the later chapter on *agape* (love) this can only mean that the revelation of God's love in the cross of Christ provides an extraordinary new measure of selflessness and humility. This is why Paul mentions the cross so early on in this letter. The cross – and the resurrection which forms the climax (1 Corinthians 15) – are the interpretative keys to many of the problems which Paul discusses in between.

iii Thorn in the flesh, or pain in the neck? (2 Corinthians)

As if 1 Corinthians were not enough, Paul wrote again to Corinth. In fact, he wrote several times to them; some of his letters have been lost, as we noted in the last chapter. Even 2 Corinthians might be two letters 'stitched' together (chapters 1—9 and 10—13). If it isn't, it's hard to understand why Paul can be so 'upbeat' about the church in the earlier part of the letter (for example, 7.16), and later on sound as if his patience with them is exhausted (for example, 13.1–3). What had happened since Paul last wrote to them?

A sub-standard apostle

It's not too difficult to work out from 1 and 2 Corinthians that Paul did not exactly measure up to their idea of what an apostle should be. Apostles, the Corinthians thought, should be eloquent; Paul wasn't: '... they say "His letters are weighty and strong, but his bodily presence is weak, and his speech contemptible"'(2 Corinthians 10.10). What is more, proper apostles live at the church's expense, rather than engaging in manual labour, whereas Paul and his colleagues '... are poorly clothed, ... and we grow weary from the work of our own hands' (1 Corinthians 4.11–12). So it seems that, in the Corinthian view, apostles should be impressive in both speech and appearance. We don't know for sure what Paul looked like, but a description from a much later period is anything but flattering: 'small, bald and spindly-legged'![1]

But to return to our question: much had happened to Paul since he wrote the letter we call 1 Corinthians. It is possible that he had come to a new understanding of human suffering, and of his own sufferings in particular, as a result of what had happened to him in Asia. What exactly that was we can't be sure, but he says himself, 'we were so utterly, unbearably crushed that we despaired of life itself' (2 Corinthians 1.8). This can only mean an experience so severe that Paul, for a time, despaired of surviving it. For a relatively poor man such as Paul, with no family so far as we know, a serious illness would have had far-reaching economic consequences. In such a culture, too, illness damaged a man's self-esteem, and even his religious standing: what unspeakable thing had he done to be punished like this? Whatever this near-death experience was, Paul writes about suffering with a new intensity in 2 Corinthians, and never more so than in chapter 4, verses 7–12:

But we have this treasure in clay jars, so that it may be made clear that this extraordinary power belongs to God and does not come from us. We are afflicted in every way, but not crushed; perplexed, but not driven to despair; persecuted, but not forsaken; struck down, but not destroyed; always carrying in the body the death of Jesus, so that the life of Jesus may also be made visible in our bodies. For while we live, we are always being given up to death for Jesus' sake, so that the life of Jesus may be made visible in our mortal flesh. So death is at work in us, but life in you.

The exchange described in the last sentence is remarkable. The apostle embraces death, and his deathly experiences give life to the Corinthians. It sounds as though he is re-living the sufferings of Christ. But, then, that seems to be exactly what he says he is doing in a later letter (Colossians 1.24). (I shall return to what Paul has to say about suffering in Chapter 5.)

Despite the severe affliction in Asia, whatever it was, the tone of the letter which makes up our 2 Corinthians 1—9 is upbeat. Titus has returned from Corinth with good news about the church there (2 Corinthians 7.5–16) – so much so that Paul can even say he had every confidence in them (v. 16). But it was a false dawn.

A *new crisis*

There is an unmistakable air of crisis about the last four chapters of 2 Corinthians. By now, it is clear that Paul is seriously worried he may lose his church at Corinth, and for him that meant losing them to the Christian faith (11.1–4) altogether. As we have seen, his own apostleship is under fire once more (10.10, but also 11.5–11). He simply doesn't measure up to the standards expected! The opposition drives him to a passionate, and bitingly satirical self-defence, which in effect says: 'If the others are going to boast about their achievements, I will boast about – my weaknesses!' And so he does (11.23–33).

This is the situation in which Paul mentions another personal matter, his 'thorn in the flesh' (12.7). After referring indirectly to the visions God had given him, he goes on: 'Therefore, to keep me from being too elated, a thorn was given to me in the flesh, a messenger of Satan to torment me, to keep me from being too elated' (v. 7b).

What did he mean? We can discount the mischievous suggestion of one scholar that 'the thorn in the flesh' was Paul's wife! The thorn is unlikely to have been a person or persons; it was probably a very trying, debilitating, and even repellent illness or disability. We can only guess: a skin disease, an eye complaint or epilepsy have been suggested. Whatever it was, it clearly didn't disable Paul entirely, or he wouldn't have been able to do what he did. But it was a problem to the headstrong, self-confident Christians of Corinth; as one New Testament scholar has put it, to them a sick apostle was a contradiction in terms.

So there were a number of things which made the Corinthians, or at least some of them, wonder: 'Is this man really an apostle?' They expected a higher standard of eloquence than they got from Paul. They were used to their teachers hobnobbing with men of status, and certainly not working to earn their keep. So what was Paul doing, working as an employee of Priscilla and Aquila in their little shop down on the waterfront, making tents (Acts 18.1–3)? We can't be absolutely certain about all of these points. But when we read what Paul says in his own self-defence in these letters to Corinth, they are probably not far from the truth.

And this is where our evidence runs out; 2 Corinthians 10–13 is the last surviving letter of Paul to the church he founded at Corinth. His thorn in the flesh was a problem to them; they were a pain in the neck to him. Yet he cannot bring himself to give up on them. Among his last words to them are an assurance that he continues to pray for them (13.9), a final appeal to them to listen and to agree with one another (13.11) and, last of all, a verse which has become one of the most well known of all: 'The grace of the Lord Jesus Christ, the love of God, and the communion of the Holy Spirit be with all of you' (13.13).

As for Paul's ailments and afflictions, by this stage of his life they have become the raw material for some remarkable testimonies. In addition to 2 Corinthians 4.7–12 (quoted earlier), we have another, shot through with paradoxes (6.3–10): for example, 'We are treated as impostors, and yet are true' (v. 8b). As for the answer Paul says he received to his repeated prayer to be relieved of his 'thorn', it was not what he had asked for. But the answer he *did* receive may be reasonably considered the secret of his entire ministry: 'My grace is sufficient for you, for power is made perfect in weakness' (2 Corinthians 12.9).

iv What happens when outsiders come in? (Galatians)

Paul's letter to the Galatians confronts modern readers with tortuous arguments, embarrassing language about 'circumcision', and not-obviously-relevant details about Paul's life. So this letter is not exactly the most reader-friendly of Paul's compositions. But scholars have illuminated Galatians in a way which makes it extraordinarily relevant for contemporary churches. In this section we shall look at some of the new ways of understanding and reading this letter.

What had happened?

Some years after Paul and Barnabas first preached the gospel in Galatia (an area of central or southern Turkey today), more Christian teachers went there. Who they were, we don't know. But, clearly, person or persons unknown travelled to Galatia and preached what, in Paul's view, was 'another gospel' (Galatians 1.6–7). In referring to these anonymous 'rivals' of his, Paul sounds at his most intolerant (Galatians 1.7–9). What was at stake?

The issue Paul addresses in Galatians was to have profound implications for the future mission and identity of the new Christian movement: did Gentile converts to Christian faith have to become Jews in order to be 'proper' Christians? Paul and Barnabas took the view that they did not. The Christian preachers who followed them to Galatia believed they did. In practice, that meant observing the law of Moses as written down in the first five books of the Jewish scriptures (our Old

Testament). Among the most important laws were keeping the Sabbath, as all devout Jews did, not eating pork, and other foods forbidden in the Scriptures (for example, Leviticus 11), and, for the men, the painful rite of circumcision, the mark of God's covenant with the Jewish people (Genesis 17.9–14).

The debate may have been sparked off by an upsurge of nationalism in and around Jerusalem. (Less than two decades later, this Jewish nationalism, in response to Roman oppression, resulted in the Jewish Roman war of AD 66–70, and the destruction of Jerusalem.) This nationalism not surprisingly affected the church in Jerusalem. So this could have been one reason why a group of Jewish Christians opposed Paul and his gospel, in that they may have felt that Paul was letting the side down by, in their view, lowering standards. Why should God keep his side of the covenant, they may have reasoned, and help his people, if we break our side of it by letting in Gentiles who aren't even going to observe the law of Moses?

Thanks to recent scholarship, we can now see these opponents in a clearer light. They were not legalists, nor should they be thought of as reactionary. They almost certainly argued from Scripture: the law of Moses required circumcision of all Jewish males, and *therefore of all Gentile converts* to God's covenant people. What is more, according to Scripture, Abraham, long before Moses, was circumcised as a mark of God's covenant with him.

It is important not to misrepresent Paul's opponents in Galatia. Whenever we represent Paul's opponents as 'legalistic' or reactionary, or caricature Judaism in the same way, we are in danger of letting ourselves off the hook. We do not serve the cause of truth, or do justice to the gospel, by denigrating Judaism. If we can see that both Jesus and his apostle Paul shocked good, religious people, rather than bigoted reactionaries, we are more likely to appreciate why the gospel was such an 'offence' to the religious. (On this, see also Chapter 3, section vi).

Paul's opponents, then, almost certainly believed that they had good biblical and moral reasons for opposing him and his 'law-free' gospel: if the law distinguishing Jew from Gentile (the 'righteous' from the 'sinner') no longer applies, they reasoned, does this not open the floodgates to moral anarchy? It would be wrong to accuse Paul's opponents at this point of being *self*-righteous; 'righteous' in the vocabulary of Judaism meant being a member of God's people – with its consequent moral obligation to keep the law of Moses.

A third reason why they opposed Paul may have been political. If nationalism back in Jerusalem and Judaea was also a factor, then Paul's opponents may have felt that, if the new Christian converts from among the Gentiles lived like Jews, they might be safer from official harassment and pressures. In any case, a new religion easily became an object of suspicion to imperial officials and, if Gentile Christian converts became practising Jews, other Jews were more likely to become Christians too. Much was at stake, in this sense: was this new Christian movement *essentially Jewish*? If so, you would be able to tell who Christians were by their diet and by their observance of the Sabbath. As Roman authors sometimes remarked, often none too politely, Jews were noted for their refusal to eat pork, and by their odd habit of not working every seventh day. So the argument in Galatians is about what a Gentile had to do to join the new Christian movement or, more precisely perhaps, what were the conditions for belonging. This is the background to Galatians: a Jew–Gentile issue, provoked by another group of Jewish–Christian missionaries who came in the footsteps of Paul and Barnabas to oppose Paul's gospel.

Paul's argument

In his passionate response, Paul insists that his gospel doesn't come from a human source (Galatians 1.1, 11–12), not even from the church in Jerusalem. It was natural for the early Christians to look to Jerusalem for leadership (Acts 15.2, 6) – most of them, after all, were Jews. But Paul points out he's hardly been to Jerusalem since he became an apostle (1.17—2.1), although, on his second visit there, a sort of apostolic 'summit meeting' established that, while Peter should head up the mission to the Jews, Paul would head up the Gentile mission (2.6).

Paul may have crafted his argument in Galatians like a speech for the defence in a court of law. If he did – and some scholars have thought so – there may be some clues to help us understand Paul's trend of thought in the rhetorical handbooks of the ancient world. (Rhetoric played an important role in Paul's world; anyone who aspired to be a man – and it would be a man – of influence and status had to be an effective public speaker.) So how might Paul have gone about his task?

First of all, the beginning (its prescript or *exordium*) states the issue: Paul's gospel versus a bogus gospel (1.6–10). This, in Paul's view, was the stark contrast facing those Gentile Christian converts; if they started observing the law of Moses in order to complete their faith, what they were doing was not completing it, but undermining it. Next, the speaker presents the facts relevant to the case (the so-called *narratio*, 1.12— 2.14) – in this case, Paul's freedom from the influence of the Jerusalem church. Then there follow the fundamental points, the so-called *propositio* (2.15–21), and a detailed argument in support (the *probatio*, 3.1—4.31). The rest of the letter is taken up with 'exhortation' (*exhortatio*) and the conclusion (its postscript or *conclusio*), a kind of judicial summing up (6.15).

So what did Paul's argument add up to? There is a 'new creation' (6.15) – that's his conclusion – brought about by the cross and resurrection of Christ (1.1; 6.14). God in Christ has 'invaded' the world, and changed it for ever, abolishing at a stroke, so to speak, its most fundamental divisions: 'neither circumcision nor uncircumcision is anything ...' (6.15a). So the old distinction between Jew and Gentile was no longer absolute or final. Nor was this the only division of the ancient world to be challenged by Christ's coming: 'there is no longer Jew or Greek, there is no longer slave or free, there is no longer male and female; for all of you are one in Christ Jesus' (3.28).

God's new world, it must be said, is taking a long time to be realized in terms of equality, freedom and justice for slaves and for women. But the world's slowness to respond to God's 'invasion' does not affect the radical nature of Paul's argument. The heart of Paul's argument (Galatians 2.15–21) may have been part of what Paul said to Peter at Antioch (2.14b). (The proverbial 'fly on the wall' would have had an interesting time there.) Paul starts with what 'we' (that is, Jewish-Christians) can all agree: we were born Jews, not Gentile sinners, but we know no one is justified by doing what the law demands. Instead, we are justified only through Christ's faithfulness to God and our faith in him. (I return to this subject in Chapter 3.)

But then, what follows? Paul's opponents said: the law still stands, including the distinction between 'the righteous' and 'sinners', Jews and Gentiles, those who keep the law and those who don't. (In the view of Paul's opponents, these were three ways of saying the same thing.) So, if the traditional distinction between God's people, the Jews, and Gentile sinners no longer holds, doesn't this make Christ himself an aider-and-abettor of sin, because his gospel leads to lawlessness and immorality (Galatians 2.17)? This was why Paul's opponents thought his gospel was both shocking and subversive. Paul counters: Christ was *not* an 'agent of sin' (v. 17). Why? Because Christ has changed everything ('there is a new creation' (6.15)). Christ's death has 'broken the mould', creating a new world in which the believer's old way of life is crucified (v. 19), so much so that 'it is no longer I who live, but it is Christ who lives in me' (v. 20). That does *not* mean, Paul says, that I am cancelling out God's grace. It's more the other way round: if, after all, being a member of the Jewish people and observing the law keeps us right with God, Christ died for nothing (v. 21).

Paul appeals (Galatians 3) to the example of Abraham in his support – perhaps because his opponents were doing so. In Paul's view, Abraham shows that God's promise came first; the law, which Paul's Gentile converts were being pressed to keep, came later. And the point was: God's promise invites faith (3.6–9, 11), whereas God's law, naturally, requires *doing* (3.10–12). So the law speaks with two 'voices', a 'faith' voice (which spoke through the Abraham story, also part of the law – that is, the five books of Moses), and a 'doing' voice: 'Whoever does the works of the law will live by them' (Leviticus

18.5, quoted by Paul both in Galatians 3.12b, and in Romans 10.5). However, as Paul argues both in Galatians and Romans, the law also speaks with another voice, pointing in the direction of faith.

So what was the point of the law? What the law did was to conduct a sort of holding operation until faith came, like a childminder ensuring a child arrived safely at school from home (vv. 23–25). Therefore the outcome is (potentially) a worldwide community in which the old distinction between Jew and Gentile no longer pertains (v. 28). So the only law that matters now is the law of *Christ*: 'Bear one another's burdens, and in this way you will fulfil *the law of Christ* [my italics]' (Galatians 6.2). Or, to put it another way, 'the only thing that counts is faith working through love' (Galatians 5.6).

The letter to the Galatians addresses a first-century question about Gentile converts to a faith which had its roots in Judaism. Therefore it was about what we might call admission requirements to the Church. So, as I hope to show in Chapter 4, this letter has much to say to contemporary churches, especially those which, perhaps quite unwittingly, impose on newcomers expectations and standards which are not an essential part of Christian faith at all.

So, according to this letter, an evangelistic controversy shaped Paul's teaching on justification by faith. Did Gentile converts to Christian faith have to become Jews in order to be truly Christian? 'No,' said Paul, 'because God's grace in Christ, *not* being or becoming practising Jews, has justified us and them.' This is part of the so-called 'new perspective' on Paul. It has challenged the traditional view that (Christian) faith versus (Jewish) works lay at the heart of Paul's gospel. Leading exponents of the 'new perspective'– especially, in Britain, James Dunn and Tom Wright – have tended to interpret 'the works of the law', referred to by Paul, very specifically. So far from being good works in general, these works were what was expected of Gentiles becoming Jews (that is, proselytes), Sabbath observance and so on. They were 'boundary markers', distinguishing Jew from Gentile, and so helping to preserve Jewish identity.[2]

So, from this new perspective, the failure of the Jews, in Paul's eyes, was not advocating salvation by works, but exercising a kind of exclusive nationalism; their 'righteousness' (Romans 10.3) was wrong precisely because it was *theirs*, and by definition couldn't be anyone else's, unless that person became a Jew, by committing themselves to living as a Jew, and keeping the law in its entirety. This new perspective has helped us see more clearly the nature of the Jew/Gentile controversies in which the apostle was engaged, particularly at Galatia. At the same time, it may have rejected too much of the old 'Lutheran' understanding. We cannot go back to the old caricatures of Judaism as 'legalistic', but we must not go to the other extreme and underestimate the difference between the parent faith, Judaism, and its 'daughter faith', the new Christian movement.

But Paul hadn't yet done with these controversies, although the issues in the church at Rome were not quite the same as those in Galatia.

v Who was here first? (Romans)

Why did Paul write Romans? He wrote it in or around AD 57 from Corinth, or Cenchreae (near Corinth), as some of the personal details at the end of the letter show (Romans 16.1–2, 23). At the time of writing, Paul was on his way to Jerusalem with relief for the poverty-stricken Christians there, before taking the gospel to Spain (15.28). For that new evangelistic venture he needs the practical support of the church in Rome (1.10, 15.28–29), but this alone doesn't explain a letter of this length!

Corinth and Galatia were not Paul's only 'problem' churches. Rome, like Corinth, had 'mixed' house churches, but at Rome their members included both Jews and Gentiles. So we look first at this background, and then at some of the tensions and questions which arose in these small Christian communities which were not only racially mixed, but also culturally and religiously mixed.

Background

To begin with, Jewish Christians were probably in the majority in Rome. It would have been natural for the new Christian movement to take root first among Jewish people wherever they lived. After all, the Christians claimed that Jesus was the Messiah and, according to Acts, the synagogue was the natural place to start preaching this message. But in Rome the arrival of Christianity seems to have spelt trouble. We noted earlier in this chapter that, according to the Roman historian Suetonius, there were riots among the Jews in Rome 'instigated' by one 'Chrestus'. Behind this garbled reference to 'Christ' there were probably tensions between the Jews living in Rome who became Christians and those who didn't.

Whatever the cause of the disturbances, Suetonius tells us that the Emperor Claudius expelled all the Jews – probably in AD 49. But if all the *Christian* Jews left the city then – and Luke tells us (Acts 18.2) that Priscilla and Aquila were among them – then for a few years the Gentile Christians presumably had the place to themselves. But the Jewish Christians drifted back, perhaps after Claudius died in AD 54, and before Nero got into his murderous stride. We know Priscilla and Aquila were back by the time Paul dictated his letter to the Romans, because he asks the church to greet them (Romans 16.3–4).

So, to put it mildly, there may have been tensions – Jew-Gentile tensions – in the house churches at the time Paul wrote. Who had pride of place now? Jewish members could have said 'We were here first; and, anyway, the Christian faith is really a Jewish faith'; the Gentiles might have said, 'You had your chance, now it's our turn'. There are a number of verses in Romans which suggest that this reconstruction may not be far off the mark. (See especially Romans 11.1 and 1.11–18.)

Conflicting Christian convictions

This is the likely scenario addressed in chapters 14 and 15, as well as in chapters 9 to 11. Paul doesn't spell out that the differences were Jew-Gentile ones, but the language and the biblical quotations of 15.7–12 suggest that they were. To those involved, the differences were not trivial, even though they may seem so to us. For example, 'some believe in eating any-thing, while the weak eat only vegetables', and 'some judge one day to be better than another, while others judge all days to be alike' (14.2 and 14.5). In this situation Christians were either 'judging' or 'despising' each other. (Those two words keep recurring.) As at Corinth, there was a great deal more at stake than hurting one another's feelings, and so much more required than being nice to one another. It is very likely that neither group regarded the other as 'proper' Christians, or at least were tempted not to do so.

But why shouldn't Jews adapt to Gentiles, and vice versa – a little bit of 'give and take' on both sides? That would not have been right, because for some (if not all) it was a matter of con-science, and Paul does not require anyone to act against their own personal convictions (14.22–23). Much more important, they were to accept one another, as Christ accepted them; that is how Paul's argument begins and ends (14.1, 15.7). There could be no question of Christians 'ex-communicating' one another. Their verdicts on one another didn't matter, and were even impertinent: 'Who are you to pass judgement on servants of another?' (14.4a). What is more, 'we will all' – whatever our view – 'stand before the judgement seat of God' (14.10c).

In this situation, neither group is privileged over the other: Paul doesn't give the weak the right of veto over the strong, and he urges the strong to exercise their freedom by not trying to defeat the weak (14.19–21). (Admittedly, the apostle doesn't use here the language of 'the weak' and, by implication, 'the strong' in the way that he did in writing to Corinth, but essen-tially the same arguments are being recycled for a different situation.) The unity of the Church was more important than individuals having the satisfaction (even if it were possible) of knowing they were right, or that their view had prevailed. In a word, says Paul, 'Let us then pursue what makes for peace and for mutual edification' (14.19).

This is the most important 'agenda', even if each group thinks the other is wrong. The personal implications now, as well as then, are far-reaching indeed. Faced with a Christian with diametrically opposite convictions (and/or practice) to mine, and whose Christian integrity and commitment I may not question (because only God 'reads' hearts), what grounds have I for saying 'I know I'm right, and you're wrong'? This is startling stuff by most Christian standards, and I return to this passage in Chapter 4 with gay people, in particular, in mind.

It's clear that the Jew–Gentile issues at Rome were different from the main question at Galatia. There the church was asking: on what terms can Gentile Christians join the people of God? At Rome, it seems, they were asking questions like: how can Jew and Gentile Christians get along together in the same church or, given that many Jews had not accepted Jesus as their Messiah, had God now rejected Israel?

If this is the background, this may be why Romans is the most Jewish of Paul's letters. Only in Romans, for example, does he refer to Jesus' descent from King David (1.3), and describe him as 'the servant of the Jewish people' (literally 'of the circumcised', 15.8). Two verses early on in the letter set out the main themes: 'For I am not ashamed of the gospel; it is the power of God for salvation to everyone who has faith, to the Jew first and also to the Greek' (1.16). 'To the Jew first, and also to the Greek' is a phrase Paul uses twice more in this letter (2.9–10). 'First' may sound like preferential treatment on God's part, but it reflects historical reality: this new universal gospel had Jewish roots; the Messiah, Jesus, was Jewish; and his coming was the fulfilment of centuries-old prophecies (1.2; 3.21; 15.12).

In Romans Paul provides the longest summary and explanation of his gospel of any in his surviving letters. He did so because he urgently needed the support of the Christians in Rome, and also because there were libellous rumours flying around about Paul's preaching. In effect, people were saying: 'Paul is preaching that people can go on sinning because God accepts sinners, and the more we sin, the more of God's grace there will be' (Romans 3.8; 5.20; 6.1). We shall look in more detail at Paul's gospel in the next chapter.

Paul returns to his 'Jew–Gentile agenda' in Romans 9—11 (as well as in 14.1—15.13). Modern readers, not surprisingly, often struggle with Romans 9—11. Coming as these chapters do between two much more familiar and comprehensible passages (8.31–39 and 12.1–21), it's tempting for readers to stay on the train, as it were, and not get off at this particular station. But Romans 9—11 are well worth wrestling with, not least for their panoramic view of God's grace and providence. But this is to anticipate.

'Predestination' and freewill

Romans 9 has some stark, even repellent, expressions of God's apparent favouritism: 'I have loved Jacob, but I have hated Esau' (9.13). This sounds bad enough, but it gets worse. Paul seems to imply that God has predestined some to salvation, and some to destruction: 'So then he has mercy on whomsoever he chooses, and he hardens the heart of whomsoever he chooses' (v. 18). And why? Because these two groups of people are simply 'objects of mercy' and 'objects of wrath' (vv. 18 and 23).

So what are we to make of these three difficult chapters? According to the 'new perspective' on Paul, the apostle may have intended Romans 9—11 to be the climax of the whole epistle, rather than, as some scholars used to think, a digression. This sounds like being told that the hymn you can't stand is the best in the entire hymnbook!

It helps to see that Romans 9—11 pick up the questions which Paul set out as far back as chapter 3 – questions which were probably exercising the minds of the Christians in Rome. If God's people, the Jews, have been unfaithful, does that mean they are not his people any more? Is God unfair? In any case, if our disobedience actually serves God's purpose, can it be wrong? Perhaps there is a case for saying 'Let's do evil in order that good may come of it?' (3.1–8). As we noted earlier, Paul was accused of preaching precisely that.

These were – and are – big questions. They have their equivalents today: why are some people Christians, and not others? Does God 'choose' people? Does it all 'work out for the best' anyway? The root question for Paul was: where do Jew and

Gentile stand now in the providence of God? Hasn't the coming of Christ – and, even more, the largely negative response by the Jewish people to his coming – changed everything?

As I mentioned earlier, it is likely that Gentile Christians in the Roman house-churches may have begun to marginalize and disparage returning Jewish Christians. Paul explicitly warns the Gentiles: 'Now I am speaking to you Gentiles ... do not become proud, but stand in awe' (11.13a, 20b). So Gentiles are not to be either proud or arrogant about their newly given Christian status. But what is Paul saying about his fellow-Jews here? It helps to begin at the end, and work backwards; as with a who-dunnit, the earlier sections make sense in the light of the conclusion, especially 11.25–32. Here Paul is gloriously positive: not only does he roundly declare that in the end 'all Israel' will be saved (11.26), but he also insists that, through all the vagaries of human faithlessness, God's ultimate purpose is unwavering: 'God has imprisoned all in disobedience so that he may be merciful to all' (11.32).

The negative-sounding 'imprisoned' is difficult for the modern reader. Paul means: God holds fast to us even in our disobedience. The Parable of the Prodigal Son in Luke 15 is the story of a father who both lets go (compare God 'handing over' in Romans 1.18–32, discussed in section iii), but also holds fast to his wayward son. Paul too, though in very different language, is writing of a waiting Father who wishes to show mercy to all. But how does this positive declaration shed light on the dark language which has preceded it?

It helps to keep in mind the situation in the house-churches of Rome after Jewish Christians, such as Priscilla and Aquila, returned. Does a Gentile Christian now say to them, 'I'm afraid your non-Christian family and friends are beyond the reach of God's mercy, because "Israel" – once God's own people – rejected God's Messiah when he came to them'? Paul is arguing throughout these chapters that God works with two groups of people: those whom he has chosen, and those whom, *for the moment*, he has not chosen. To begin with, those groups were represented by Isaac and Ishmael, Jacob and Esau respectively (9.6–14). The language, as we saw, is difficult: 'I have loved

Jacob, but I have hated Esau' (v. 13). But this was a Semitic way of saying 'I *preferred* Jacob to Esau',[3] and even that, as Paul's conclusion shows, was a temporary preference. God's ultimate purpose is to have mercy on everyone.

But now, with the coming of Jesus, roles have been reversed: Jacob, we might say, is 'out' and Esau 'in'. (This is what Paul is wrestling with here.) But this is not the final state of affairs. God works on: just as Israel's rejection of Jesus was instrumental in Gentiles coming to faith, so the Gentiles, in turn, will be the means of Israel coming, in the end, to faith in Jesus (11.13–27).

Or will they? Here we touch on one of the most sensitive and hotly debated points of all in the study of Paul. Does Paul mean that his fellow-Jews will one day come to faith in Jesus? Or does he mean that they will be reconciled with Gentile Christians in a new community centred on God, rather than on Jesus? If the latter, is it wrong for the Christian evangelist to seek to convert Jews? Some scholars have argued that it is, pointing out Paul's positive statements about Israel in Romans 11.25–32, including a quotation from Isaiah (Isaiah 59.20–21), where – and this is one of the much-debated points – it is not clear whether 'the Deliverer' is a reference to God or to Christ: 'Out of Zion will come the Deliverer ...' (Romans 11.26). A sentence later, Paul insists, with reference to Israel's ultimate destiny, 'the gifts and the calling of God are irrevocable' (v. 29). It is this passage especially which has led some scholars to outline a 'two covenant' view: according to this, Paul envisaged God saving Israel without faith in Christ, for his 'old' covenant with them still stands (11.29), and the 'new' covenant – with Christ's saving death at its heart – is God's covenant with the Gentiles.

Such an interpretation of the New Testament, and of Paul in particular, is understandable in the light of Jewish–Christian sensitivities after the Holocaust. In any case, Christians will do well to abandon the aggressive proselytizing which has so alienated, and even frightened, not only Jews, but also people of other faiths. Tragically, there has been far too much in Christian history of the Gentile arrogance Paul warns against here – and much, much worse than arrogance. But in the light of this letter to the Romans, and Paul's other major letters, we must surely conclude that Paul saw the gospel as a truly universal gospel – for Jew and Gentile alike.

Before we leave Romans 9—11, we look briefly at the underlying theme of 'predestination'. This, like other words we have already discussed in this book, is unhelpful and misleading. But it has found its way into Christian vocabulary, and for that reason we address it here.

Many readers of the New Testament (not just Paul) are troubled by language which suggests that God predetermines everything: in particular, that God decides who will become Christians, and who will not. It all sounds monstrously unfair and, if God *does* do this, what place is left for human freewill?

It is vital, if we are to understand this language of predestination properly, that we recognize that it is *the language of grace*. Grace is that mysterious quality of love and respect for the other person which gives the other person space. Grace works within our human freedom without undermining it or manipulating it. The best illustration of this comes from our own human experience, especially marriage and friendship. We use both the language of predestination and human freewill of marriage: 'they were meant for each other' *and* 'they decided to get married'; 'this was a marriage made in heaven' *and* 'they got married at St Andrew's Church'.

So, in Romans 9—11, we have a kind of 'sandwich'. In between what Paul says in chapters 9 and 11 about God's mysterious grace at work in all the ups and downs of human history there is, in chapter 10, the other side of the coin: the space for human freedom and responsibility.

Conclusion

As with Galatians, the 'new perspective' on Paul has helped us to see more clearly how much Jew–Gentile relations helped to shape his letter to the Romans as well. But it is in this letter that we can see Paul's teaching beginning to 'outgrow' the original controversies in which it was forged. If that were not so, or if the early Church had not seen that, Paul's letters would never have come to form part of the Christian Scriptures.

vi 'The powers that be' (1 Thessalonians, Philippians, and later letters)

Half a century ago, George MacLeod, the founder of the Iona Community in Scotland, wrote these words about the churches of his day: '... the greatest criticism of the Church today – and this goes for all of us – is that no-one wants to persecute us. The reason is a little frightening: there is really nothing to persecute us about'.[4]

That could not be said of Paul's churches, especially the churches at Thessalonika and Philippi, where Roman influence was strong. Although we don't know very much about the persecution of Christians in Paul's day, we can be quite sure that the young Christian communities would have felt very vulnerable and exposed. Jewish communities must have been; and Christians, as members of a new, strange, and even offensive faith, would have been even more so.

Some scholars of earlier generations were inclined to extol the benefits that the Roman Empire brought. But that was to take the propaganda statements of Roman writers, such as the poets Virgil and Horace, at face value – or, if such scholars had opined that the British Empire was a good thing, to imagine that the Roman Empire was similar. It is true that the Empire, established by Caesar Augustus from 27 BC, replaced civil war with a kind of peace, but this *pax Romana* was imposed and maintained by oppression and terror (including crucifixions), and the Empire itself benefited only a small elite at the expense of the many.

Thessalonika

Roman 'law and order' was also kept by religious means (as we saw in the introduction to this chapter). This was very evident at Thessalonika. Archaeology has brought to light not only relics of pagan cults: the cults of Serapis, with its sexual symbolism, of the wine god Dionysus, with its accompanying orgies, and of the local hero/god Cabeirus, but also relics of the civic cult. In 27 BC, the effigy of Emperor Augustus replaced that of Zeus, the father of the gods, on the coins of Thessalonika, and the emperor was venerated as divine.

So Roman influence at Thessalonika was probably strong, and Luke himself seems to have thought so. Paul and Silas, according to Acts, were accused of acting 'contrary to the decrees of Caesar' by saying that 'there is another king, named Jesus' (Acts 17.7). Although Luke goes on to say that the city authorities, the 'politarchs', let them out on bail, the Christians were clearly taking no chances: they packed Paul and Silas off to Beroea, a little further south that very night (v. 10).

This background helps to explain many of the details in 1 Thessalonians, Paul's earliest letter. It is full of anti-imperial language. What matters, Paul says in effect, is not Caesar's victories, but God's. It is God's *euangelion* (2.2, 8) – a word used in imperial propaganda – which is 'good news', not Caesar's. And more important than any visit from Caesar, or even meeting with him, is the coming of Jesus, and their meeting with Jesus (1 Thessalonians 4.15, 17, where Paul uses political words again: *parousia* ('coming') and *apantesis* ('visit'): both these words tended to be used with reference to visiting dignitaries and even emperors).

So we must imagine a young church socially, politically and religiously exposed in its community. It seems that some had already died even in the short time since Paul had been there (1 Thessalonians 4.13–14); had they been martyred for their faith? The 'politarchs', the local authority, were responsible for administering the oath of loyalty to the emperor, and dealing with violations of it. There is evidence that, in other parts of the Roman Empire, Romans and non-Romans alike were expected to inform on those suspected of disloyalty to the emperor, and even to help track down such offenders. It is no wonder that Paul tells them, 'encourage one another' (4.18). Did they feel Paul had left them in the lurch? Paul sounds on the defensive at one point, and seems to make a point of saying, 'though we had already suffered ... at Philippi, as you know, we had courage in our God to declare to you the gospel of God in spite of great opposition' (1 Thessalonians 2.2). It is no wonder, either, that Paul uses warlike language (1 Thessalonians 5.8); they are up against it, and they know it. Their faith, it seems, was holding, and their love for each other, but what of their hope? One scholar has noted that Timothy reported back to Paul that the Thessalonians were doing fine in faith and love, but perhaps they were beginning to lose hope.

If we are right in imagining the situation of the Christians at Thessalonika as vulnerable, and even dangerous, Paul's concluding words are all the more remarkable: 'See that none of you repays evil for evil ... Rejoice always ... give thanks in all circumstances ... may your spirit and soul and body be kept sound and blameless at the coming of our Lord Jesus Christ. The one who calls you is faithful, and he will do this' (1 Thessalonians 5.15a, 16, 18, 23b, 24).

Philippi

Philippi was another city where Roman influence was strong. It was a colony, so there was a strong military presence. So, again, it's not surprising that Paul uses plenty of political imagery when writing to the Philippians. This is the only letter, for example (apart from the later letters – almost certainly not Paul's – to Timothy and Titus), where Paul calls Jesus *soter*: 'saviour'. This may have been another borrowing from imperial propaganda (Philippians 3.20). The reference comes, significantly, just after Paul had reminded them of where their own 'government' was – in heaven. The letter to the Philippians is, on the whole, Paul's happiest. His references to them seem more carefree, despite the abrupt, crude warning about 'Judaizers': clearly, there was still pressure on Gentile converts to become Jewish Christians (3.3). The best-known passage in Philippians, however, is theologically the richest: the hymn which Paul quotes in chapter 2:

Let the same mind be in you that was in Christ Jesus, who, though he was in the form of God, did not regard equality with God as something to be exploited, but emptied himself, taking the form of a slave, being born in human likeness. And being found in human form, he humbled himself and became obedient to the point of death – even death on a cross. Therefore God also highly exalted him and gave him the name that is above every name, so that at the name of Jesus every knee should bend, in heaven and on earth and under the earth, and every tongue should confess that Jesus Christ is Lord, to the glory of God the Father (vv. 5–11).

There has been a lively debate among scholars about the meaning of this hymn (whether composed by Paul himself or not, we don't know). Many think this is the earliest reference to what the Church later called the doctrine of the Incarnation: God sharing human life as a human being. Others have suggested that verse 6, 'in the form of God', is another way of saying 'in the image of God'. If so, the hymn is contrasting Jesus with Adam, also made in God's image (Genesis 1.26). But whereas Adam reached upwards to grasp divine status, Jesus humbled himself. (Ezekiel's words about the prince of Tyre provides an interesting commentary here – Ezekiel 28, especially verses 1–2 and 11–13.)

The incarnational interpretation is, on balance, the more probable of the two, but here we note again the subversive potential in the Roman Empire of a poem like this: a crucified man, whose voluntary humiliation is both a pattern for humans and a reflection of God's character, was raised by God to the heights.

The heavy Roman presence at both Thessalonika and Philippi shows how 'the powers that be' were a threatening, daily reality for the small Christian communities there. So to affirm 'Jesus is Lord', rather than 'Caesar is Lord', when this same Jesus had suffered the ignominious death of crucifixion, was to make a breathtakingly subversive affirmation. It flew against all perceived reality.

Colossians and Ephesians

Other letters, bearing Paul's name, also have things to say about 'the powers'. There are (at least) two schools of thought about the letters to the Colossians and the Ephesians. Some scholars see a real difference between these letters and the ones we have looked at in the earlier sections of this chapter. So did Paul really write them? Would the Paul who declared 'in Christ there is neither slave nor free, male nor female' (Galatians 3.28) really have told wives to obey their husbands, and slaves their masters (Colossians 3.18—4.1, Ephesians 5.21—6.9)? We can't be sure, and the uncomfortable fact is that these 'Household Codes', as scholars call them, are in the New Testament, whether they were written by Paul or not.

But these letters to the Colossians and Ephesians also have things to say about 'the powers'. A verse in Colossians is remarkably positive about them: 'for in him [that is, in Christ] all things in heaven and on earth were created, things visible and invisible, whether thrones or dominions or rulers or powers – all things have been created through him and for him' (Colossians 1.16). Whoever wrote these words (part of another powerful hymn – verses 15–20), it is a staggering claim – for a 'Christ' who had been crucified, at the most, a mere half-century ago. And what a surprise to find these words written by Paul, or in the name of Paul, the very man who had accused 'the rulers of this age' of crucifying this same Christ (1 Corinthians 2.6), and who assured the church at Rome that no 'rulers' or 'powers' would be able to separate them from God's love in Christ (Romans 8.38–39). The hymn here in Colossians gives us, well and truly, 'the big picture': the Christ celebrated here is a cosmic Christ. So whatever Paul was thinking of when he referred to 'the powers' here, they fall within, not outside, the creative purpose of God in Christ.

The letter to the Ephesians, thought by many scholars to be modelled on Colossians, is also quite clear that Christ risen and ascended has put the powers, including every 'rule, and authority and power and dominion', in their place (Ephesians 1.21–22). But who and where are these powers according to Ephesians? Whatever they are, they are not human – so a warning, perhaps, against demonizing political leaders, however unsatisfactory they may be: 'our struggle is not against enemies of blood and flesh, but against the rulers, against the authorities, against the cosmic powers of this present darkness, against the spiritual forces of evil in the heavenly places' (Ephesians 6.12).

So the different letters bearing Paul's name give us several different perspectives on 'the powers that be'. The letters to the Thessalonians and to the Philippians provide graphic 'cameos' of life for small vulnerable Christian communities under the Roman Empire. To adapt George MacLeod's words, there would have been plenty of people poised to persecute them, and much, in the view of those people, to persecute them about. These are 'the rulers of this age' responsible for the public execution of Jesus of Nazareth outside Jerusalem in the year AD 29. These are the authorities whom, if the Christians in Rome are to live discreetly and responsibly, they must obey (Romans 13.1–7), unpleasant though they are.

And yet – such is the all-embracing worldview of this apostle and those who wrote in his name – even these powers were somehow created in and for Christ, however much they have forgotten, or abused, their original remit. Like most other biblical writers, Paul will not abandon the world to the devil or anyone else. It is God's, and so, in the end, are its rulers. So even though Ephesians may seem to some a 'cop-out', transferring 'the powers' to a metaphysical, spiritual realm, it carries a healthy reminder to Christians to demonize no one. But that still requires open-eyed realism.

Conclusions

Scholars, of course, do not have a monopoly of insights. But they are among the best qualified to tell us about the historical background of Paul's letters, and what the words he used would have meant both to himself and to his contemporaries. The task, though, of interpreting Paul for today falls to everyone who reads his letters. Here I wish merely to draw out the implications of one very sensitive area of debate, which we have touched upon in this chapter, before preparing the way for our exploration, in Chapters 4 and 5, of Paul's relevance for us today.

Paul's Jewish background

As we have seen, scholars have radically re-assessed what New Testament writers say about 'the Jews'. (Some scholars use quotation marks here to indicate the danger of stereotyping an entire people.) They have been led to do so, not only by the terrible events of World War Two, but also by a growing realization that many New Testament statements about 'the Jews', particularly in the Gospels of Matthew and John, are both *rhetorical* and *polemical*. So what earlier generations took to be straightforward factual descriptions of, for example, the Pharisees, we are now having to re-think as weapons in a sort of first-century propaganda war, as relations between Jews and Christians tragically worsened.

It is clear from the Gospels that Jesus offended Pharisees, almost certainly on religious and moral grounds. This was not because the Pharisees were 'legalists' in the way that that term is often understood; rather, the Pharisees may have thought that Jesus, by actively seeking out, and eating with, the likes of Zaccheus, was undermining the religious and moral fibre of the nation, and so delaying the coming of God's kingdom.

In Paul's day, and for some time afterwards, Christians and Jews were still members of the same religious family – which was far from monolithic, as the Dead Sea Scrolls have shown. True, real differences were emerging, and Paul himself must have contributed mightily to them in his insistence that Gentile Christian converts should not have to 'Judaize'. The observation that Jew and Christian were still part of the same family helps to put the harsh language and the polemics of the New Testament writings in a different perspective. They cannot properly be called 'anti-Semitic'; different Jewish sects who disagreed passionately about points of religious practice would often 'trade insults' in this way.

In interpreting New Testament texts critical of Israel and 'the Jews', Christian readers might bear in mind the old adage 'If the cap fits, wear it!' A recent commentator on Luke's Gospel observes how Luke introduces the Parable of the Pharisee and the Publican (Luke 18.9–14): the parable was directed 'at those who were sure of their own goodness'. She writes: 'it is natural to think that the Pharisees were in mind. Yet Luke does not say this, and his more general phrasing suggests that he knew that such could be found elsewhere, perhaps even within his church.'[5]

Paul for today

Why did Paul's writings become part of the Church's Scriptures? It can only have been because the whole Church had recognized that what he had had to say to the churches in Galatia and all the other places to which he wrote was important for the Church everywhere. And if everywhere, then, presumably, for always – even, perhaps, today.

In the second half of this book we explore in what ways Paul's writings may have something to say to the churches and the wider world of the twenty-first century. Here it will be useful to recognize that this is not a straightforward matter, and two viewpoints need to be challenged at the outset. First, a fundamentalist or literalist approach to Paul will not do. The Bible itself, surprising though it may sound, does not support such an approach to its sacred texts. (I return to this in the section of Chapter 5 entitled 'Paul and modern fundamentalism'.)

The Bible bears witness to an incarnational faith. That is to say, biblical faith is always enculturated in the language, concepts and speech-forms of its day. Its writers were inspired *and also* were men of their day. (One widely perceived problem with the Bible today is the likely fact that all its writers, as far as we know, were male.) Those two qualities – being inspired and being human – belong together; divine inspiration makes a person not superhuman, but more fully human than before. What that means when we come to interpret particular passages of Paul takes some teasing out. But it needs to be done.

At the opposite extreme, we need to be wary of an unquestioning approach to the norms and values of our own culture, including an uncritical view of our human experience. We cannot judge Paul at the bar of our own experience, however much we value that experience. It is not enough to seek to 'apply'

74

Paul's message, and make him relevant for our time. As Dietrich Bonhoeffer once observed, the Bible does not need to be made relevant; its relevance is axiomatic. So what is needed?

I suggest a conversation between ourselves and St Paul. But it has to be a proper conversation. If we do not 'listen' to him by paying attention to what he really said, as opposed to what we think he said, or would like him to have said, that is not really to converse at all. On the other hand, if we suppress what we are really thinking, express our misgivings, even our objections to what our conversation-partner is saying, that is not a genuine conversation either.

Does such an approach do justice to the status of Paul's writings as part of the Christian Bible? That depends a great deal on what we bring to the conversation. If we bring only suspicion, rather than a suspicion which we are prepared to replace by love, Paul will have little for us. If we bring an unquestioning approach because we have decided in advance that Paul agrees with us, Paul may not persuade us otherwise. We might prefer to say that we agree with Paul, but how can we tell the difference?

Notes

1 Description of Paul from the second-century Christian writing, *The Acts of Paul and Thecla*, quoted in M. J. Harris, *The Second Epistle to the Corinthians* (NIGTC Commentaries), Eerdmans/Paternoster, 2005, p. 699.

2 For further reading on this 'new perspective' on Paul, see the suggestions in the Bibliography.

3 Compare the more Semitic version of a saying of Jesus in Luke 14.26 with its less Semitic version in Matthew 10.37.

4 G. MacLeod, *One Way Left*, Iona Community, Iona, 1956, p. 130.

5 J. Lieu, *The Gospel of Luke*, Epworth, Norwich, 1997, p. 141.

3

God's New World

So what was Paul's life's work? What were the fundamental convictions behind his mission? This is what we now need to explore, not least because his message, like the man himself, has often been misunderstood or misinterpreted. Even interpretations of Paul which were appropriate enough 100 years ago may not be so now. We explore, first, Paul's core beliefs about the cross and resurrection of Jesus, contrasting them with some contemporary misunderstandings about both. In section ii of this chapter we turn to what Paul teaches about faith, a much over-used and misunderstood word today. This will include a discussion of a relatively new question: when Paul talks about being justified 'by faith', whose faith does he mean? A third section takes a fresh look at the Christian life according to Paul, noting differences from some of our contemporary ideas. After a more personal question, 'Did Paul practise what he preached?', we look in section iv at his language about the future, asking how it is to be understood today. A final section asks why Paul's gospel shocked many religious people of his time, suggesting that it should have a similar impact today.

i Christ crucified and risen

We begin where Paul's life began again. Although we cannot recapture exactly what happened to him on the Damascus Road, he and the author of the Acts of the Apostles both believed that he had encountered the risen Christ. So we need to begin with the resurrection. But many people today – both in and outside the churches – have questions and doubts about the resurrection, so some preliminary ground-clearing may be useful.

The meaning of the resurrection

The American-born theologian Dan Hardy said that when he came to the UK he found that nobody was able to preach the Easter message. Apart from telling the Gospel stories, and saying that you had to believe in the resurrection in order to be a Christian, no one (it seemed) could say what it *meant*.[1] I think this observation is broadly correct, although in the churches the problem may be more serious still.

First, many professing Christians are unsure about the resurrection and, as at Christmas, choose to repress their doubts and forget their questions, concentrating instead on spring and the new life returning to gardens and countryside. After all, they reason, we can surely have 'kingdom values' and an inspiring creed without a supernatural, even incredible event, at the heart of our faith. Some may also be aware that the Gospel narratives don't match up in every detail. So what kind of evidence is this? Or, if people retain some kind of faith in the resurrection of Jesus, that resurrection is often misunderstood. We talk of Jesus 'coming back to life' – which is not the message of Easter at all. In the Gospels, there are stories of people such as Lazarus and the daughter of Jairus coming back to life, but they came back to *this* life. What the New Testament says is that God raised Jesus into *eternal* life. This helps to explain why his appearances to his disciples seem so mysterious: he is not always recognized, he comes and goes without warning as it were. At the same time, the Gospel writers stress that this was real; the risen Jesus was no ghost.

Paul can help us to understand not so much what happened as what it all means. But it is important to say that, in Paul's view, *something* happened. It is Paul who gives us the earliest evidence for the resurrection, in a letter he wrote in AD 54 or 55 (the Gospels being written some years later):

For I handed on to you as of first importance what I in turn had received: that Christ died for our sins in accordance with the scriptures, and that he was buried, and that he was raised on the third day in accordance with the scriptures, and that he appeared to Cephas, then to the twelve. Then he appeared to more than five hundred brothers and sisters at one time ... Last of all, as to someone untimely born, he appeared also to me (1 Corinthians 15.3–8).

This is a very early tradition about the resurrection. Paul says it was a tradition he 'in turn had received', and that was likely to be soon after his own conversion in the early 30s – within a few years, at most, of the original events. Paul is summarizing the experiences and testimonies of the first apostles. The Church has never claimed to have more 'evidence' for the resurrection than that.

For Paul, then, the resurrection of Jesus was utterly real, as real and as life-transforming as God's existence. (The resurrection, in many ways, is another way of talking about the power of God.) It was the foundation of everything else Paul came to believe, and the starting-point in many of his letters. It's as if he were saying to his listeners (his letters would be read aloud): 'Hear everything that follows in the light of this!' It's especially noticeable how the beginning and the end of Galatians connect: 'Paul, an apostle ... through Jesus Christ and God the Father who raised him from the dead' (1.1), thus bringing about 'a new creation' (6.15).

The first verses of Galatians show that the resurrection is not just about what happened to Jesus; it is also about God, and what God did ('... who raised him from the dead'). Other letters show the same pattern. So Jesus can now be called 'Lord' because God raised him to 'God's right hand' (Romans 8.34), which, as Luther taught, meant everywhere. So what, according to Paul, does it all mean? The resurrection was a kind of victory: a victory over death, certainly (1 Corinthians 15.54), but it was more than that. Paul came to see that God raising Jesus from the dead cast a flood of light on what had happened before – above all, a flood of light on Jesus' death by crucifixion.

The resurrection is, as it were, God's signature across the life and death of Jesus. So, without the resurrection, the life and teaching of Jesus, like those of Socrates or Gandhi, might inspire, but his death would be at best a tragedy, and at worst a contradiction of all that he had taught about God. For there is a difference between Jesus, on the one hand, and Socrates and Gandhi, on the other. Unless Jesus was completely deluding himself about the God he talked about, we have to say that he and his God were 'hand in glove'. So the death of this 'Son of God' raised profound questions about his God. Had his God abandoned him? Or, if God had somehow willed or permitted that terrible crucifixion, was that God's last word? Was there nothing but silence from heaven?

The resurrection can be made to sound like a 'happy ever after' story, and we must not make it that. The crucifixion was real, humiliating and agonizing, and no resurrection could ever alter that. But the resurrection transformed Paul's understanding of the cross, and so to that we now turn.

The meaning of the cross

We don't know for certain why Paul persecuted the first Christians, but we can be sure that he would have found their claim that a crucified man was God's Messiah profoundly shocking and offensive. What Paul would have thought about the executed Jesus can be gauged from a verse he quotes from the Old Testament in one of his letters: a crucified man is under God's curse (Deuteronomy 21.23, Galatians 3.13). So the resurrection of this man, condemned as a criminal under the law of Moses, could only mean that God had overruled the verdict of the law.

So a revolution began in the life and the thought of Paul. It was as if a staunch Protestant at the height of the troubles in Northern Ireland had suddenly discovered that a man lynched as a republican criminal was in fact a holy man of God. But with Jesus it was more than that. It was all or nothing. Either Jesus really had died a criminal under the curse of God, or God had vindicated him as God's own Messiah and right-hand man (part of what was meant in calling Jesus 'Lord'). And this revolutionary alternative was precisely what Peter, according to Acts, proclaimed on the day of Pentecost (Acts 2.36).

The way in which the resurrection turned upside down the

meaning of the cross helps to explain why Paul has so much to say about both. People who come to Paul from the Gospels are often puzzled by how few references there are to the life and teaching of Jesus, compared with what Paul says about the cross and resurrection. He never mentions the miracles or parables of Jesus; he refers twice to other teaching of Jesus (1 Corinthians 7.10, 9.14), tells the Corinthians that he received the tradition about the Lord's Supper 'from the Lord' (1 Corinthians 11.23), and seems to echo the words of Jesus in a few other places as well (for example, Romans 14.14). But that is about all.

This is one reason why so many people struggle with Paul, but one way to look at the cross is to think of it as not apart from the life of Jesus, but as the summary of that life. The death of someone for a cause to which he has devoted his life could be fairly described as his last and greatest sacrifice. In a similar way, the death of Jesus was his most important statement. Like his teaching, it expressed the mystery of the kingdom of God. The cross was also the climax of his mission and healing ministry. Through Jesus' death and resurrection, according to Paul, people came into the kinds of experiences that characters in the Gospels – such as Zaccheus, a leper, the woman accused of adultery – found: acceptance, healing, forgiveness, and a new beginning. So the cross of Jesus represents the summary and climax of his whole life; and across both that life and death, as God's 'yes' to Jesus, was the resurrection.

What the cross does not mean

At this point we need to look at one widely held view of the cross which is wrongly attributed to Paul. Some hold that the death of Jesus was the necessary sacrifice which had to be made in order to satisfy the justice of God – otherwise, God, in his love, could not forgive us. This is a serious misunderstanding of the cross. Jesus' death can, and should, be understood as paying the penalty for human sin. You could say the same about the death of Socrates, who also paid the penalty for human sin – in his case, the idolatry of Athens in the fifth century BC. In the Christian view, however, it is *who Jesus was* that makes all the difference.

We can't properly understand Paul without appreciating the deep gulf which, in his view, has opened up between humankind and their Creator. But Paul nowhere sets up a tension between the love and the justice of God. The New International Version misleadingly translates the same Greek word (*dikaiosune*) in Romans 3.21–26 as God's 'righteousness' in verses 21 and 22, and God's 'justice' in verses 25 and 26. It is an important principle of translation that you don't always translate the same word every time in the same way, but here it is simply misleading. We need to ask what this key word means.

God's 'righteousness' in the Bible really means God's consistency: God's faithfulness to himself. And that, in turn, means two things: God's commitment to the moral order, which reflects his own will and purpose, and also God's commitment to putting things right when they go wrong. God keeps his word and lives up to his obligations, which, according to the Old Testament, include God's promise to be Israel's God even when Israel was faithless. For Paul, what has happened is that these commitments of God have been revealed in Jesus (Romans 1.16).

So the cross, according to Paul, is God's 'righteousness' *in extremis*. God in his righteousness comes into 'the far country' (to use an image from a parable of Jesus) in order to find us. God's commitment to humankind and the world was tested as far as it could be tested: 'he became what we are ...' with all that that involved. By sharing our life, God transformed, and goes on transforming, the human situation. But the cross did not transform or change God's attitude, as if God's wrath had to be appeased, or God's justice satisfied. That is not Paul's theology.

Paul's own teaching about the cross varied according to the situation he was addressing. He told a church intoxicated by a heady mixture of wisdom and rhetoric that the cross of Jesus turned their cultural values upside down (1 Corinthians 1.18–25). That same church, which seemed to think that the cross was just an embarrassing episode in the life of God, learned that all true Christian living is cruciform (2 Corinthians 4.7–12). A church which thought it had to comply with the old way of being religious learned that the cross and resurrection of Jesus liberated them into a brave new world of faith, freedom and love (Galatians 2.19–20, 5.1, 6.14–15).

The list could go on. But there is a family resemblance to Paul's many different ways of talking about the cross and resurrection. They all, in their various ways, proclaim God's new world into which anyone may step through faith, baptism and the gift of the Holy Spirit. (I return to this subject later in this chapter.) There is, though, another basic theme in Paul – again richly variegated – which puts the cross and resurrection of Jesus in a wider framework. One of Britain's leading New Testament scholars, Morna Hooker, has drawn attention to what she has called the divine 'interchange' in Paul's writings. This is so important that we need take a little time to explore what this means.

The divine interchange

A picture may help. A few years ago Michael Buerk fronted a television series about emergency rescues. One programme re-constructed the rescue of passengers from a stricken ship. Their 'saviour', in a quite literal sense, was an RAF man winched down on to the deck to join them. He calmed the panic-stricken passengers, and winched them all up, one by one, to safety. A passage from the writings of Simone Weil can serve as a commentary on this story, before we return to Paul: 'When the whole universe weighs upon us there is no other counterweight possible but God himself ... That is why on the balance of the cross a body which was frail and light but which was God, lifted up the whole world.'[2]

Paul writes about this interchange in which God in Christ shared our life and death in order that we might share *God*'s life, in many different ways. Again, Paul chooses language appropriate for the situation he is addressing – another example of different 'sermons' for different congregations. In discussing money with the Christians at Corinth, he explains the divine interchange like this: 'For you know the generous act of our Lord Jesus Christ, that though he was rich, yet for your sakes he became poor, so that by his poverty you might become rich' (2 Corinthians 8.9). When, in Galatians, he is arguing that Gentile Christian converts should be free from the obligation to keep the law of Moses, he says, 'But when the fullness of time had come, God sent his Son, ... born under the law, in order to redeem those who were under the law, so that we might receive adoption as children' (Galatians 4.4–5). There is yet another example in 2 Corinthians 5.21: 'For our sake he [God] made him [Christ] to be sin who knew no sin, so that in him we might become the righteousness of God.'

In looking more closely at Paul's interchange language, we find that its centre is the cross and resurrection of Christ, and it is these which, above all, transformed Paul's inherited understanding of God – our next theme in this section.

Paul's understanding of God

Here we need to be careful that we do justice to Old Testament and Jewish convictions about God. We cannot say that Paul suddenly discovered the love of God; the Jewish Scriptures and, above all, the book of Psalms bear witness to God's 'unfailing' love. Nor should we ignore some of the universal statements of the Old Testament, such as Psalm 145.9: 'The Lord is good to all, and his compassion is over all that he has made.' But there can be little doubt that the cross and resurrection, from Paul's conversion onwards, came to shape his basic convictions about God. They were the heart of God's 'saving action' (literally, his 'righteousness', Romans 1.16) for the world.

So although Paul, as a devout Jew, already believed in the love and grace of God, as the Psalms, in particular, so clearly show, he now bore witness to the love and grace of God in a way which he would not have done before. What changed Paul's life was not so much new information about God, but a revelation which changed his life (for example, Romans 1.16, 2 Corinthians 4.6). It was a new *experience*, and, with this experience he gained the conviction that something world-changing had *happened*. This is why the words 'every' and 'all' occur so often, as in 2 Corinthians 5: 'For the love of Christ urges us on, because we are convinced that one has died for all; therefore all have died. And he died for all, so that those who live might live no longer for themselves, but for him who died and was raised for them' (vv. 14–15). This seems to mean that God in Christ has changed everything: there is a new world, incorporating everyone, or potentially everyone ('all have died'). But that new world has to be realized through a personal response: '... if anyone is in Christ, there is a new creation ...' (v. 17a).

So while we cannot doubt that Paul the Pharisee believed in God's love for Israel, and perhaps even for Gentiles, we may wonder whether he could have made the affirmations about God's love which he expresses, for example, in Galatians 2.20 and Romans 5.8: 'And the life I now live in the flesh I live by faith in the Son of God, who loved me and gave himself for me' (Galatians 2.20) and 'But God proves his love for us in that while we still were sinners Christ died for us' (Romans 5.8). Similarly, Paul, as a Jew, did not need to be told of the *hesed* ('loving-kindness'), by which, according to the prophet Hosea, God had drawn 'Ephraim' to himself. (Since Hosea's imagery here is female, perhaps we should say 'herself', Hosea 11.1–4.) But even though, as a devout Jew, Paul cannot have been a stranger to the grace of God, we may wonder whether he would have spoken quite so confidently of grace 'superabounding' even where 'transgression multiplied' (Romans 5.20).

There was yet another way in which the life and death of Jesus, if not his teaching, almost certainly changed Paul's understanding of God. Paul may have seen more clearly in the light of the cross that nothing at all could damage or contaminate, still less destroy, the holiness of God – that is, God's essential being. God redeemed even the curse and apparent God-forsakenness of a crucifixion. So a remarkable change has occurred in Paul's language of holiness, compared with that language in the Old Testament. He refers often to the 'Holy Spirit', now operative far beyond the 'holy' land, and given to hitherto unclean Gentiles. These Gentile converts he even describes as 'holy' (for example, 1 Corinthians 1.2), not because they were perfect, but because God loved and called them as he had Israel. So one of the marks of God's *Holy* Spirit in Paul's teaching is transforming previously 'unclean' people and, by implication, 'unclean' territory.

This is the very picture the first three Gospels give us of a Jesus who touched and healed people whom no one else would touch, who associated with and so transformed the likes of Zacchaeus, whom most others had ostracized. Jesus wasn't polluted by such contact. Rather, the influence went the other way; the lives of the people he touched were transformed and this was a new understanding of God's holiness. Whereas some devout people took care to protect their holiness, Jesus lived in the conviction that God's holiness not only did not *need* protecting, but could actually transform what was unclean and impure. So Paul could tell those Christians married to people who did not share their faith to remain married if his or her partner so wished; 'the unbelieving husband' and 'the unbelieving wife' are thereby 'made holy' (1 Corinthians 7.14).

Because the cross and resurrection of Jesus were now so central to Paul's understanding of God, he saw and experienced God's grace, love and holiness in new ways. But can we be more precise about how this became good news for Paul and his contemporaries? What *happened* in the cross and resurrection?

Sacrifice and victory

These are Paul's key themes and the two belong together. This is what the divine 'interchange' means: God sacrificially places himself where we are, but does not leave us there. God does not get 'stuck' in the same mess as humankind; instead, he remains, victoriously, the same God. On the whole, Paul uses the language of sacrifice about the cross, and the language of victory about the resurrection. But they are two sides of the same coin; neither can be fully understood without the other. The resurrection was, in some mysterious way, God's victory.

We have to say 'in some mysterious way' because that victory wasn't obvious to everyone. It never has been. But it forms the basis of Paul's triumphant conclusion in Romans 8: 'For I am convinced that neither death, nor life, nor angels, nor rulers, nor things present, nor things to come, nor powers, nor height, nor depth, nor anything else in all creation, will be able to separate us from the love of God in Christ Jesus our Lord' (vv. 38–39).

Summary

When we ask what drove Paul, this is where we must look: his fundamental convictions about God and Jesus, revealed in the cross and resurrection. His encounter with Christ was a life-changing experience for him, and from then on he understood God's love, grace and holiness as Christ-like. He lived and preached the divine love, grace and holiness in the light of Christ. And his preaching took him deep into Gentile lands, because he believed that, through the death and resurrection of Jesus, the Holy Spirit was now 'let loose in the world' (to echo the poet John Masefield) 'where no one can stop him'.

As for Christ, now at 'God's right hand' (Romans 8.34), he 'intercedes' for us. 'Intercede' cannot mean trying to persuade a reluctant God; God has already declared for us, and so needs no winning over: 'If God is for us, who is against us?' (Romans 8.31). The 'intercession' of Jesus is best understood as an extension of the divine interchange: God in Christ is with us, and for us, always and everywhere. This was the driving force behind Paul's mission.

ii An open invitation

How does a person come to faith? The short answer to that question is that we don't really know or, at least, we never know the whole story. Coming to faith is a bit like falling in love, or 'clicking' with someone else in such a way that that person becomes a firm, lifelong friend. You can explain it up to a point; for example, we might say that two people in love were meant for each other. But even if they *were* meant for each other, they also fell for each other in a way that we can't entirely account for. Faith is rather like that, and people's journeys to faith are many and varied. But we need to say more. For all sorts of reasons – upbringing, life experience, temperament and, for better or worse, church experiences – our capacity for faith varies too. Here we are concerned with how Paul understands this important Christian word.

What is faith?

Faith is often misunderstood. 'Faith' is an 'umbrella' term which can cover several things: belief, trust and commitment, as well as a person's entire religion. In Paul's writings, the word 'faith' has a special importance and meaning. In the phrase of a famous twentieth-century theologian, Paul Tillich, faith, according to Paul, means 'accepting that you are accepted'. It means reaching out a hand to grasp God's hand stretched out in friendship to you. Faith, according to Paul, also includes commitment and obedience ('the obedience of faith', Romans 1.5), but the commitment grows out of the initial acceptance and trust. What Paul's message that we are 'justified by faith' means is that there is nothing we can do to earn this friendship or mercy of God. The hand is simply there, waiting for us to grasp it. How do we know? Paul's answer to that question is: Jesus Christ and, above all, the cross and resurrection of Jesus.

But now we need to ask a question which might seem surprising. Ever since the Reformation, Christians have tended to see 'justification by faith' as the heart of Paul's gospel. But whose faith are we talking about here? By whose faith are we 'justified'? We assume that it is *our* faith, but that is probably to misread Paul – and to distort the Christian gospel.

So whose faith saves?

Many have observed how easily 'our faith' becomes a 'work': we think we 'qualify' for God's forgiveness on the basis not of good deeds, but our faith in response to the gospel. Christian preachers have often declared 'Unless you believe, you will not be saved'. It sounds biblical, but it is possible to put the emphasis in quite the wrong place. Another great twentieth-century theologian, Karl Barth, writing of the church at Corinth, referred to their belief 'not in God, but in their belief in God'.[3] Paul himself:

> ... did not believe in faith. He believed in God and emphasized faith – not because faith is powerful but because God is. ... Had Paul been interested in the power of faith ... he might have organized 'faith clinics' in which he taught people how to 'believe harder' so that their faith would be more powerful.[4]

So we are not, strictly speaking, justified by 'our' faith, but by God. God reached out his hand before we even made a move. We grasp Paul's meaning more accurately if, instead of asking 'Justified by what?', we ask 'Who justifies?' Paul's answer to that question is very clear: 'It is God who justifies' (Romans 8.33). The later letter to the Ephesians makes the same point in saying that the faith we do have is the gift of God (Ephesians 2.8). That is the scriptural basis for Tillich's gospel invitation: 'Accept that you are accepted'.

To return to the question 'Whose faith justifies us?', Paul comes up with a surprising answer. At least, such is the belief of a growing number of scholars. They argue that, according to Paul, 'our' faith was the faith of Jesus himself before it could be ours. If this relatively new understanding of Paul is correct, it gives new meaning to the words of an old hymn, 'nothing in my hand I bring ...': 'nothing' – not even my faith, because it was his (that is, Jesus') before it could be mine.

Is this a correct understanding of Paul? That we are justified by the faith (or faithfulness – the Greek can mean either) of Jesus? Is this really a scriptural idea? In several places (Galatians 2.16, Romans 3.22, and Philippians 3.9), the apostle uses a phrase which is ambiguous. The Greek can mean either '[our] faith *in* Christ' or '[the] faith *of* Christ'. It is possible that Paul meant to say both things at once. Paul clearly says, in Galatians 2.16, '... and we ourselves have put our faith in Christ ...'. That is *not* ambiguous either in translation or in the original. But what Paul probably meant in this verse as a whole is this: we know that a person is not justified 'except through the faith of Jesus Christ'; we ourselves have put our faith in Jesus, so that we might be justified 'by the faith of Christ ...'. In other words, our faith rides on (piggybacks?) Christ's; and faith becomes ours only because it was first his.

Is the idea of Jesus' faith 'sound'? Does the New Testament talk in this way? At first sight it appears not. Yet Paul places great emphasis on Christ's *obedience* (Romans 5.19, Philippians 2.8; cf. Hebrews 2.13 and 12.1). Although the Gospels nowhere speak explicitly of the faith of Jesus, it is surely implied from start to finish, and his *faithfulness* found expression supremely in his going to the cross. So was Paul referring in these passages to 'the faithfulness' of Jesus? The Greek word *pistis* can mean 'faith' or 'faithfulness', and faith and faithfulness in the Christian life should not be too sharply distinguished anyway. Jesus' faith, because it was continuous and unbroken, became faithfulness as well. So, too, should the Christian believer's, although there is no doubt in Paul's mind that the believer's faithfulness begins as trust in God and in Christ (once more, the outstretched hand). The entire Christian life is lived on this basis: 'the life I now live ... I live by faith in the Son of God, who loved me and gave himself for me' (Galatians 2.20). So our faith stands on his; the faith, faithfulness and obedience of Jesus make possible ours.

The place of faith

This discussion may seem technical, and a far cry from contemporary church life. Yet is it? The place of grace, freedom and choice in the Christian life is fundamental. What we believe about these things profoundly affects how we see not only ourselves, but also those who do not share the Christian faith or come to church. Are such people to be condemned because they have made the wrong choice? Or are some people beyond the pale anyway because God has not chosen them? Only an experience of grace, I suggest, can save us from both these errors of judgement. And believing that 'our faith' isn't ours in the first place at all, but ours only because it was first Christ's, can save us from both presumption and complacency.

So was justification by faith part of what I earlier referred to as Paul's mission statement? Yes, it was. Even though we have learned to recognize that justification by works was not Judaism's central creed, that does not de-throne justification by faith from its central place in Paul's experience, mission and preaching. Its centrality does not depend on having its opposite in Judaism. Jesus lived and preached it, too. Where he extended the hand of a 'transforming friendship',[5] particularly to religious and moral outsiders, he was living out the gospel that a person is justified by faith: accept with gratitude that you are accepted.

iii A Church without 'Christians'

The word 'Christian' has many negative connotations today. Just as the name 'Protestant' became tainted by the troubles in Northern Ireland, so 'Christian' is in danger of becoming another sectarian name in a deeply divided world. 'Christian' has other negative 'vibes': many people, especially outside the churches, assume that the first thing to be done when a person becomes a Christian is to stop doing things, especially if they used to enjoy them.

This is not where Paul starts, or where he himself started. Writing of his own Christian experience, Paul said, '... I have come to regard everything as loss because of ... the surpassing value of knowing Christ Jesus my Lord' (Philippians 3.7–8). In modern parlance, we might talk of 'the expulsive power of a new affection', or the transforming power of a new allegiance. Paul's Christian life began as a personal experience of God's mercy and grace, and so, for him, thankfulness pervades the whole of Christian living. It was normal practice in those days to start a letter with thanks, but with Paul the conventional thanksgiving has become much more. As well as the opening thanks, which occur in most of his letters, he several times urges his churches to be thankful – even 'in all circumstances' (1 Thessalonians 5.18a).

Why there are no 'Christians' in Paul

Paul never uses the term 'Christian'. The word 'Christian' probably came from outside the Church; Roman officials may have needed a label for this strange new sect. Instead, Paul talks of people being 'in Christ': 'if anyone is in Christ, there is a new creation' (2 Corinthians 5.17); he writes of people belonging to 'the Lord': 'whether we live or whether we die, we are the Lord's' (Romans 14.8b), and, thirdly, he describes the Christian life as life in the Spirit: '... you are in the Spirit, since the Spirit of God dwells in you' (Romans 8.9a). This is strange, unfamiliar language to us, or at least it is less familiar than our modern labels: 'Christian', 'Catholic', 'Baptist', 'Anglican' and so on. But Paul's language reminds us that the Christian life is not just an outward allegiance; it is an inward reality, an affair of the heart. This is why it is a matter for constant thanksgiving and joy ('Rejoice in the Lord always; again I will say, Rejoice', Philippians 4.4).

Correcting the received picture

This is an important correction to how Christian faith is often seen, and to how, unfortunately, Christians sometimes present themselves. A member of the cleaning staff at a theological college, observing the long faces of the students one day in Lent, was heard to say, 'I thought Christianity was supposed to make you happy'. There is a paradox here: a faith which calls disciples of Jesus to take up the cross doesn't sound, at first hearing, like the way to happiness. But this paradox of finding life by losing ourselves runs throughout the New Testament, including in Paul's letters.

So this is the first alteration we must make to a widely held view of Paul on the Christian life: he is profoundly positive; joy and thanksgiving have a central place in this 'affair of the heart'. But the word 'heart' in Paul's writings means more than it does for us. A drawing of a heart these days tends to represents romantic love, as on Valentine cards. For the people of the Bible, Old and New Testaments alike, the heart is utterly central to all that a person is. Not least, it is where the will resides. So when Paul talks about our 'hearts', that is what he means. This is why he can say, for example, that God sent his Spirit *into our hearts* – the very centre of a person's being (Galatians 4.6). Such an experience begins to affect what a person *wants* – out of life, for themselves, for their loved ones, for the world.

There is another characteristic fundamental to the Christian life as Paul saw it. A person cannot be a Christian on his or her own. In Paul's view, a person doesn't become a Christian and then decide whether or not to join the Church. In becoming a Christian, a person by that very fact joins not only the Church in general, but the local church down the road, whether it met in Gaius' house in Corinth, in Priscilla's and Aquila's house in Rome, or wherever. This is where, in a very concrete, human way, the green shoots of God's new creation are appearing – or should be, if Romans 12 may be our guide here.

The heart of a church

So can we say what a church really is, according to Paul? Yes, we can; his language is very clear. A church is the church *of God* (for example, 1 Corinthians 11.16), and it normally has a very specific geographical name: the church in Corinth (1 Corinthians 1.2), the churches in Galatia (Galatians 1.2), and so on. So we might say that what matters most about a church is who it belongs to – that is, God – and where it is earthed – for its worship, life and witness. Paul's word for church, *ekklesia*, keeps the focus on another essential characteristic: a church is an assembly. The word *ekklesia* had both a Greek and a Jewish pedigree, but for Paul it's an assembly of people gathering in the name of Christ. It is difficult to think of a more important characteristic.

What else characterizes a church, in Paul's view? It is a

community of the Spirit. There is no church, no Christian life, without the Holy Spirit. A Christian without the Spirit is like a sailing boat with no wind; it's impossible to get started at all. The Spirit enables us to call God 'Father' (Galatians 4.6, Romans 8.15); without the Spirit we can't even pray (Romans 8.26), and the Spirit is the source of all the qualities which should mark a Christian's life: love, joy, peace, and so on (Galatians 5.22–23). But here we need to be careful. Christian experience may become the basis for spiritual one-upmanship, as it did at Corinth. Whether the church there asked Paul about spiritual gifts or spiritual people (1 Corinthians 12.1 could mean either), it is significant that, at the heart of his long discussion (chapters 12 to 14), is a hymn about love (13.1–13): 'If I speak in the tongues of mortals and of angels, but do not have love, I am a noisy gong or a clanging cymbal' (v. 1).

From the old to the new

For Paul, two images in particular express the change from the old life to the new. One image is that of cross-and-resurrection. As always, we need to recall that the two go together in Paul, even though the Christian experiences resurrection in two stages. So here and now the person coming to faith (putting his or her hand into the hand of God), makes the cross of Christ that person's own. That last phrase paraphrases Paul's own language of 'being crucified with Christ' (Galatians 2.19, Romans 6.6). By making Christ's cross theirs, the person of faith begins to share the life of Christ (for example, Galatians 2.20, Romans 6.4). By the life of Christ, Paul means the resurrection life of Christ, in the power of the Spirit. This may be why some of the first Christians thought that they would not die; Paul more than once explains that our experience now is a foretaste of what is to come on the far side of death (for example, 2 Corinthians 5.1–5).

The other image which Paul uses to express the transition from the old life to the new is baptism. This, of course, was more than an image. We know very little about early Christian baptisms, but it is likely that people being baptized were totally immersed, where that was practicable, in a river or in the sea. Whether the earliest Christians baptized children is impossible to prove or disprove. Two arguments suggesting they may have done are worth considering. Paul says that, among the small number of people he baptized on his first visit to Corinth, was the household of Stephanas. It is possible, even probable, that that meant everyone – slaves and children included. In a patriarchal society where the male head of the household really did rule, a new convert like Stephanas might well have decided that his new faith was for everyone who lived and worked under his roof. It's also possible that the Christians baptized their children from very early on because, like the people of Israel in the Old Testament, they regarded their children as being members of God's covenant people. But we can't prove it, and there is no need to. The Church holds confirmation services, but there are no examples of such services in the New Testament. Not all the Church's traditions can have, or need to have, a basis in the Bible.

More important than the practical details was what baptism meant. It signified the transforming power of a new allegiance – the beginning of life 'in Christ', 'for the Lord', 'in the Spirit'. And that meant the renouncing, or leaving behind, of the old life.

The cost of this for Paul's converts was often enormous, as we began to see in our look at the oppressive character of the Roman Empire. The extent to which they became social outcasts may have depended on where they lived, and their attitude to the largely pagan life around them. The Corinthian Christians varied in their practice: some took a more 'worldly' view than others. But for all of them it must have been a very brave thing to do. That is why we should not lose sight of the profoundly positive experience at the heart of their new-found faith: in discovering God's grace, they had been 'surprised by joy'.[6]

With this we come to another fundamental way in which Paul corrects our limited view of the Christian life. We tend to place a lot of emphasis on our own efforts, on New Year resolutions, giving up things for Lent, and so on. Paul is quite clear that self-discipline plays a major part in the Christian life, but above and beneath the self-discipline, is the Christian's experience of grace. The Christian life simply cannot be lived at all without the grace of God and the help of the Holy Spirit. In the words of a former New Testament teacher of mine, Kenneth Grayston, grace is that power which enables us to be and to do what otherwise we would not be able to be and do. So the answer Paul received in answer to his prayer about his 'thorn in the flesh' can serve as a motto for the Christian life in general: 'My grace is sufficient for you, for power is made perfect in weakness' (2 Corinthians 12.9).

Does all this make the Christian life one long success story? Some contemporary versions of Christian faith can easily give that impression ('Come to Christ and all your problems will be over'). Such versions tend to downplay the centrality of the cross in the Christian life. If we understand Christ's death primarily as a penalty and a substitution, we might draw the wrong conclusion: that Christ suffered in order that we might not have to suffer. In a sense that is true, but it is equally true to say that Christ died on the cross in order that we might make that cross of Christ our own. That, as we have seen, is Paul's teaching. In Paul's view, the Christian never leaves the cross behind; Christian existence remains *cruciform* from beginning to end.

A *new creation*

Paul's language can sound very otherworldly: 'being crucified with Christ' and 'receiving the Holy Spirit' can seem a long way from our workaday, humdrum experience of being a Christian. We should not trivialize this language, but, at the same time, we need to recognize that many people grow into such experiences very gradually over many years. Not for them a dramatic 'Damascus Road' experience. What really matters is not how a person's Christian life began, but whether it is for real. And, once again, Paul not only elevates and challenges our understandings of the Christian life, he well and truly earths them as well, not least in the detailed advice of Romans 12, with its opening, 'I appeal to you, therefore, brothers and sisters, by the mercies of God, to present your bodies as a living sacrifice, holy and acceptable to God, which is your spiritual worship' (Romans 12.1). Some versions have 'present your *selves*', rather than the more literal 'present your *bodies*' (the Greek is *somata*). That is fine, provided we realize that for Paul the Christian life is nothing less than our total *embodied* existence. Nothing can be left out of that, least of all difficult relationships (vv. 14–18) and politics (13.1–7).

In fact, Romans 12 is the positive counterpart to the picture of humankind, 'hooked' on idolatry and sin, which Paul gives in Romans 1.18–24. According to Paul, sin has two far-reaching effects on human communities: it clones, and it fragments. This is why a drably or fearfully uniform social group, or a divided one, is the very opposite of a community of the Spirit. The Spirit of God at work in human society accomplishes the opposite effects: the Spirit creates communities which are united and diverse – both at the same time. In such a community, the relationships between the members are key, and we shall need to return to this subject in our next chapter. These days, especially in Western Europe and North America, Christian faith has been both individualized and privatized. Christians more readily think of their faith in personal terms, rather than social and political ones. So, before we leave this survey of what Paul taught about the Christian life, we must widen the scope still further: from the Church to the wider world.

Paul, in his conclusion in Galatians, focused on 'new creation' (6.15). By definition, a 'new creation' is a universal concept: it is potentially all-embracing. Here on earth it anticipates something ultimate (eschatological). This doesn't mean that the new creation is basically 'otherworldly' in the way in which that word is normally understood. The new creation represents God's ultimate purpose for the world, and it is underpinned and characterized by his justice. (I return to this important theme in Chapters 4 and 5.)

Several times Paul gives expression to the universal scope of God's new creation; for example, 'as all die in Adam, so all will be made alive in Christ' (1 Corinthians 15.22, Romans 5.17f.). This does not necessarily mean that Paul was a universalist, believing that everyone in the end will be 'saved', but at times he comes close to sounding like one; 2 Corinthians 5.14 provides a good example of a verse whose universalist implications are frequently overlooked: 'For the love of Christ urges us on, because we are convinced that one has died for all; therefore all have died.' It is not easy to say what Paul meant by 'all have died', but commentators are surely right to argue that 'all' here must be the same 'all' as in the preceding clause: 'one has died for all'.

So the 'new creation' inaugurated by Jesus is, according to Paul, universal in scope. But it finds expression in the faith, love and hope of a person 'baptized into Christ' who has found – or, better, been found by – the transforming power of God's grace. God's new creation finds expression in the unity and diversity of a new community whose quality can be seen most of all in the way its members relate to one another, and by the way in which they seek to share God's mission to the world (2 Corinthians 5.18–21).

iii Did Paul practise what he preached?

One of the most searching tests of any person's faith is whether, by the way they live their lives, they make it easier for other people to believe in their god. The popular writer Edgar Wallace once wrote of a Christian he knew: 'he was a perfect man ... I believe that much of the good that is within me came because I knew him. He is an everlasting barrier between me and atheism.' Did Paul have that effect on people? The question may seem laughable when we read some of his angry, intolerant language. But it needs to be pressed, for this reason: Paul speaks of himself in language which suggests he thought of himself as an *ikon* ('image') of God.

Icon or megalomaniac?

How good an 'advert' was Paul for his faith? With the fragmentary evidence available to us, we can't be sure of the answer to this question. Paul may not always have practised what he preached. As we saw when we tried to look at his life with fresh eyes (Chapter 1), his relationship with at least two of his churches, or groups of churches (Corinth and Galatia), was anything but straightforward. That, however, was not always Paul's fault. And yet he won converts; most of his surviving letters were written to churches which he founded. So, for them, he had the authority which went with being their founding apostle; he was their role model, as this command to the church at Corinth shows: 'Be imitators of me, as I am of Christ' (1 Corinthians 11.1).

Was this a sad case of apostolic megalomania, religious delusion on a grand scale? It might appear so, but other passages also reflect, directly or indirectly, Paul's imitation of Christ. Just as Christ Jesus 'emptied himself' in the service of the world, so his apostle Paul emptied himself; the hymn which Paul quotes in Philippians 2.5–11 refers to Christ's self-emptying, and Philippians 3.5–11 describes the apostle's self-emptying (with several verbal echoes of the hymn).

So the sequence is simple, but vital for understanding Paul: the apostle was, or sought to be, an 'icon' or image of Christ, just as Christ was the image of God (2 Corinthians 4.4). Paul sought to represent, in his own person, both the cross and the resurrection of Jesus. This is absolutely central to Paul's understanding of himself. In the last chapter I drew attention to Paul's testimonies (1 Corinthians 4.9–13, 2 Corinthians 4.7–12 and 6.3–10). What Paul says about himself, and his fellow-apostles, is extraordinary: fools for Christ, poorly clothed, beaten, homeless … like the rubbish of the world (1 Corinthians 4.9–13); always carrying in our bodies the dying of Jesus (2 Corinthians 4.10), '… sorrowful yet always rejoicing, as poor yet making many rich; as having nothing, and yet possessing everything' (2 Corinthians 6.10). If these descriptions of himself are anywhere near accurate, then we must say that the apostle who preached 'Christ crucified' practised what he preached.

Yet Paul may not *always* have done so. He was only human, after all. But the apostle's sufferings, humiliations and poverty – not to mention his 'thorn in the flesh' – were a *problem* for the Corinthians, as we saw earlier (Chapter 2, section iii). They could not understand why an apostle of Christ should live in this way; most other teachers and philosophers did not! Paul might have impressed them more if he had *not* tried to embody the message of the cross, so there is likely to be much truth in these self-portraits. Paul, in all kinds of ways, really lived the gospel of Christ crucified.

That is the most important answer we can give to our question 'Did Paul practise what he preached?' We should, though, take a closer look at his relationships with his churches, since most of the evidence relevant to our question centres on these. In an earlier chapter we looked at his most angry and apparently intolerant statements, and to be fair to Paul, we now need to look at the affectionate language in his letters as well. It is plentiful. A verse in his earliest letter is typical: 'So deeply do we care for you that we are determined to share with you not only the gospel of God but also our own selves, because you have become very dear to us' (1 Thessalonians 2.8). He writes in similar vein to the church at Philippi (1.8); to the church at Corinth, despite all the ups-and-downs of his relationship with them (for example, 2 Corinthians 7.3); and he writes with affectionate longing to a church he has not yet seen (Romans 1.11–13, 15.23). Even at the end of his tether, Paul can still write like a mother to the churches in Galatia: 'My little children, for whom I am again in the pain of childbirth until Christ is formed in you, I wish I were present with you now and could change my tone, for I am perplexed about you' (Galatians 4.19–20).

On the level?

What are we to make of emotional language like this? To us it sounds 'over the top' – especially, we might say, coming from a man. It would not, I think, have come across so oddly then, but the expressions of affection are still remarkable, and, of course, we don't know how they were received.

So the modern reader of Paul has a decision to make! Is this man 'on the level'? Does he mean what he says? Is he genuine?

Some have accused Paul of being manipulative, but, for all his rhetorical skill and adaptability, I find very little evidence of this. The nearest he comes to this occurs in his arguments about the collection in 2 Corinthians. Two successive chapters, 8 and 9, are devoted to this subject. (Some scholars have wondered whether these were also separate letters originally; the first verse of chapter 9, for example, could read as though Paul was introducing a new topic.) We might accuse Paul here of promoting some inter-church rivalry. Which church is going to raise more money? In the first chapter (8.1) Paul tells the Corinthians how well 'Macedonia' is doing; in the next chapter he tells them, in effect, that that was the argument he used when he was in Macedonia – 'Come on! Achaia [that is, Corinth] is ahead of you!'(9.2). But at least he is 'above board' about what he is doing.

To return to the decision we have to make as readers of Paul: how genuine was he? There is really no halfway house here. Several times, especially in the letters to Thessalonika and Corinth, he protests not only his innocence, but also his integrity and transparency: '... we have behaved in the world with frankness and godly sincerity, not by earthly wisdom but by the grace of God – and all the more towards you' (2 Corinthians 1.12; cf. 2.17, 4.2 and 5.11). Most telling of all are his frequent assertions that he is open to the scrutiny of God. Of course, there are examples galore, inside and outside the Church, of people who have protested their honesty and piety when their hand was in the till or the collection box. Ultimately, of course, we have to make up our own minds as to whether Paul practised what he preached. To this reader, at least, he doesn't come across as a self-deceiving liar or charlatan. But there are other questions to be asked.

Team player?

How well did Paul get on with others? That isn't always an accurate test of the genuineness of someone's faith, but it may tell us something! In Chapter 1, I tried to offer some explanations for some of Paul's intemperate, angry language, but that doesn't alter the fact that he had a row with Peter – or, at the very least, a frank exchange of views (Galatians 2.11–14). He also quarrelled with Barnabas, when he refused to accept John Mark on the team. Paul doesn't tell us so, but Luke does (Acts 15.37–39).

Was Paul in the right, or in the wrong? And how many other rows did he have?! We cannot tell. But a church culture which tends to prize being 'nice' as the greatest of Christian virtues is not a good measure by which to assess Paul's behaviour. There is nothing necessarily wrong with a quarrel. And there is, as it happens, another example of a conflict Paul was involved in. This time, he seems to have been on the receiving end; someone at Corinth, on Paul's second visit there, insulted or humiliated him (2 Corinthians 2.5–11). Paul wrote a tearful letter to the whole church, but by the time he wrote again, it is Paul himself who is urging the church to 'go easy', and to forgive the offender.

Of course, we cannot tell whether Paul practised what he preached, when we have only his writings nearly two millennia after he lived. We know, though, that he brought many people to Christian faith. Even if the churches to which he wrote were small, there were no doubt many more converts whom we simply do not know about. That alone suggests that his message and his life were not entirely at odds with each other. His relationships with his churches were certainly rocky at times. Paul may not always have been as tactful as he might have been – how well did his sarcasm go down at Corinth? (1 Corinthians 4.8). The church at Corinth might have also wondered why he could accept help from the church at Philippi, but not from them (1 Corinthians 9.12–18, Philippians 4.15–16). Nevertheless, most of the problems in his churches were due to misunderstandings or outside interference rather than Paul's own mistakes or shortcomings.

Imitator of God?

Before we leave this question, we should note one particular way in which he sought to 'model' his life and mission on the

Christ he served. I suggested in the last chapter that when Paul said he was 'all things to all men', he meant something far more sacrificial and costly than we mean by that phrase. 'To the Jews I became as a Jew, in order to win Jews' says Paul (1 Corinthians 9.20). But that probably got harder and harder, as negative rumours about Paul spread among his fellow-Jews. 'To those outside the law I became as one outside the law ...' (v. 21), a policy which left Paul wide open to misunderstanding. 'To the weak I became weak, that I might win the weak ...' (v. 22). 'The weak' were the people of low social standing, without power, influence, status or wealth. Is it significant that Paul does not say 'To the strong, I became strong, in order to win the strong'? We should be right, I think, in detecting here what people have recently called 'God's bias to the poor'.

Who is Paul's role model here? There can be little doubt about the answer to that. It was Jesus himself or, to put it in Paul's own language, Paul sought to reflect the God who became what we are that we might become what God is. Paul's strategy of 'being all things to all people' was the apostle's embodiment of the divine interchange. That is what the apostle actually says, in a verse almost universally mistranslated. In effect, he says: 'I do all this for the sake of the gospel, in order to be a "sharer" (*synkoinonos*) in it' (1 Corinthians 9.23). (There is no reference in the original Greek to sharing 'in the gospel's blessings' as every translation I know of renders it.)[7]

I submit that Paul, for all his faults, comes across in his letters as an authentic human being. The passion, affection, anguish and anger are unmistakable, but so too is the genuineness of a man who sought to embody in his own life the message he proclaimed of Christ crucified and risen.

v What did Paul believe about the end of the world?

Soon after the bombings in New York on 11 September 2001, I heard of a church at which the preacher told the congregation: 'Don't worry! Whatever happens to everyone else, Jesus will come for us, and take us to be with him in heaven.' I paraphrase, but that was the gist of it. The preacher was referring to 'the rapture', an event which, in their view, Paul describes in his first letter to the Thessalonians. In the USA, though not only there, many devout Christians believe in 'the rapture'. The word derives its meaning from the Greek word 'to seize' (1 Thessalonians 4.17); Christ will return on the clouds of heaven to carry (literally, 'seize') the elect to heaven, leaving everyone else behind.

Was Paul a literalist?

Most Christians find such a literal understanding of this passage in 1 Thessalonians incredible, but are not sure how else to interpret it. In practice, most of us ignore this difficult 'end-of-the-world' language. But this is a mistake, because it is so central to Paul's thought and, indeed, to most other New Testament writers. New Testament scholars call this language 'eschatological'. The word comes from the Greek word *eschatos*, meaning 'last', and eschatology has been traditionally described as 'the doctrine of the last things'. But that is another kind of literalism which isn't very helpful, although it points us in the right direction.

'Eschatological' language isn't confined to the New Testament. It is there in the prophets of the Old Testament, and in Jewish writings penned after the Old Testament period, particularly in the centuries around the time of Jesus and of Paul. It occurs in the book of Jeremiah:

I looked on the earth, and lo, it was waste and void; and to the heavens, and they had no light. I looked on the mountains, and lo, they were quaking, and all the hills moved to and fro. I looked, and lo, there was no-one at all, and all the birds of the air had fled. I looked, and lo, the fruitful land was a desert, and all its cities were laid in ruins before the LORD, before his fierce anger (Jeremiah 4.23–26).

The Old Testament prophets contain many examples of both 'eschatological' and 'apocalyptic' language; and much of it, like this passage, is clearly poetic. The two words 'eschatological' and 'apocalyptic' are not identical, but they are closely related. Eschatological language is best understood as language about what is *ultimate*, a word which has two meanings. It can refer to what is final: what there will be when this life, this world and its history are at an end. It may also mean what ultimately matters: what is ultimately important.

As for 'apocalyptic', the word derives from the Greek word meaning 'revelation'. Such language, in Jewish and Christian writings, implies that there is more to this world than first meets the eye, especially in situations where evil appears to triumph. In fact, anyone writing apocalyptic literature, such as the John who wrote the last book in the New Testament, is claiming to be drawing back the curtain of history to disclose the ultimate truth and purpose behind it.

It is no accident that this kind of literature flourished when the Jewish and Christian worlds were wracked by a series of terrible crises, bringing with them much suffering and persecution. When the armies of Babylon or of Rome rampaged into the holy land and ransacked Jerusalem, and even the temple of God, God's people needed to know that such arrogant powers did not have the last word. Or, to return to 1 Thessalonians, when some of the first Christians died, those who mourned them needed to know that, in the light of Christ's resurrection, not even death is the last word: 'Therefore encourage one another and build up each other, as indeed you are doing' (1 Thessalonians 5.11; cf. 1 Corinthians 15.12–19, 54–58).

So what did Paul believe about the future? Eminent scholars, including C. H. Dodd, have suggested that Paul began by expecting the return of Jesus in his lifetime, and later changed his mind. But there is not enough evidence to prove or disprove this theory. In any case, we cannot be quite sure that Paul, and other Jewish and Christian writers who used 'end-of-the-world' language, would themselves have understood it literally. What really matters is the fundamental conviction behind the language, and that can be summarized in four words:

In the end, God.

Paul's future hope, however, was not only God-centred, but also Christ-centred. He writes of the 'coming' (*parousia*) of Christ, as in 1 Thessalonians 4.15, of 'the day of our Lord Jesus Christ' (for example, 1 Corinthians 1.8), and of 'the revelation' (*apokalypsis*) of our Lord Jesus Christ' (1 Corinthians 1.7). So eschatological language in Paul (and most New Testament writers) can be expanded to:

In the end, God – who is like Jesus Christ.

It is impossible to be sure how exactly Paul thought of this future 'day', 'coming' and 'revelation' of Christ. We need to avoid over-literal interpretations which are likely to contradict other biblical images, but we need to take seriously the centrality of Paul's Christ-centred hopes. But whether Paul understood this literally or not, whether he changed his mind on the subject or not, what are we to make of it today?

Beginning and end

In the Bible, including Paul, the beginning and end of the world are linked. This is just what we should expect if the same God who created everything is also working ultimately to fulfil his creative purpose. So what Paul says about the future appearing of Christ has to be related to his other convictions about Christ, particularly the role of Christ in creation. In opening his long discussion of what the Christians at Corinth should do about meat offered to idols, Paul sets out his basic creed: first, his belief in 'one God, the Father, from whom are all things and for whom we exist', and then his belief in Jesus: '... one Lord, Jesus Christ, through whom are all things and through whom we exist' (1 Corinthians 8.6).

For most people today, this creation language, in the light of recent discussions about science and religion, is no less difficult than Paul's language about the end of the world. But the two need to be kept together, even if at first that appears to make for two problems, not one. What Paul is talking about here is not only the source or origin of the world, but what we might call its constitution. 'Origin' here does not mean *how* the world began, but rather *why* there is a world at all, and what its purpose and meaning are. So three things belong together: the origin, the constitution and the end of the world. They are held together by God or, more precisely, the God who expresses his purpose and utters his 'word' in Jesus Christ. The hymn in Colossians, noted briefly in the last chapter (section vi), expresses this more fully:

> He [that is, Christ] is the image of the invisible God, the firstborn of all creation; for in him all things in heaven and on earth were created, things visible and invisible, whether thrones or dominions or rulers or powers – all things have been created through him and for him. He himself is before all things, and in him all things hold together. He is the head of the body, the church; he is the beginning, the firstborn from the dead, so that he might come to have first place in everything (Colossians 1.15–18).

This, I hope, helps to show why scholars have written about 'realized' or 'inaugurated' eschatology in the New Testament. They mean that, in Christ, the ultimate has dawned and that, in him, the goal of creation has been anticipated. So Christ is the key to the three things which, in Paul's view, belong together: the origin, the constitution and the end of all things. We might say that the very genesis and purpose of creation lies in the mystery of the relationship between 'the one God' and 'the one Lord', but that would be to take us way beyond our remit here!

This still begs the question of whether you should take Paul's language about the 'appearing' or 'coming' of Jesus literally or not. Down the centuries, many Christians have interpreted it literally, and still do today. In November 2007, a small group of Russian Christians barricaded themselves into a cave to await the end of the world, which they fully expected in a few months' time. This has been a recurring phenomenon in Christian history.

Two things need to be said. The first concerns biblical interpretation. The Bible gives many different pictures and images of the end of all things, and to take them all literally is impossible. Instead, we need to look at the context in and for which they were first written, as also with 'the rapture' of which Christian fundamentalists today make so much. Paul, when he used this language, was writing to a young church faced with severe persecution, probably from the oppressive might of the Roman Empire. This is why this letter has so much imperial imagery. Words like 'coming' (*parousia*, v. 15) and 'meet' (*apantesin*, v. 17) were associated with emperors and kings (Chapter 2, section vi). Paul uses the language to remind the Thessalonians that they have a lord and king far greater than Caesar, and meeting that lord and king is part of Christian hope now, as it was then. But we should not literalize, and thereby make incredible, this one image among many others.

The second thing to be said is this: a literal understanding of Christ's future coming can tie us up in contradictions: how can an event in history be the end of history? What happens after the return of Christ, because, if Christ's coming ushers in eternity, there can be no 'after'? Equally difficult, if Jesus descends from the sky, as the imagery of Mark 14.62, for example, seems to suggest, how will everyone in the entire globe see him at the same time? It is facile to talk of miracles here, as if God engages in a round-the-world transmission of some kind. Third, the so-called 'second coming' (though not Paul's terminology) has been traditionally thought to mark the end of the distinction between the visible and the invisible. A collect often used at funeral services suggests that we are attempting here to conceptualize and to visualize what is not susceptible to either:

Bring us, Lord our God,
at our last awakening,
into the house and gate of heaven ...
Where there shall be
no darkness nor dazzling,
but one equal light;

no noise nor silence,
but one equal music; ...
no ends nor beginnings,
But one equal eternity ...[8]

Paul said as much in referring to 'What no eye has seen, nor ear heard, nor the human heart conceived, what God has prepared for those who love him' (1 Corinthians 2.9). Paul goes on to say that God has revealed these very things to us now, through the Spirit (v. 10). This is a good example of how, in Paul's view – and that of other New Testament writers – the mystery of Christ is the golden thread binding together the origin, the constitution and the end of the universe.

Hope in God's future

So what, according to Paul, should we hope for? His answer might well be 'all things', which God has already wished upon us in Christ (1 Corinthians 3.21–23). More precisely, his answer seems to be: the glory of God (our lost birthright) is what we should hope for. The recovery of that birthright begins with our baptism, and will be completed after death. Yet, true as this is, it opens the door for other misunderstandings of what Paul is saying about the future.

The preacher whom I quoted at the beginning of this section had seriously misunderstood the message of the New Testament. Tragically, Christians have sometimes given the impression that they are more interested in the redemption of their souls than in the salvation and renewal of creation. Yet the Bible testifies again and again to God's care for his creation. There are, indeed, messages of doom and destruction; biblical writers sometimes appear to despair of the world and wash their hands of it (implying, perhaps, that God does too). But this is not the main theme. Instead, the Bible insists God keeps faith with the world he is making.

The Bible looks forward more than it looks back, and in spite of all Israel's failures in the Old Testament, the prophets look forward to a new creation (for example, Isaiah 11.9).

That is the note on which the Bible ends: the vision of 'a new heaven and a new earth' (Revelation 21.1). So Paul is singing from the same hymn sheet as the rest of the biblical choir when he, too, speaks of a 'new creation' (Galatians 6.15, 2 Corinthians 5.17). Paul uses this phrase only twice, but each time he speaks of being 'in Christ' (which he does so often), that is what he means: God's new world, embodied, improbable as it may sound, in those tiny Christian communities. Each time he refers to the work of the Holy Spirit, or encourages his converts to bear each other's burdens and to bless those who persecute them, he is describing that new creation.

So, Christian hope in God's future, according to Paul, is not confined to this world, but at the same time it cannot write off the world. (The Christian does not believe that God has.) Because the clue to the origin, constitution and end of the universe is the victoriously sacrificial God revealed in Jesus Christ, we may have hope. But Paul would be the first to say: to discover the secret of *that* hope, you have to make the cross of Christ your own.

vi The gospel according to Paul – a shock to the religious system

No generalizations

We can be quite sure that Paul's gospel for today will not be the same as his gospel for yesterday. A wise old scholar once said that the gospel hasn't really been preached until it's been heard. Every preacher worth his or her salt knows that if you want to share the same message with two completely different congregations, you don't preach the same sermon – or, rather, *exactly* the same sermon. If both congregations are to hear the gospel, the preacher will need two sermons, not one. Otherwise, the preacher may think he or she has preached the gospel, but only one of those congregations is likely to have heard it. I risk over-simplifying, but that seems to have been Paul's approach. All his surviving letters – except the personal one to Philemon – were addressed to particular congregations with their own specific questions, so discovering the heart of his message isn't easy. It's like having the spokes of a wheel without the hub from which they emanate. According to Paul, there is no gospel in general, only the gospel for Corinth, the gospel for Philippi, and so on. We can't isolate from his letters a grand summary and entitle it 'the gospel according to Paul', as if Paul hawked only one sermon all the way round the eastern Mediterranean.

First principles

Paul, however, keeps going back to 'first principles' and two passages in particular get us as near as any to the heart of things. (But it's important to emphasize that there are other passages as well, such as Romans 3.21–26, 2 Corinthians 5.14–21 and Philippians 2.5–11.) Both of these two passages are to be found in 1 Corinthians.

The first is a reference-point to steer Paul and the Corinthians through the complex issue of whether Christians should eat meat which had been offered to idols. It's especially significant because it contains two words fundamental to Paul's gospel, whatever form that gospel took. Those two words are 'one' and 'all': '... yet for us there is one God, the Father, from whom are all things and for whom we exist, and one Lord, Jesus Christ, through whom are all things and through whom we exist' (1 Corinthians 8.6). It would be difficult to exaggerate the importance in Paul's theology of 'one God' and 'one Lord'. Even today, many of us live as though we believe in 'many gods and many lords' (v. 5). Monotheism isn't just what we say we believe, but what we do. But here is Paul's Christ-centred monotheism, which may fairly be described as the heart of his theology.

Towards the end of 1 Corinthians comes the other key statement that I call Paul's 'first principles': 'Now I should remind you, brothers and sisters, of the good news [gospel] that I proclaimed to you ... that Christ died for our sins in accordance with the scriptures, and that he was buried, and that he was raised on the third day in accordance with the scriptures ...' (1 Corinthians 15.1, 3–4, quoted more fully in section i of this chapter).

So these two passages give us an indispensable framework: the heart of the gospel is the cross and resurrection of the one Lord Jesus, the saving revelation of the one God, whose creative and redeeming work embraces everything and everyone. But this can only be the beginning as we explore Paul's gospel for today: no gospel in general, only the gospel realized in particular contexts for each person or group.

There is a question of method to look at, however, before we go any further. Protestant Christianity, starting with Luther, has tended to concentrate on the letter to the Romans only. This, I think, is the origin of the view that in preaching the gospel you first argue that everyone is a sinner (Romans 1.18–3.20). If we take his letter to the Romans as our guide, it does look like that. But even if Romans is the fullest expression of what Paul thought and preached, we mustn't let it overshadow the other letters.

Paul, then, adapted his gospel, depending on whom he was writing to. So we can expect to find something fresh and different in all his letters. In writing to a church facing persecution and even martyrdom, because they had refused to give the oath of loyalty to Caesar, Paul concentrates on the coming of a 'Lord' far greater than Caesar, and on the hope of life after death with Christ (1 Thessalonians 1.9–10 and 4.13–18). To Gentile converts wondering whether they should observe the Jewish law (including, for the men, the painful physical rite of circumcision), Paul tells them that God sent his Son to free them from the law (Galatians 4.4–5). To Athenians religiously worshipping 'the unknown god', Paul – or Paul according to Luke – begins where they are. (This sermon at Athens, so far from being a 'dud', as some people argue, is a good example of Paul's adaptability as he describes it in one of his letters (1 Corinthians 9.19–23; see Chapter 5, section iii, for a further discussion of this).)

A shocking gospel

But now to the second part of our exploration: why should Paul's gospel have been 'a shock to the religious system', as the title of this section states?

The Church is always in danger of losing touch with the gospel and, in Paul's terms, 'gospel' can become 'law' at any time. Since the Reformation, Christians have tended to caricature the Judaism of Paul's day as 'legalistic'. In an earlier chapter (Chapter 2, section iv), I tried to show that such caricatures are neither accurate nor fair, but we need to return to what Paul taught about the law to grasp what was, and is, so shocking about his gospel.

A New Testament scholar has helpfully defined 'legalism' as the following of laws for their own sake, rather than God's sake. But if, in that definition, we replace the phrase 'the following of laws' by 'going to church and working for the church', it begins to sound more pertinent. Is it a fair parallel? It is not an exact parallel; going to church is not necessarily legalistic at all. But whether or not there were Jews in Paul's day who followed their laws for their own sake rather than for God's sake, certainly contemporary forms of Christianity can decline into being church-centred without being God-centred. In Paul's language, a church, or an individual Christian, may cease to live by the Spirit, and live 'according to the flesh'.

When this happens, attitudes may harden, and the religious person's view of humankind becomes polarized. 'Outsiders' are perceived not so much as those for whom Christ also died, but as people who may (or may not) contribute to the Church. Similarly, the preaching of the gospel may be replaced by moralistic exhortations to support a particular localized church because, for instance, refurbishing the premises has come to dominate the immediate horizon. Consequently, it becomes easy to dismiss 'outsiders' as people who are just not 'interested' (that is, in the Church).

Paul's gospel-centred world is very different. We have already noted Paul's fondness for the words 'all' and 'everyone': for example, 'one man died for all' (2 Corinthians 5.14) and 'as all die in Adam, so all will be made alive in Christ' (1 Corinthians 15.22). But what is also noticeable is how infrequent in Paul's letters are contrasts between opposite groups: the righteous and the unrighteous, the holy and the unholy, believers and unbelievers. This last contrast does occur in the letters

to Corinth, notably in the unusually rigorous 2 Corinthians
6.14—7.1: 'Or what does a believer share with an unbeliever?'
(v. 15b).⁹

Why does this – to us – fundamental contrast between the
religious and the irreligious not dominate Paul's writings? It
was not because Paul did not care about a person's response
to the gospel. He clearly did. He contrasts those 'being saved'
with those who are 'perishing' (1 Corinthians 1.18). But this
urgency does not result in a sharp contrast in his letters between 'the righteous' and 'sinners', between the moral and the
immoral, between Christians and non-Christians, churchgoers
and non-churchgoers. It is worth asking why.

In Paul's day the difference between those who had been
baptized and those who had not would have been crucially important, and, at least to the local Christians, obvious. But the
issue here is attitudes and perceptions, and they in turn derive
from the basis on which anyone is 'in' at all. If, as Paul said to
the Corinthians, they had nothing which they had not received
(1 Corinthians 4.7), then they had no reason to pass judgement
on anyone. Above all, they had no grounds for 'boasting'. In
fact, the only legitimate boast is a boast which really stands
boasting on its head: boasting in a crucifixion: 'May I never
boast of anything except the cross of our Lord Jesus Christ, by
which the world has been crucified to me, and I to the world'
(Galatians 6.14).¹⁰ So the cross was why Paul's gospel shocked
the religious (1 Corinthians 1.23). It abolished the existing
distinction between the righteous and the sinner (that is, Jew
and Gentile). Paul's own conversion, no doubt, brought home
to him the realization that the distinction between the religious and the unreligious was not as straightforward as he had
thought. Paul can only have experienced his encounter with
the risen Jesus as an overwhelming experience of forgiveness.
Was that the origin of one of the most radical and subversive
verses he ever penned: '... where sin increased, grace abounded
all the more' (Romans 5.20b)? In Paul's argument in Romans
it led naturally to the question 'Should we continue in sin in
order that grace may abound?' (Romans 6.1, cf. Romans 3.8).
When religious people start to ask questions like that ('What is

the point in going to church, and trying to lead a good life?'), it may be a sign that Paul's subversive gospel is being heard once more.

Notes

1 D. Hardy, *God's Ways with the World*, T. & T. Clark, Edinburgh, 1996, p. 370.

2 S. Weil, *Gravity and Grace*, Routledge, London, 1963, p. 85.

3 Quoted in A. C. Thistleton, *The First Epistle to the Corinthians: A Commentary on the Greek Text*, Eerdmans, Grand Rapids, Michigan/Cambridge, UK, 2000, p. 74.

4 L. E. Keck, *Abingdon New Testament Commentaries. Romans*, Abingdon Press, Nashville, 2005, p. 133.

5 *The Transforming Friendship* was the title of a book by the popular writer and preacher Leslie Weatherhead.

6 The title of C. S. Lewis's autobiography, *Surprised by Joy*, Geoffrey Bles, London, 1955.

7 I owe this point to Professor Morna Hooker's lecture to the Methodist Conference of 1994.

8 Collect from the order of service for a funeral in the *Methodist Worship Book*, Methodist Publishing House, Peterborough, 1999, p. 470.

9 But when Paul briefly refers to marriages in which a believer is married to an unbeliever, he clearly believes that the 'holiness' of the believer 'rubs off', as it were, on the unbeliever (1 Corinthians 7.12–15).

10 Paul implicitly criticizes his fellow-Jews for 'boasting' in God and in the law (Romans 2.17 and 2.23). It is not difficult to find contemporary Christian parallels.

4

Re-thinking Church

Church experiences

Many people, whether members of a Christian church or not, will not see a ready connection between the apostle Paul and the renewal of the Church. Paul, it might be thought, is more of the problem than the solution. Certainly, reading Paul in a literal, wooden way, without regard to historical context, has done damage enough; 'wives obey your husbands', 'slaves obey your masters', and so on have been oppressive texts in the past, and may still be in the future.

Some people may respond: 'Best leave Paul well alone!' But I want to argue that the Church today suffers immeasurable loss by its neglect of Paul's teaching. We need to interpret Paul in such a way that we unlock the enormous potential in his writings for deepening and renewing the life of both the Church, and the individual Christian. But before we begin, it might be helpful to me as I write this chapter – and therefore helpful, I hope, to whoever reads it – if I begin by trying to imagine the experiences which readers of this book will have had of reading Paul and of the life and worship of the Church.

Such experience will be immensely varied. There will be readers who have attended church for most or all of their adult lives and for whom the letters of Paul have long been a puzzle, a sort of grumbling appendix in the background. There will be others reading this book as members of a study group looking for a book which seeks to make a connection between the Bible and our contemporary world. Others may be preachers who have begun to feel a little guilty about sidestepping the epistle every Sunday, and concentrating on just the Gospel or the Old Testament reading (on the odd occasion when it looks promising, that is, or is read at all).

But, aside from the Bible itself, what experiences of the Church have people had, and continue to have? To start at the positive end, I hope there are many who find their local church and its worship a continuing joy and source of nurture for their Christian life. If, for some, that is not true all of the time, I hope at least that it proves true on more Sundays than not. But there are other attitudes and experiences I can easily imagine as I write these words. Many people in the churches – in Britain at least – are tired. They have lived the whole of their Christian lives during a period of numerical decline. They have shouldered responsibilities in their local church for many years, and find it difficult to be as enthusiastic and hopeful as they once were. Still others may be just hanging on. By that I mean that some, perhaps many, have had a less positive experience of the Church. For them, it has been too liberal, or too conservative, or simply irrelevant. Even worse, their local church may not be exactly the best advertisement available for loving your neighbour as yourself. (I recall hearing of a small church with a membership of five which was split three ways. The giving of the peace in that church must have been a sight to see.)

It is more than likely that the preceding paragraphs have hardly begun to do justice to the range of people who may be reading this. But I hope that I have imagined enough for us to explore profitably together what the writings of Paul might have to say to the churches in our day.

i Joining the human race

It may not be immediately apparent, to someone crossing the threshold of a church for the first time, what it's all about. Notice boards, both internal and external, sometimes give an accurate impression, but not always. The notice sheet given to you at the door on a Sunday morning may be just as bewildering, raising in even sharper form the question 'What is this strange organization *for*?' Those of us who have been members of the Church for years may sometimes get the feeling that we can't see the wood for the trees. So what is it really all about?

The way in

In Paul's view, there are three 'gateways' into the Church and the Christian life. First of all, as we saw in Chapter 3, section ii, faith means accepting gratefully God's 'Yes' to us in Christ. Second, God gives us the gift of the Holy Spirit, without whose help we cannot live the Christian life. And, third, we are baptized 'into Christ'. (We tend to think of baptism as a public way of joining the Church or, in the case of a small child, his or her parents making promises on his or her behalf. But Paul's phrase, 'baptism into Christ' (Galatians 3.27), points us to the Church's real centre.)

These three gateways into the Christian life – faith, the gift of the Holy Spirit and baptism – show that there is a 'Trinitarian' foundation to the Church. Paul is constantly going back to first principles: what God has done through Jesus Christ, God's gift of new life in Christ, and God's Spirit who places us in a new community of Christ. So, in case the crowded notice board or the busy midweek programme of our church sometimes obscures 'the Church's one foundation', we begin where Paul began.

Its God-centred character makes the Church different from all other human organizations or societies. True, the Church has a lot in common with other organizations as well, and I'll come to that in a moment. But being God-centred, however imperfectly, makes all the difference. A Roman Catholic scholar recounts the story of how an enthusiastic guide was once showing a group of tourists round the Vatican. When they reached the offices of the Curia, he said, 'And now we come to the very centre of the Church.' A priest in the group was heard to say, 'I thought that the centre was back home, whenever I celebrate the Mass.' It would only be fair, ecumenically speaking, to imagine other scenarios. For example, as a Methodist, I might say: 'I thought that the heart of Methodism was its annual Conference', only to be reminded that its real heart is elsewhere: a small congregation worshipping and witnessing faithfully against all the odds in a place where such a witness is desperately needed.

Of course, the Church – and most local churches – bears a striking resemblance to other organizations. It's always raising money! It's always having committee meetings and, these days, it seems to be constantly re-structuring itself. But Paul reminds us that the Church will only survive by being faithful to its true self – that is, by being God-centred, Christ-centred and Spirit-centred. A church-centred Church, according to Paul, is a contradiction in terms.

More human than religious?

This may sound daunting, even rather narrow to some, so we need to remind ourselves of another important characteristic of the Church. I refer to Paul's teaching about the Church as a truly human community. Admittedly, Paul never uses the phrase 'truly human', but it is implied in what he says about Jesus. Jesus is 'the last Adam' (1 Corinthians 15.45), the 'image of God' (2 Corinthians 4.4), and what Jesus has started is a 'new creation' (Galatians 6.15). Martin Luther saw what this meant when he described Jesus as 'the proper Man', although we should now want to say, instead of 'the proper Man', 'a human being as God intended human beings to be'. This is why baptism (into Christ) may be described as joining the human race. Of course, we join the human race biologically at birth, but Christianity points us towards joining the human race in a fuller, deeper way. Sebastian Moore, in his book *God Is a New Language*, describes Christian experience as 'first, the basic experience of being a human being, being alive to all around you'. This includes being alive to other people, and to all the different ways in which you relate to them. It also means being alive in other ways as well: to the whole world, to the passage of time, to the unfolding of both our lives and the lives of those in whom we are interested, and, finally, to the fact that we shall one day die. And then Moore says this: 'Christian experience is all the above with the co-ordinating sense of unity and growth mysteriously intensified.'[1]

To many people, this quotation may seem a far cry from Paul, or to say far too little about the wonder and depth of the Christian life. But I once heard a monk (of all people, we might think) remark, 'It is more important to be human than religious.' It is all too easy to imagine that the Church stands for a remote and irrelevant 'religious' world which impinges on real life very little. That is not the gospel of Paul. We saw in our discussion of Paul's teaching about idolatry that the difficult language points to how a less-than-God-centred life becomes less than fully human. That problematic word 'sin' means not just losing touch with our true centre – that is, God – but losing touch with our real humanity, often in ways which can be very damaging and destructive. From start to finish, the Bible insists that the Creator is that power which both shapes and renews (redeems) our humanness. God's quest to shape and renew us culminated in the death and resurrection of Jesus, so to be baptized into Christ is to become part of God's new creation, to join the human race as God intended it to be.

Community of Christ and Spirit

No reader of Paul can fail to notice how often he uses the phrase 'in Christ'. 'Christ' here means the mysterious depths in every human being where the human and the divine meet. To put it another way, 'Christ' is the threshold we cross to find communion with God. This, in my view, sheds light on Paul's use of some verses from the book of Deuteronomy in the Old Testament:

> But the righteousness that comes from faith says, 'Do not say in your heart, "Who will ascend into heaven?"' (that is, to bring Christ down) 'or "Who will descend into the abyss?"' (that is, to bring Christ up from the dead). But what does it say? 'The word is near you, on your lips and in your heart' (that is, the word of faith that we proclaim) (Romans 10.6–8).

Paul has other phrases which describe this life lived out of the depths where human and divine intersect. He calls it life 'in the

Spirit' – particularly in Romans 8.1–11, where life in the Spirit is contrasted with 'life in the flesh'. That language is misleading, understood literally. Living in the Spirit does *not* mean living some kind of otherworldly, disembodied life. Living 'in the flesh' means living on the surface of things, allowing the superficial 'me' to call the tune, instead of the Christ who is hidden in the depths. Christian hymns and prayers sometimes use different imagery, like the popular Christmas carol:

> O Holy Child of Bethlehem
> Descend to us we pray.
> Cast out our sin, and enter in,
> Be born in us today.

But whether we imagine the new life being unlocked in the depths of our hearts, or coming to us from outside, the reality is the same: life in Christ, which is also life in the Spirit. (Paul uses yet another phrase which points in the same direction: 'in the Lord', a phrase which occurs when he is giving instructions about Christian living, and so the emphasis falls on obedience.)

The mysterious reality of Christ – where God and humankind met and still meet – is humanity's template. So, seeking to live by that mystery and 'joining the human race' is, in Paul's view, what it's all about. In the Church at its best, or at its heart, that is precisely what we *do* see: for example, when a congregation of all ages, races and backgrounds comes to the communion rail to receive the bread and wine. This is the Church's heart, rather than the premises, the meetings, and the structures – however useful and even necessary they may be. Paul would, I think, have agreed with my monastic friend: 'It is more important to be human than religious.' He had tried being religious – in the wrong sort of way. (Romans 10.2–3, with its reference to an unenlightened 'zeal for God', almost certainly reflects his own experience.)

Being a human community is not simply an airy-fairy idea, and it is no accident that the words 'each other' occur so frequently in Paul: 'bear one another's burdens' (Galatians 6.2), 'encourage each other' (1 Thessalonians 5.11), 'consider each other better than yourselves' (Philippians 2.3) – the full list is a long one. It shows that, in Paul's view, the key to this new life 'in Christ' isn't just, by the grace of God, in the depths of our own hearts, but somehow *in each other*. Because we are the body of Christ, 'we are members of each other' (Ephesians 4.25).

At this point, some readers might be saying to themselves 'If only … If only the Church were truly human!' As with everything fundamental about the Church, God gives it as his gift and, at the same time, calls the Church to get on with realizing it. A New Testament scholar once summarized Paul's instructions to his churches as 'Be what you are!' Another summarized the apostle's teaching even more challengingly: 'Be what God is!' ('… be imitators of God … and live in love' (Ephesians 5.1).)

Paul's contrast between life in the Spirit and life 'according to the flesh' is a particular challenge to the Church. A church living 'according to the flesh' is one which allows the outward, tangible things of its life to call the tune. They may be the premises, practicalities about worship (what kind of music, how much IT, etc.), or it might be money: the lack of it, how to raise it, what to do with it. When the outward, tangible things shape, or even dominate, the life of the Church, rather than the Spirit, then the Church is in trouble.

No competition

But there is another practical result of trying to see the Church in the way that Paul saw it. The Church is distinctive, if not unique, in not defining itself over against any other organizations. Whatever a congregation may sometimes think, their church is not in competition with anyone or anything else: not the church down the road, not the local mosque, not even the local supermarket. Why? Because its mandate is simply to be God's universal human society in the way I have tried to outline – and the human race can't be in competition with itself!

Paul's way of looking at this is what scholars call 'eschatological', a word we came across in the last chapter. To say that the Church is an eschatological reality is what is implied in Paul's language about a new creation. This new thing is what God in his love purposes for everyone. Whether everyone will one day join the Church is a different matter. As Paul saw when he reflected on the destiny of his own people in Romans chapters 9–11, the ways and the purposes of God soar way above what we can imagine. But in the meantime the Church has a responsibility to model God's new creation, and to share it with as many people as it can. It is not in competition with anyone, and should never behave as if it is.

ii What does a person have to do to sign up?

The lady put her head rather diffidently round the church door. It was a weekday, she was collecting her child from the play-group meeting in the hall adjacent to the church, and she had never set foot in the church before. Someone was arranging the flowers. 'Can anyone come to this church?' she asked.

Do people who don't attend church not realize that church services are open to anyone who wishes to go? It is difficult to know whether or not that lady was typical of many, but the story certainly raises the question of what I will call 'admission requirements'. We need to look at these from two directions. From inside the Church, as it were, it is important not to water down the demands of Christian faith. The Church must go on saying, as honestly and clearly as it can, 'This is what we take on if we are serious about being Christians'. But it would be misleading, even downright wrong, to call this invitation to faith and discipleship an admission requirement. You don't have to believe anything to set foot inside a church. Becoming a committed, or confirmed, member is another matter, and I shall return to that.

Admission requirements

To begin with, we are concerned with admission requirements as seen not from inside the Church, but from outside. There are all kinds of misunderstandings, ranging from the frankly comic to the very serious, about what a person has to be or to do to join the Church. I recall an example of the more comic kind of misunderstanding when, many years ago, my wife-to-be informed her colleagues at the school where she taught that she was to marry a Methodist minister. 'Does that mean', asked one, 'that you'll have to wear hats, and things like that?'

There are many other misperceptions about what is required from people seeking to join the Church, or even attending a church service. Many still appear to believe that you have to be a teetotaller to be a Methodist, for example. Many who haven't been to a church service for a number of years may think that you have to 'dress up' if you are not to appear the odd one out. In fact, these days it is the person who dresses up to go to church who is more likely to be the odd one out! Much more serious are the misgivings which stem from a feeling of unworthiness: 'I have been divorced, so I may not be welcome', 'I am a single parent, so I won't fit in', and so on. Experiences of this kind are, sadly, only too numerous.

Tragically, misgivings like these have on occasions proved only too well-founded. Sometimes what people mistakenly think they have to do to join the Church finds confirmation in the attitudes, conscious or otherwise, of a local congregation. When that happens, such people have encountered the Church at its worst, rather than the Church at its best. The point I am making is this: apart from what we might call legitimate requirements – for example, a person can't really be confirmed if they don't believe anything – there are also illegitimate, or illusory, admission requirements. From the inside a congregation may, wittingly or unwittingly, impose its own qualifications for joining: 'we want people who will fit in, people who are "one of us"', or 'we would rather not have scruffily dressed people in our church' or 'we approve of children and young people only if they know how to behave', and so on.

What has all this to do with Paul? To coin a phrase of the apostle himself, 'Much in every way!' In Chapter 2 we looked at the crisis addressed by Paul in his letter to the Galatians. It was a crisis about admission requirements or, more precisely perhaps, the conditions for being members of the Christian movement: should Gentile converts to Christ become practising Jews in order to be 'proper' or 'fully fledged' Christians? It was natural to think that they should. After all, the Scriptures (that is, our Old Testament) said that God's people should not eat pork or work on the Sabbath (to mention just two of the most important hallmarks of the people of God). So surely Gentiles, like their Jewish-Christian brothers and sisters, should keep the law of Moses where these commandments of God – and many more – were to be found? This was the young Christian movement's first big identity crisis. What was it? A kind of Jewish sect? Or what? To Paul's everlasting credit, he seems to have been the first to see, or the first to see and to argue so cogently, that Gentile converts did not have to become practising Jews in order to join 'the church of God'. Scholars call this crisis at Galatia the 'Judaizing' crisis. (Paul uses the Greek word 'Judaize' in Galatians 2.14; it's normally translated as 'live like Jews'.) This major crisis in the life of the infant Church suggests that there is a world of difference between 'proselytizing' and evangelizing and it is worth taking a moment to consider this difference.

Proselytizing and evangelism

Proselytizing today can mean a number of different things. In particular, it can be used to describe the activity of one religious faith in poaching adherents from another faith. They are 'proselytes'. But the situation at Galatia suggests a slightly different meaning. In view of what Paul's rivals were trying to do, persuading Gentiles to become Jews, we can describe 'proselytizing' as 'making Christians in your own image'. In other words, such evangelists, for whatever reason, seek to turn their converts into the same kind of Christians as they are.

The churches today constantly confuse proselytizing and evangelism. We think we are talking about evangelism when we are really talking about getting new members – people like ourselves, who will do their bit in supporting 'our' church. Or, more subtly perhaps, we think that anyone becoming a Christian has to believe all that we believe. As a university chaplain, I encountered this kind of Christian proselytizing quite often. Some Christian groups supposed that you could not be a proper Christian unless you accepted a particular view of the atonement, and of the inspiration of the Bible. On one occasion, I recall, it was made very plain that even a chaplain wasn't welcome to address one of these groups unless he first signed up to such beliefs! Of course, Christian groups and Christian churches have a right, within reason, to establish their own boundaries. But what they may not do, if Paul is to be our guide, is to imply that their boundaries are the threshold to, or the admission requirements for, Christian faith. That would be to repeat the mistake of Paul's rivals at Galatia, and to imagine that the only conceivable kind of Christian was one like themselves.

Paul's letter to the Galatians presents a particular challenge to congregations. Let members of a congregation ask themselves, 'What really holds us together as a church?' 'What do we, as members of this church, have in common?' The answer to questions like that is likely to be what I have called 'admission requirements' which, perhaps quite unwittingly, they impose on 'outsiders' or would-be newcomers. To take an extreme example, I have encountered churches (usually small chapels) where the duty steward has said to me, as the visiting preacher, 'You might as well start the service; we're all here.' What held that congregation together? I hope I am wrong, but I fear it may have been habit or loyalty: they had all been coming to that chapel for 20 years and more. That is what they had in common. It can be very difficult, as many who are reading this will know, for newcomers to join such a congregation. A church in which the characteristic feature of all its members is long attendance is in danger of being a closed shop. How can anyone join them if being one of them, by definition, is to have been attending that church for 20 years?

I do not wish to paint too gloomy a picture, and, thank goodness, the grace and warm-heartedness of a genuine welcome can encourage a newcomer at the most unprepossessing-looking of churches. But the challenge of Paul's letter to the Galatians stands: are we trying to turn newcomers and outsiders

into Christians like ourselves, by getting them to conform to
a particular church identity or culture? Or are we giving them
the space to find themselves in Christ?

This brings me to the question of what evangelism really
is. I am suggesting that Galatians challenges us to distinguish
between proselytizing – which I have tried to illustrate – and
evangelizing, which I have not yet defined. But, first, we should
remind ourselves of the ground-breaking revolution which
Paul sparked off as a result of this crisis.

All the first disciples were members of the Jewish race, and
for a number of years that seems to have been true of the
Church as it grew in numbers in places like Jerusalem, Judaea
and Galilee (Acts 9.31 – perhaps Samaritans were counted as
'borderline'). Even if a disciple like Peter had been a rather lax
Jew, and Matthew the tax-collector certainly was, their following of Jesus may have made them better Jews. Luke paints a
picture of Peter as a devout, law-abiding Jew (Acts 3.1, 10.14),
so the notion that you could be a Christian *without* observing
the Sabbath, refraining from eating pork, and so on, must have
seemed to many revolutionary indeed.

Evangelism according to Paul challenges members of a
church, like the first Jewish Christians, to welcome Christians
not like themselves, but *different* from themselves. How different they can be is a critical question for the churches today,
and I return to that question in section iv of this chapter. But
Paul has more to teach us about evangelism, and for this we
turn to another of his letters, 1 Corinthians.

Evangelism in 'weakness'

Paul's description of his first visit to Corinth is surprising. He
says '... I came to you in weakness and in fear and in much
trembling' (1 Corinthians 2.3). 'Weakness' here means a
weakness which Paul chose, rather than a natural weakness.
He chose not to speak in the fine rhetoric of the average Greek
sophist, and so, to many, he may have seemed distinctly un-
impressive. 'Weakness' may mean he also chose not to find
the patronage of a wealthy man, as many teachers did at that

time. Paul may not have been able to, anyway, and the 'weakness' Paul chose may simply have been the choice to earn his living at the humble trade of tent-making (Acts 18.3). That was not the style sophisticated Greeks would expect from a philosopher-teacher!

According to Acts, Paul divided his time between the workshop and the local synagogue (Acts 18.3–4), which would have been, at best, a very modest building – or perhaps not even a building at all, but simply a meeting-place. In both places Paul would have been in a somewhat exposed position as the teacher not of a recognizable brand of philosophy, but of a strange oriental sect which was puzzlingly like, yet unlike, Judaism.

Paul at Corinth – and Paul at Athens for that matter (Acts 17.16–33) – embodies something profoundly important about authentic Christian evangelism. Evangelists choose 'weakness' in this sense: they make themselves vulnerable for the sake of the gospel by moving out of what we might call a religious comfort zone – which, in our situation, means church premises. In footballing terms, the evangelist plays not on his own turf, but away from home.

One of the best modern illustrations I know of this comes from a Catholic priest called Vincent Donovan, who evangelized the Masai tribe in east Africa. He chose to go – that is the point – into unknown territory where no Christian teacher had previously gone. His description of his first visit is worth quoting:

> Here I was, at last, face to face with an adult pagan people, with nothing between me and them but the gospel of Jesus Christ ... Each day, in that brisk, early morning hour ... as I stood waiting for them to gather, I was conscious of the knot in my stomach, wondering if this were the day it would all blow up in my face, with Christianity being utterly rejected by these sons of the plains. Many is the time in that lonely, nomadic setting that I wished I were back in the comfortable company of familiar and acquiescent Christians.[2]

This is what Paul meant in 1 Corinthians by 'weakness'. Donovan's story is quite a dramatic example; the setting for many of us today is more likely to be the workplace or the pub – anywhere which is not a religious comfort zone, and where the would-be evangelist is likely to find himself or herself in a minority. Like the football team playing away which knows that their own supporters comprise only a small minority among the watching spectators, the evangelist knows he or she is out on a limb for the sake of the gospel. That is evangelism according to Paul.

It is a more vulnerable activity than proselytizing will normally be. Evangelism, according to Paul, turns upside down some commonly held views about the subject. Take this extract from a document produced some years ago by the World Council of Churches:

> can a person ... Or a church, indeed a whole people, who holds human power over others truly evangelize? I think not. If I hold power over others, I can feed them, I can protect them ... or manipulate their will ... I can lead them. I can even offer my life for them. But I cannot challenge them ... To repent, or to stand up and walk, or to take up one's cross and follow Jesus ... As long as I hold power over others, I cannot share the gospel of Jesus Christ with them and expect an authentic response. There is no evangelism. There is only proselytism.[3]

That, I think, is why Paul had to go to Corinth 'in weakness', and why he has so much to teach us about evangelism.

iii 'Seven whole days, not one in seven'

We are so used to there being seven days in a week, it's very difficult to imagine time being organized in any other way. But it could be. We could re-design diaries, calendars and working weeks in accordance with a nine- or ten-day week. This was tried both during the French Revolution, which was obsessed with decimalization, and during the Russian Revolution, but in both cases it had to be abandoned as it simply did not work.[4] As it is, we have a seven-day week, and though times are changing, three of the world's great faiths observe one of those days as their holy day: Moslems observe Fridays, Jews Saturdays, and Christians Sundays.

In Paul's time, the seven-day week had been long established. In the Jewish world, there was a seven-day week, with strict observance of the Sabbath – that is, our Saturday; in the wider Graeco-Roman world there was the 'planetary' week, though the planets known then were only five in number, and the sun and moon were included as well.

But what happened in Paul's churches? As we've seen, he fought hard for the principle that his Gentile converts did not have to keep the Jewish law of Moses. So among other things, they were not obliged to observe the Sabbath. In fact, it's hard to see how a Gentile slave in, say, Corinth, could observe *any* day, since he would be at his master's beck-and-call 24 hours a day. The best he could probably hope for would be a bit of free time either before daybreak, or else at the very end of the working day. It may not be just a coincidence that when 'the first day of the week' is mentioned in the New Testament, it's often at those times (for example, Acts 20.7–8). We don't know when the first Christians began to meet on the day we now call Sunday, but Paul gives us the earliest reference of all. He urges the Christians at Corinth to put aside what they can for the collection 'on the first day of the week' (1 Corinthians 16.2). That doesn't prove that the church at Corinth met on that day, but it makes it likely that they did. And yet – and this is one of the many startling things Paul has to say to the contemporary Church – in the apostle's view most worship happens outside 'church', not inside it.

Life as worship

Of course, to say 'church' here is misleading. Paul's young Christian communities didn't have church buildings; they met in people's homes: Priscilla and Aquila hosted one such house-church in Rome (Romans 16.3–5), and Gaius, so it seems, hosted the 'whole church' at Corinth (Romans 16.23). It's also clear from Paul's letters, particularly 1 Corinthians (chapters

11 and 14), that they met in such homes for worship. But Paul's language shows that their worship on those occasions was only the tip of the iceberg. Their daily lives were their worship.

A chapel in the city of Lincoln illustrates the principle very well. As you enter, you can see above the doorway, inscribed in the stonework, '*Orare est laborare*' ('To pray is to work'). As you leave the chapel, you can see, in the stonework now facing you, a complementary message: '*Laborare est orare*' ('To work is to pray'). Paul writes of seven-day worship more than once, but never more clearly than in Romans 12.1: 'I appeal to you therefore, brothers and sisters, by the mercies of God, to present your bodies as a living sacrifice, holy and acceptable to God, which is your spiritual worship.'

This isn't the only language of this kind Paul uses. Remarkably, he tells the motley collection of Christians at Corinth (almost certainly all Gentiles): 'Do you not know that you are God's temple and that God's Spirit dwells in you?' (1 Corinthians 3.16). And this from an erstwhile Pharisee who had been schooled from birth to regard a building in Jerusalem as God's temple!

The theme of worship which is 'seven whole days, not one in seven' runs throughout Paul's letters. In the light of his description of the churches to whom he writes, this should not surprise us. They are 'the holy ones' (for example, 2 Corinthians 1.1, Philippians 1.1). That is what the word literally means. Many modern versions prefer the translation 'saints' or, in the case of the Contemporary English Version, 'God's people'. This last translation at least makes the contrast between being holy and the behaviour of some of the church at Corinth rather less stark!

Holiness today is an offputting concept to most people. We are more familiar with the expression 'holier than thou' than with more positive ideas. But for Paul it was, above all, a God word. Behind the word is the experience of God's grace: no one ever becomes a member of God's people except by the generous invitation and call of God. So there is no such thing as DIY holiness. But that didn't mean that God's people at Corinth could rest on their laurels; they were called to live up to the status God had generously lavished on them, reflecting in their daily lives the character of God, a theme to which we shall return in the next chapter.

So a community variously described as God's temple and God's holy ones might be thought to live in a little religious world of its own! We could hardly be more wrong. Demetrius, my fictional slave in Thessalonika, had to work all day, every day; perhaps Marcella, wife of Rufus who wasn't a member of the church at Philippi, would have had a household to supervise. So life had to go on. That was the message of 2 Thessalonians, which, even if not by Paul himself, was written in his name: '... we hear that some of you are living in idleness, mere busybodies, not doing any work. Now such persons we command ... to do their work quietly and to earn their own living' (2 Thessalonians 3.11–12).

What must the pressures on the likes of Demetrius and Marcella have been? We can only imagine. Paul frequently refers to the sufferings of Christians; at the very least, that means the pressures they were under solely because of their faith. They must have been tempted many times to give up this strange new Christian faith, or merge chameleon-like with their environment to the point where the question of a modern advert would apply: 'Can *you* tell the difference?' This is why, in the second half of a major appeal to Christian living which we've already quoted from, Paul makes it clear that God's people are to be a 'contra-flow' people: 'Do not be conformed to this world, but be transformed by the renewing of your minds, so that you may discern what is the will of God – what is good and acceptable and perfect' (Romans 12.2).

A contra-flow life

Where did Christians such as Demetrius or Marcella find the inner resources to go against the flow of the pagan society in which they were immersed? In important ways, of course, they could not. A Christian slave obeying his pagan master, or a Christian wife obeying her pagan husband, must have been involved in compromises. But unless Paul was completely wasting his breath – and Tertius' ink (16.22)! – in urging the Christians at Rome not to be conformed, we must assume that, in ways which could be seen and ways which could not be seen, Demetrius and Marcella were different. There were points at which they would have taken a stand; Paul's most uncompromising statement on the subject we have noticed before: 'Therefore come out from them, and be separate from them, says the Lord' (2 Corinthians 6.17).

Is the habit of churchgoing the only real 'contra-flow' characteristic of Christians today? Or, if it is not, how do contemporary Christians find the wherewithal not to be conformed to the prevailing norms of the society around them? Sometimes the voice of God speaks through that wider society. The move towards greater equality between women and men began outside the churches, and the churches are, it seems, playing 'catch-up'. On the gay issue, the churches have yet to make up their minds whether society at large is ethically ahead of them, or whether they should be a counter-cultural minority resisting the pressure to judge homosexual and heterosexual relations by the same standard. (I return to this indirectly in the next section.) For examples of this, most churchgoers in developed countries are likely to spend more time reading newspapers, and watching or listening to news bulletins, than reading the Bible. This is not surprising, and the way we read a newspaper and the way we read the Bible are likely to be very different. But we can't escape the challenge: which of the two has the greater influence on us – our newspaper or the Bible? This is an important question to ask, not least because of the moralistic and often intolerant tone of some of our newspapers. Take, for example, this summary of the creed of one popular newspaper:

> ... against welfare (and what it describes as welfare scroungers) and for standing on your own feet; more concerned with punishment than the causes of crime; against public ownership and for the private sector; against liberal values and for traditional values, particularly marriage and family life. It puts achievement above equality of opportunity and self-reliance above dependence.[5]

As this summary was published in another newspaper, we must be careful! What may be said about one paper may be said about the others, too. I am not, of course, suggesting that the philosophy summarized here is wholly wrong. My concern is that churchgoers who read this paper (the *Daily Mail*) each day, but not their Bibles, may unwittingly have their lives shaped more by the *Mail* than by the gospel. The challenge for contemporary Christians stands: which will have greater influence on their lives – their newspaper (or television) or the Bible?

So how is worship to be sustained all day every day? It may seem an impossible ideal, but it is the direction in which Paul points us. We find a number of clues in his writings. Being vigilant – not the same thing as watching for the end of the world – and praying 'without ceasing' (1 Thessalonians 5.6 and 17) provide the ground bass of Christian living. Putting our whole selves into whatever we have to do is another major theme (Colossians 3.23). So, too, are the many reminders that the Christian life is not like the card game of patience: there are others to encourage and to be encouraged. Here it would be worth exploring why most Christians find it easier to offer to carry someone else's burden than to admit they need help in carrying their own (Galatians 6.2).

There is one expression, repeated in 2 Corinthians, which points us to the heart of Paul's Christian experience and discipline: 'We are speaking in Christ before God' (2 Corinthians 2.17, 12.19). Paul is answering criticisms here, and he points to the One to whom he is finally answerable. Yet, in so doing, is he hinting at the daily discipline of practising the presence of God? He would surely have been the first to say that these words of his could be extended: we are *living* in Christ, in the presence of God. That is both gift and discipline.

iv What Paul didn't say about gay people

How much diversity should the Church tolerate?

In recent years, it seems that the only occasions when the Church makes headlines is when Christians can't agree – whether about women's ordination, women bishops or, above all, the gay issue. Yet, surprisingly, we seem to have taken very little notice of what Paul advised in a situation where a church was sharply polarized by contradictory convictions.

In our discussion of 'What does a person have to do to join?' (section ii), I raised the question of how different Christians can legitimately be. If we aren't able to say, 'In the church, anything goes – believe what you like, do your own thing', what *can* we say? Paul teaches us that there is a place in the Church for conflict. He opposed Peter at Antioch (Galatians 2.11–21) for the sake of what he, Paul, clearly believed was 'the truth of the gospel'. Therefore it can be right for Christians to confront one another if a person believes that the other has violated that fundamental truth. But it's also important to notice that Peter and Paul did not excommunicate each other; they remained fellow-apostles. (If some refused to recognize Paul as an apostle, we have no evidence for supposing that their number included Peter.)

What of other differences in the Church? Within many churches individual beliefs differ a great deal, and that may be a very healthy sign. It's good that people are welcome to come to church whatever, or however little, they believe. Becoming a confirmed member is different, of course, although even here there is room for diversity. For example, Christians may have – within certain limits – different understandings of the Bible, of the death and resurrection of Jesus, and so on. It's important to say that there are some articles of faith by which the Church stands or falls, including the doctrines of the incarnation and Trinity, which imply also a belief in the atoning death and resurrection of Christ. These form a central part of every basic Christian creed. None of us understands them fully (how could we possibly do that?), and we may differ in our interpretation even of these central affirmations. But the point is that they are the central beliefs from which everything that matters about the Church derives. So, in discussing what happens when Christians disagree, I am not suggesting that anything goes, or that Christians can take opposite views on the fundamentals of the Christian faith and it really doesn't matter.

Let's consider first how we know whether a person is a Christian or not. We don't often ask that question, and for good reason. Jesus told his followers not to assume the prerogative of God in judging others (Matthew 7.1), and the Bible keeps on reminding us that only God reads people's hearts. Sometimes, however, the question has to be put, particularly when the Church is in crisis. But most of the time, if people confess the faith, and avail themselves of the means of grace as often as they can, we don't say to them 'Prove to me that you are a Christian'. Normally, unless a person is consistently behaving in a way which is damaging the Church, or which is blatantly at odds with the faith, we accept them as they present themselves. So what should we say to one another, when, for example, we take opposite viewpoints on an important (even emotive) moral issue, such as gay partnerships? How much diversity of conduct may the Church embrace? How many conflicting convictions can, or should, the Church tolerate about Christian behaviour?

Paul's teaching doesn't allow for diversity on everything. All Christians are called to show qualities like faith, hope, love, humility, forgiveness, obedience, vigilance, self-control, concern for the poor ... The list could go on. Paul says as much about, by implication, the opposites of these qualities: all Christians are called to avoid greed, anxiety, disregard for the poor, etc. So Paul is a long way from telling his converts to 'do their own thing', as if he were an early exponent of post-modernism. But in two passages he offers us a wealth of guidance about what Christians should do when, as with the gay issue, they find themselves taking diametrically opposite viewpoints. I shall come to those two passages in a moment. But first we need to ask whether, in these disputes, being able to quote the Bible in your support settles the issue; that is, when you can quote a text or two to back up your view, but your opponent can't – or, at least, you think their use of the Bible is suspect, to say the least.

Interpreting the Bible

So, how are we to use the Bible? We can't avoid this question if we are going to answer our basic question of how much Christians are, as it were, 'allowed' to differ. The Bible itself does not tell us directly how we should use it, and contrary to what many suppose, contains no theory of inspiration, and makes no claims of inerrancy or infallibility. (Even if 2 Timothy 3.16 were relevant here, it simply assumes that the Scriptures are inspired, but the writer doesn't say what he means by that.)[6] St Paul says of the Hebrew Scriptures that they were written for our instruction (Romans 15.4 and 1 Corinthians 10.6). The way Paul used *his* scriptures (that is, our Old Testament) in those two passages suggests that we should use the Bible – as the record of God's transforming revelation – to enrich and, where necessary, correct the life of the Church.

That's only a start, of course, and we'll need to come back to the very complex question of how we use the Bible. (People who don't acknowledge that it is a complex question are likely either to be picking and choosing parts of the Bible to suit themselves, or else not taking the Bible seriously enough to have noticed.) For now, we should note that when Christians disagree, it is insufficient and unhelpful simply to quote the Bible, and to assume that that should end the argument.

Doesn't Paul do precisely that – quote the Scriptures to back up his arguments? It seems he did, but it is very likely that his opponents did so too. After all, they were Jewish Christians, like him. So, for example, the rival missionaries in Galatia who tried to persuade Paul's Gentile converts to become Jews would almost certainly have quoted Scripture in their own support. The issue then, as now, was not who accepted the authority of the Bible and who did not, but which interpretations of the Bible were to be accepted, and which not.

Instead of speaking of the authority of Scripture in a general or absolute way, we should rather ask, 'Where do we *locate* its authority? What is the heart of the Bible?' The question needs to be asked because even the most ardent fundamentalist does not take every verse literally, since that would be impossible. We all *interpret* the Bible; we don't simply quote it. And even if we do, our selection of quotations is, in itself, an interpretation. For myself, I try to interpret the Bible on the working hypothesis that the heart of its authority is the saving revelation of God in Christ.

After these preliminary reflections about the Bible, its authority and interpretation, I come to the two key passages in Paul's writings about how Christians should proceed when they hold opposing convictions, particularly – as with issues relating to gay partnerships – on fundamental issues of Christian behaviour. We are concerned mainly with a passage from Romans which we looked at briefly in Chapter 2 – namely, Romans 14.1—15.7. But it's useful to notice first that this passage had a predecessor in the form of 1 Corinthians, chapters 8 to 10.

Conflicting convictions at Corinth and Rome

The background to these chapters we explored in Chapter 2, section ii, but it may be helpful to summarize briefly that discussion here. Paul was addressing a situation similar to that at Rome – Christians couldn't agree. How differences among Christians arose at Corinth is fairly clear. The stronger, more self-confident Christians were probably those of higher social status. Paul quotes two of their slogans (1 Corinthians 8.4 and 10.23): they did not believe in the reality of idols, and so meat which had been used in pagan sacrifices could be eaten without harm by Christians – even in the dining-rooms attached to pagan temples. The 'weaker' members were not so sure. (And these were probably poorer Christians who, in their pre-Christian days, may only ever have eaten meat at pagan festivals.)

Paul is concerned that the faith of the weak might be damaged or even destroyed – probably by the example or the pressure of the strong. In this long discussion, he offers himself as a role-model (1 Corinthians 9): don't simply exercise your freedom as a Christian, not even your freedom of conscience if it's going to damage someone else's faith. The whole argument shows that the needs of the other, rather than the freedom of the individual Christian, should be what determines Christian conduct. This was what guided Paul's own evangelistic strategy, and it gives a very surprising picture of Christian integrity – in Paul's case, 'all things to all people' (9.22).

The situation at Rome was similar to that at Corinth, but

there the conflicts almost certainly arose from Jew/Gentile differences. Some scholars have questioned this; 'the weak' who
are described here ate only vegetables (Romans 14.2), and ab-
stained from wine (14.21), and we've no other evidence for
such practices among Jews in Paul's time. But the letter to the
Romans as a whole is so much concerned with the mutual
understanding of Jew and Gentile in the purposes of God and
the Church of Christ that it is likely that Paul is addressing
another Jew/Gentile issue here as well. The biblical quotations
with which the section concludes (15.8–12) make this even
more likely. But socio-economic differences – as at Corinth
– may have been a factor at Rome as well, and this may be why
Paul does not specifically address the two groups as Jews and
Gentiles.

Paul's starting-point in Romans (and conclusion, 15.7) is
God's acceptance of us all in Christ (14.3). So *both groups
in these disputes belong to Christ* (14.6–9). It would be difficult to over-emphasize the importance of this, and that is
why the question I raised earlier is so important: how do we
know whether a person is a Christian or not? It is no part of
the Christian life to cross-examine one another in destructive
ways, which is the meaning, perhaps, of an obscure phrase in
14.1 (New Revised Standard Version: 'Welcome ... but not for
the purpose of quarrelling over opinions').

This mutual acceptance, however, does not imply an easy-
going 'live and let live' attitude. Paul's teaching here rests firm-
ly on two things:

1 He believes that Christ is the common Lord of all Christians.
2 All Christians are accountable, both now and in the future,
  to God.

So two attitudes, in particular, are out of place in the Church:
judging or despising Christians who hold a conviction contradictory to yours (14. 3–4, 10, 13). In these conflicts at Rome,
both sides belong to Christ. How dare anyone say otherwise?
We may disagree sharply with someone, but how dare we say
that someone who confesses the faith, and seeks to live by it,

even if with different convictions from yours, is not a Christian? (This does not, of course, include those foundational beliefs which I identified earlier as those by which the Church stands or falls.)

Paul does not say that at the judgement it will be revealed who was right and who was wrong, although that no doubt will be true. Instead, he insists that, until then, we all live and die to the Lord (14.8), and so, in the meantime, judging and despising are inappropriate and unwise, because 'we will all stand before the judgement seat of God ... each of us will be accountable to God' (14.10c, 12). But Paul rules out judging and despising one another – the characterizing attitudes of the weak and the strong respectively – not only because it's inappropriate in the church, but also because it is destructive. In 14.13, he continues: 'Let us therefore no longer pass judgement on one another, but resolve instead never to put a stumbling-block or hindrance in the way of another.'

What was a stumbling-block? Subsequent verses show that putting a 'stumbling-block' in someone's way was tantamount to damaging or destroying their faith (vv. 15 and 20–21). How might this happen? First, destructive attitudes in a church (notably judging and despising) are damaging. But, second, a Christian, or a group of Christians, might have put pressure on those fellow-Christians who disagreed with them, either by their arguments, or because of their superior status (in the church or in society), or, if they were in the majority, simply by the pressure of numbers. A third way in which someone's faith might be damaged could be by example (cf. 1 Corinthians 8.9–10). A 'weaker' Christian sees a fellow-Christian sitting down to a meal in the precincts of a pagan temple, and allows himself to be persuaded, against his own conscience, to do the same.

Paul sets an enormous premium here on personal responsibility. In effect, he gives a Christian brother or sister the right to be wrong – or wrong in his view. This seems very clear from Romans 14.14: 'I know and am persuaded in the Lord Jesus that nothing is unclean in itself; but it is unclean for anyone who thinks it unclean.' Paul has already said that each must act according to his or her own convictions (v. 5), and he goes on to express this even more strongly in verses where the word 'faith' seems to function in a way similar to the word 'conscience' in 1 Corinthians 8—10. So, remarkably, it is faith here, not the law, which defines sin: 'The faith that you have, have as your own conviction before God. Blessed are those who have no reason to condemn themselves because of what they approve. But those who have doubts are condemned if they eat, because they do not act from faith; for whatever does not proceed from faith is sin' (14.22–23). So, as a great German scholar observed, in this passage Christ remains the only measure for all. No one must make his or her faith a norm for others as they seek to serve Christ. The weak want uniformity by making their law binding for others, and the strong seek uniformity as well by trying to impose their own 'freer' ways on the weak. So we end up trying to make others in our own image. When we do that, we fall into sin, because Christian faith is about people conforming to the image of Christ, not ours, or anyone else's.[7]

Gay relationships and the Bible

Before I draw some conclusions from this passage for our situation today, it might be helpful to recall the title of this section: 'What Paul didn't say about gay people'. We know that Paul condemned the homosexual practices of his day. That seems clear from 1 Corinthians 6.9 and Romans 1.26–27, although we noted in Chapter 1 that what Paul condemned was almost certainly promiscuous, abusive sexual practices. What none of us knows, or can know, is what Paul would say now. With our greater understanding of human sexuality – and it *is* greater, not just different – would a twenty-first-century Paul take a positive view of a faithful, lifelong same-sex partnership? Some will say that we have no reason for supposing that at all. Fair enough, but the argument cuts both ways. We might equally well conclude that he would, given his readiness to adapt and change in his own lifetime to the leading of the Spirit. Who would have forecast that the zealous Pharisee would one day sit down to share a meal with a Gentile in pagan Corinth?

Instead of debating what Paul would, or would not, say if he were to come back today, we would be wiser to concentrate on what he *did* say to Christians with opposing convictions at Rome: 'Accept one another, as God in Christ has accepted you'. So what conclusions may we draw from Romans 14.1— 15.7? The issues which Paul addressed at Rome were not trivial. Questions about whether Christians today should eat vegetables may not be important, but they were in the church at Rome. The language Paul uses about 'destroying' a brother or sister shows that the matter was serious. But there is another point. When the Church finally recognized that a certain writing, whether a gospel or an epistle, should be included in its Scriptures, it implied that that writing had a message for the Church anywhere at any time. So the fact that Romans is in our New Testament means: its teaching transcends its original context. What Paul said then applies to other situations where Christians cannot agree, so can we relate it to current debates about gay partnerships?

We need to return briefly to the question of how we use the Bible. In a number of ethical issues, such as the blessing or re- marriage of divorcées, the possession of wealth, and the just war, the Church has seen fit to go beyond the literal application of certain biblical texts. The issue here is not the Bible's author- ity – for the Christian that cannot be in doubt – nor how many verses we can find in the Bible to support our point of view. Rather, there are two questions, both to do with the Bible:

1 What is the heart of the Bible's authority? Is it, as I sug- gested, God's transforming revelation in Christ?
2 How are we to *interpret* the Bible, and find the grace to lis- ten to others' interpretation of it?

So it cannot be sufficient to respond, 'Scripture says ...' when in many other issues we have set the letter of Scripture aside on the grounds that God's transforming revelation recorded in the Bible leads us to do so. For example, if we allow people who have been divorced to receive communion, or to re-marry in church, or if we permit a millionaire to receive communion, gladly accepting his generous donation for church funds, what is our scriptural foundation? And what verses from the Bible will an army chaplain use to reassure young soldiers in Iraq or Afghanistan that they are doing God's will? Interpreting the Bible is truly a complex matter, but it is a task vital for the health of the Church.

So, if Paul is to be our guide, we are faced with a stark choice when we encounter confessing Christians with convictions contradictory to ours on a particular moral issue. We may, in effect, 'excommunicate' them, by denying that they are Christians at all, but that would be a grave step to take. If such a person is not denying an article of faith by which the Church stands or falls, and is not living a life flagrantly in contradiction of the faith or destructive of the Church, we have no grounds for declining to recognize their status as a fellow-Christian.

Some will say that a life flagrantly at odds with the faith or destructive of the faith is precisely what is at stake in the gay issue. Romans 14.1—15.7, though, invites us to take another course of action. Attitudes to each other are, according to Paul, absolutely crucial. We may not judge or despise; we may not impose our own convictions on others, whether by threat or pressure. Nor should we damage another's faith by our own example, our attitude, or in any other way. There is, according to Paul, no basis at all for being angry with, or intolerant of, another Christian because she or he has a conviction contrary to yours unless – and it is an important 'unless' – that person is damaging 'the weak'. But in contemporary debates that does not often seem to be the cause of the anger and moral indignation, and it also begs the question of who are 'the weak' in this situation. Accepting one another, and building one another up (14.19), is central to Paul's agenda for the Church. Within these parameters, each must follow his or her own conscience, or must (to do justice to Paul's language in Romans) be answerable before God both now and at the end for their convictions and their actions (14.12 and 22).

Who are 'the strong' and 'the weak'?

How do we identify 'the strong' and 'the weak' in any given situation? Romans 14—15 offer important guidelines. Who are the victims of attitudes comprehensively condemned by Paul here – namely, judging and despising? Who feel threatened or marginalized because they comprise a minority, or because they are vulnerable in other ways? Who is exercising, and who is on the receiving end, of inappropriate pressure to conform? In the complex situation we face today, where contradictory convictions spread across different nations, cultures and races, it is not easy to answer these questions. But Paul's teaching suggests these are the questions we should be asking. It is particularly important to ask 'Who are "the weak"?', not because their convictions should be imposed on everyone else (Paul makes it clear that must not happen), but because 'the weak' – in Paul's definition – are those whose faith is more fragile and vulnerable than that of others.

Can Paul's argument about not causing damage to Christian brothers and sisters be extended to people outside the Church? What 'stumbling-blocks' or 'hindrances' (14.13) which may stop someone from coming to faith should we take care to remove? Paul urged the Christians at Corinth to avoid giving offence to three groups of people – two, presumably, outside the Church: 'Give no offence to Jews or to Greeks or to the church of God' (1 Corinthians 10.32). How many 'offences' can and should be removed from the path of a potential convert to Christ? The New Testament seems to say there is only one 'offence' which should not be removed, and that is the offence of the cross (1 Corinthians 1.23). So are there no moral conditions attached to being a Christian? Of course, Christian conversion must lead to a new way of life, or it is spurious. A faith which does not show at least some sign of finding expression in love (Galatians 5.6) would be an empty sort of faith. But moral consequences are not the same thing as moral conditions. So it follows that the evangelist does not normally 'lay down the law' to 'Gentiles' coming to faith. We do not say to the rich person, in spite of Mark 10.25 and Luke 14.33, 'First give your money away'. Zaccheus gave much of his wealth away after he had been accepted, not as a condition of it (Luke 19.1–10). We do not say to someone who has re-married after a divorce – in spite of Luke 16.18 – 'first renounce this unscriptural marriage ...'

There is a role here for individual self-understanding and conscience. If a teenager has come to the conclusion that he or she is gay, for that is the way God made him or her, would it not be more helpful if the Church were to allow that youngster to follow his or her own conscience? If two committed Christians of the same sex have a clear conscience before God about their committed, faithful relationship, should any other Christian be so inquisitorial or censorious as to query what they should or should not do in the personal privacy of that relationship?

This is a painful time for churches wrestling with this, and other, divisive issues. The situation of the early Church, nearly torn apart by issues relating to the presence in the Church of both Jew and Gentile, has much to teach us. But perhaps there is no lesson more challenging and helpful than Paul's teaching in Romans 14.1—15.7 – above all: 'Let us then pursue what makes for peace and for mutual edification' (14.19).

The limits of Christian pluralism

Does it mean that, in the Church of Christ, anything goes: pluralism unlimited? No – but Paul 'pushes' it a long way here in Romans. His own adaptability is remarkable, and so is the far-reaching accommodation (making room for the other) which he urges on the Christians at Rome. What is at stake here is 'my' recognition of a fellow-Christian with whom I profoundly disagree – to the point where I find it hard to comprehend that he can be a Christian at all. How far can such a principle be taken? Paul does not imply that Christians can agree to differ over Christian fundamentals. But what are these fundamentals? Not as many as we might think. The building-blocks of Paul's own arguments tell us: the death (for us all) of Christ and his resurrection and, by implication, what a later generation was to call 'the incarnation' (Romans 15.3).

To these fundamentals we must add the experience arising out of them: the welcoming, accepting grace of God in Christ (Romans 14.3b, 15.7). These are the articles of faith by which the Church stands or falls. They presuppose two (and, I suggest, only two) more: belief in one God (as expressed in 1 Corinthians 8.6), and the shared experience of the Holy Spirit in the fellowship of the Church. For Paul, these fundamentals are the framework within which members of the Christian Church accommodate one another.

v Paul and the renewal of the Church

The challenge of Paul's language

Paul puts some searching questions to every church, and his very language prompts some self-examination. We no doubt mean well when we say, 'You are welcome to our church', but Paul never talks about 'our church' or 'your church'. It is the church *of God*, and each church is the church in a particular place – at Thessalonika, Philippi, and so on. Even though small communities of Christians met in the homes of people like Priscilla and Aquila, I think we can safely assume that Paul would never have referred to 'Priscilla's and Aquila's church'. Nor does he ever use the expression 'joining the church', perhaps because it is God who does the 'joining' – in ways which are not entirely visible.

The biggest challenge of Paul's language, however, lies in the words and phrases he uses to describe Christians. As we have seen, he never uses the word 'Christian'. Instead, he addresses, or refers to, God's 'holy ones', to those who live 'in Christ'. He writes of life 'in the Spirit', and of relating to one another 'in the Lord'. I am not suggesting that such language becomes part of everyday Christian discourse in the churches today, for it can be both misunderstood and abused. But we neglect it at our peril. 'Christian' was a label, probably attached by people outside the Church to the early disciples. As such, it is an external and potentially superficial description. Paul's words are deeper, denoting, as they do, the internal reality of all Christian living: Spirit-centred, Christ-centred, God-centred.

The challenge of each letter

Not only does Paul's language challenge us, each letter does so too. Paul's first letter to Corinth challenged a church compromised by the prevailing social culture. Their attitudes, relationships, and even their celebrations of the Lord's Supper, owed more to contemporary values and aspirations than to the gospel. Self-centred spirituality was damaging and dividing the church. Paul re-calls them to the counter-cultural message of the cross, and to the self-denying Christ who is the image of God (1.18–25).

The second letter to the Corinthians is more personal in its challenge, not least because of Paul's recent near-death experience (2 Corinthians 1.8), his humiliations at Corinth (2.4–11), and his 'thorn in the flesh' (12.7–10). It is a letter which puts searching questions to churches and ministers whose relationship is strained, and to any Christian tempted to view the Christian life or Christian ministry in any way which is not cruciform (for example, 4.7–12, 6.3–10). This letter is a stark reminder that a life centred on the cross is the authentic mark of both Christian ministry and Christian life. At the same time, this letter challenges contemporary churches to recover their vision and lose their despair by, paradoxically, sharing in the sufferings of Christ (for example, 1.3–7). Although Paul's thorn in the flesh was a weakness which he did not willingly embrace, by 'weakness' Paul normally means (section ii above) weaknesses which Christians voluntarily assume for the sake of the gospel. (Again, the fundamental 'model' is the crucified God – 1 Corinthians 1.25.) In the light of the cross and resurrection, Paul is convinced that churches will, paradoxically, experience power in the weakness they have embraced for the gospel (for example, 12.10, 13.4; cf. 1 Corinthians 2.1–5).

Here is another counter-cultural message from the apostle for our time. We tend to confuse hope with optimism, basing our 'hope' for the Church and its future on membership statistics, church attendances and the like. These are not unimportant, but hope for the Church, according to Paul, seems to be directly related to its readiness to embrace weakness, and even suffering, for the sake of the gospel. Only a Church which shares the 'fellowship of Christ's sufferings' will experience the power of his resurrection.

The letter to the Galatians challenges a church in danger of forgetting that the gospel is for the people we mistakenly refer to as 'outsiders'. A church is more likely to remember that point if it is Christ-centred; what holds a congregation together is not long-standing friendships, or a common loyalty to a church building, but life together in Christ. Being law-centred comes perilously close to replacing Christ as the centre with a religious culture. So a good test of a church's health is how readily it welcomes people who are different without expecting them to fit in to a prevailing church culture.

The letter to the Romans challenges a church to model God's new creation, by the way the people relate to one another (Romans 12), especially to fellow-Christians who are very different (14.1—15.7). And Romans, too, summons the Church to be a counter-cultural community (12.1–2), over against all life-sapping forms of idolatry. But there are internal challenges for the Church, too. A church is called to live by 'the Spirit', not 'the flesh', even though 'the flesh' can take some very devout forms (chapters 7 and 8)! Paul seems to admit as much about his own pre-Christian – or even Christian – past when he says he once knew Christ 'according to the flesh' – that is, in an all too human way (2 Corinthians 5.16). When tangible, visible things, such as the premises, money, or numbers start to matter more, or to exercise greater influence than relationships with one another and with God, then such a church is beginning to lose its way.

I have alluded so far only to a few themes in the major letters of Paul. His shorter letters, too, have much to say. Colossians, for example, invites us to a Christology as large as the cosmos itself (Colossians 1.15–20), and Philippians reminds us that a radical self-emptying lies at the heart of Christian living every bit as much as it lay at the heart of the life and death of Jesus. There are many parallels between what Paul says about Jesus in Philippians 2.5–11 and what he says about himself in the following chapter (3.4–11).

But Paul's twofold message of both challenge and encouragement can be found not just within an individual letter, but across several of them. In the rest of this section I shall try to offer a few examples.

The renewal of leadership

First, Paul has much to say about Christian leadership. One of the defining characteristics of a Christian leader, according to Paul, is that person's suffering for the gospel and for the Church. That must not be taken to mean that a Christian leader goes looking for suffering, but he or she may assume that it goes with the territory. The apostolate is cruciform; that is the stark message of the Corinthian correspondence. Paul's letters remind the Church of the leader's fundamental role: to help people to grow in the life of Christ or, in the words of one letter, to enable the formation of Christ in them (Galatians 4.19, a verse where Paul strikingly applies feminine imagery to himself). Not surprisingly, then, Paul is uncomplimentary about 'super-apostles' (2 Corinthians 11.5 and 12.11). Whether he meant apostles who couldn't resist encroaching on others' territory, seeing their ministry in imperialist terms ('wider still and wider shall thy bounds be set'), or whether they simply enjoyed competing with other apostles, we cannot be sure.

Contrary to popular perception, Paul himself was a team player. He may have been a dominant member of every team he played in, but he needed the ministry of others to complement his own. Where would he have been without the ministries of Timothy, Titus and Epaphroditus (Philippians 2.25–30), who travelled between his churches? Or his key partners in each church? Two verses in Philippians refer to two such people: Euodia and Syntyche. They, unfortunately, are in danger of falling out, but Paul asks a third person, 'my loyal companion', to help patch up the quarrel (4.2–3); Gaius, Chloe and Stephanas seem to have been valuable colleagues based at Corinth (Romans 16.23, 1 Corinthians 1.11, 14–16).

Perhaps greater attention to Paul will lead us to examine some of our long-standing assumptions about ordained ministry. There is something topsy-turvy about our situation, in which questions about ordination form a far bigger obstacle to Christian unity than differences about baptism. Paul says nothing about ordination, but a great deal about baptism. We cannot conclude from that that ordination does not matter, but we may reasonably wonder whether many of our contemporary churches are too hierarchical in their leadership structures, and too clergy-dominated, in their day-to-day life and worship.

That is not to say apostolic leadership is an optional extra. The first apostles were witnesses to the resurrection of Jesus, and everyone in the apostolic succession (that is, the whole Church) is committed to continuing that witness. That is why an apostle's life is cruciform, bearing witness both to the cross and to the resurrection which, as always in Paul's theology, belong inseparably together.

The renewal of pastoral care

The renewal of leadership in the Church goes closely with the renewal of pastoral care, a defining mark of the apostle is his 'anxiety for all the churches' (2 Corinthians 11.28). This does not mean that Paul lay awake night after night wondering how Philippi would balance their books, or whether Thessalonika had large enough premises in which to meet (not that these are unimportant issues). The next verse shows what Paul's anxiety entailed: 'Who is weak, and I am not weak? Who is made to stumble, and I am not indignant?' (v. 29).

Paul's overriding concern is the Church's growth in the life of Christ, but his concern clearly has a bias to 'the weak'. The acid test of a church's health is its care for 'the weak'; as we have seen, 'the weak' in Paul's letters are those Christians whose faith was vulnerable, and/or those Christians from the poorer classes of society (1 Corinthians 8—10, Romans 14—15.7).

Another defining mark of Christian pastoral care is bearing one another's burdens; that, says Paul, *is* the law of Christ. The context here (Galatians 6.1–2) shows that Paul is talking about heavy burdens – so heavy, in fact, that those carrying them might sink beneath them unless they get help. Loneliness, a bereavement, an illness, a period of unemployment – all these, and other equally heavy burdens, can submerge a person's faith without support from fellow-Christians. Paul's definition of 'the law of Christ' is a word for our very individualistic society where Christian faith has become such a private matter.

In view of what Paul writes about the Christ whom God sent 'in the likeness of sinful flesh' (Romans 8.3), and even of the Christ whom 'God made to be sin' (2 Corinthians 5.21), Paul would have understood, and probably agreed with, the twentieth-century American Cistercian Thomas Merton when he wrote, 'If we want to know God, we must learn to understand the weaknesses and sin and imperfections of others as if they were our own.'[8]

The renewal of worship

One far-reaching result of our exposure to Paul will be his gentle, yet relentless questioning of our church priorities. We set great store by a church's busyness; the more activities a church has, the more lively, generally speaking, it is reckoned to be. Or we count heads, on the assumption that increasing attendances bode well for the Church's future. Yet, according to Paul, and particularly his several 'each other' commands (for example, 'Encourage each other', 1 Thessalonians 4.18), the quality of the relationships within a church are more important than either busyness or numbers. Similarly, we tend to evaluate worship by its 'liveliness' – whether it is 'modern' and 'relevant'. These are some of today's 'buzz' words, and I acknowledge the genuine concerns behind them. The young person who said that he had found most church services either trite or dead may have been speaking for many of his generation. But what might Paul contribute to this vital discussion?

Paul's most extended discussion of worship occurs in 1 Corinthians 14. Space precludes a detailed discussion, yet some pointers are clear. Will a newcomer readily discover that 'God is really among you' (v. 25)? Will everything that happens 'build up' the Church (v. 26; cf. Romans 14.19)? 'Building up' the

Church involves more than providing worship 'for all tastes' (as if a church were a kind of spiritual supermarket); in Paul's book it means deepening a church's corporate life in Christ, strengthening the faith, hope and love of all its members, their relationships with one another, and so, by implication, their evangelistic effectiveness.

Lastly, under the heading of worship, we need to recall an earlier discussion in this chapter, 'Seven whole days, not one in seven' (section iii). Worship is the Christian's daily offering of her or his life to God (Romans 12.1), so what everyone brings to public worship matters profoundly. It is true that the pace, noise and busyness of modern life do not make preparation for worship easy either for those who lead it or those who share it (a distinction, by the way, not to be found in Paul's letters – 1 Corinthians 14.26), but such preparation, and listening to Paul, can help the churches today stop their worship of God from becoming corrupted and trivialized by a consumerist culture.

Finally, we must not overlook the obvious – at least, obvious to Paul. The Church lives by the gospel (1 Corinthians 15.1–3); one could say: no gospel, no Church. For Paul, though, there was an important corollary to this – no preaching, no gospel either: 'And how are they to believe in one of whom they have never heard? And how are they to hear without someone to proclaim him? ... faith comes from what is heard, and what is heard comes through the word of Christ' (Romans 10.14 and 17). This is yet another of Paul's unfashionable messages for our time: there can be no renewal of the Church without the renewal of preaching.

The subject of 'Paul and the renewal of the Church' merits a book to itself! Paul both challenges and encourages, in a way similar to the author of a recent book about the Church (*After Our Likeness: The Church as the Image of the Trinity* by Miroslav Volf).[9] In his preface, Volf describes two basic church lessons which he learned in his earlier years. First, there is:

> no church without the reign of God. The church lives from and toward something that is greater than the church itself.

When the windows facing toward the reign of God get closed, darkness descends upon the churches, and the air becomes heavy. When the windows facing toward the reign of God are opened, the life-giving breath and light of God give the churches fresh hope.[10]

Paul rarely talks about 'the reign (that is, kingdom) of God'; his language is different. But his message is the same. Only the Church which is Spirit-centred, Christ-centred and God-centred will have energy and hope.

But Volf's second church lesson is equally important, and equally Pauline. There is no reign of God without the church.

... We come to recognize the fresh breath of God and the light of God that renew the creation only because there are communities called churches – communities that keep alive the memory of the crucified Messiah and the hope for the Coming One.[11]

A hymn by Charles Wesley has the improbable line, 'The Church can never fail'. The Church can and does fail – again and again – and the Paul who wrote to the churches at Corinth and Galatia (to mention only two of his churches) knew that as well as anyone. But Paul's conviction about Israel applies to the Church: 'the gifts and calling of God are irrevocable' (Romans 11.29). That does not apply to individual 'branches' – as Paul's earlier remarks show (11.17–24) – but the Church will not fail ultimately, completely and irredeemably (and that is probably what Wesley meant). Paul remained buoyant and resilient, not because of any successes which came his way, but because of the risen and coming Christ.

Notes

1 S. Moore, *God is a New Language*, DLT, London, 1967, p. 162.

2 V. J. Donovan, *Christianity Rediscovered*, SCM, London, 1978, p. 24.

3 From the WCC's Monthly Letter on Evangelism, nos 4/5, April–May 1986.

4 I owe this information to my editor, Natalie Watson.

5 From 'Why middle England gets the Mail', *Guardian*, 20 August 2007.

6 See also Chapter 5, section v, for a brief discussion of 2 Timothy 3.16.

7 E. Kaesemann, *Commentary on Romans*, English translation: Eerdmans, Grand Rapids, Michigan, 1980, p. 379.

8 T. Merton, *No Man is an Island*, quoted in the *Merton Journal*, Eastertide 2007 (14, no. 1), p. 61.

9 M. Volf, *After Our Likeness: The Church as the Image of the Trinity*, Eerdmans, Grand Rapids, Michigan, 1998.

10 Volf, *After Our Likeness*, p. x.

11 Volf, *After Our Likeness*, p. x.

5

Paul and Contemporary Issues

In the Introduction to this book, I described Paul as an apostle whose time had come. That may sound a dramatic exaggeration, but there are several important ways in which Paul can speak today, not just to the Christian Church, but to the wider world. His vision of the righteousness of God, and of a universal human community brought into being by Christ, is profoundly relevant for our time, faced as we are with global crises more serious than humankind has yet encountered. So, too, is what he has to say about suffering in a world where we are more aware of it than ever before. (The suffering in the world is a commonly cited reason for not believing in God.)

There are other ways in which Paul has much to say to us. As the apostle to the Gentiles, he was a man who crossed and re-crossed racial, cultural and religious boundaries, so his is a significant voice in our multi-faith, multi-cultural world. Then there is Paul's use of his Bible: what can he teach us about the interpretation of sacred texts in a world of strident fundamentalisms? But underlying and over-arching all issues is, quite simply, the question of God as the ultimate source of truth, value and meaning. In a final section we shall return to some of Paul's fundamental convictions. In the so-called 'developed' world, however, we tend to have a lop-sided view of the gospel. I once heard an American minister say, 'My congregation finds it easy to relate their faith to their personal lives, much harder to relate it to social and national issues, and harder still to relate it to international issues.' The minister could have been British, or a citizen of another affluent nation. Tragically, we have privatized and individualized Christianity to the point where we have almost turned ourselves into heretics. After all, heresy has been defined as treating part of the faith as if it were the whole.

Other pressures today conspire to make churches safe havens for Christians. The world as we experience it has always challenged belief in God, and today, as it changes with bewildering and ever-increasing speed, awkward new questions emerge for the person who seeks to make sense of the Bible and his or her faith. Some of these questions are global in their scope, and to these we now turn.

i God's justice and a universal society

God's righteousness

It is not immediately obvious that Paul has anything at all to say about justice, but those of us living in the so-called developed world may have a blind spot here. Some years ago, a South African church leader gave a lecture on Paul's letter to the Romans at the college where I taught. I was startled to hear him say, in response to a student's question, that the righteousness of God in Paul's letters meant social justice. Nothing, in all the New Testament commentaries I had read by British, German and American scholars, had ever led me to think that! I had learned that God's righteousness was his salvation, effected through Jesus, bringing people back into a right relationship with himself.

Had I got it all wrong? No – although the language I have used here is traditional, my commentaries were not wrong. But they were one-sided. If I had paid more attention to what the Old Testament says about God's righteousness, I should have realized that my South African colleague had a point – to put it mildly. A mere glance at Old Testament prophets such as Amos and Isaiah shows that God's righteousness and human righteousness go together. Where the word 'righteousness' occurs, the word 'justice' is never far away, as in Amos: 'But let justice roll down like waters, and righteousness like an ever-flowing stream' (Amos 5.24; cf. Isaiah 61.8–11). Paul himself describes God's righteousness as something to which 'the law and the prophets' bear witness (Romans 3.21). So

God's salvation includes God's justice, and that in turn must include – in the light of the prophets – social and economic justice. So we need to rescue Paul from his ecclesiastical captivity, and from one-sided interpreters, especially those of us in the developed world. How can an apostle who preached a new *creation* not be globally significant? If Paul, standing in the tradition of the law and the prophets, preached the righteousness of God, how can he not have a message of justice for today?

God's righteousness is the nearest equivalent in Paul's letters to 'the kingdom of God' in the teaching of Jesus. It denotes God's character, God's saving activity, and God's faithful commitment to the healing and well-being of the world. In the Old Testament, that righteousness is directed to the healing and well-being of Israel. In the New Testament, God's scope is now seen to be what it always was – universal. The cross and resurrection of Jesus represent God's utter commitment to complete his creative purpose: to make time and room in the mystery of God's own being for a world – that includes ourselves.

The word 'righteousness', of course, is hopelessly old-fashioned, but the problem is that there is no single word in English which can possibly describe, or refer to, God's character, saving activity and faithful commitment to his world all at the same time. But that is what God's righteousness means in the Bible, including Paul's writings, notably in Romans 1.16–17 and 3.21–26. Similarly, it would be hard to find another image or metaphor to replace 'the kingdom of God'. But since, as I have tried to show, one of the practical results of God's righteousness in human society is justice, the theme of this section, as its title shows, is the justice of God.

From 'flesh' to a body

Against this theological background, we now explore the practical consequences for human life – and therefore for our globalized world – according to the teaching of Paul.

There are two crucial words which will help us in our exploration. The first is the word 'flesh' (*sarx*). In Chapter 1, I pointed out that 'flesh' in Paul does not mean what it appears to mean. Against its Old Testament background, it comes to mean 'human life apart from God'. The question for us here is this: what effect, according to Paul, does the malign power of sin have on 'flesh' – that is, human life apart from God? An important part of Paul's answer is that sin fragments, so a church living 'according to the flesh' will be a divided, fragmented church (for example, 1 Corinthians 3.1–3), as will human society at large (Galatians 5.19–21, Romans 1.28–32).

What kind of society begins to emerge out of this 'fleshly' morass when humans move from life 'according to the flesh' to life 'in the Spirit' – one of Paul's fundamental contrasts? Paul's answer is that 'the flesh' begins to be 'a body (*soma*) – the second crucial word in this discussion.

Of course, everyone has a body – or *is* a body. Paul acknowledges that our bodies have ambiguous potential: for good and evil. Through baptism and the Spirit, a person is called to leave the old 'body' behind (Romans 6.6 and 8.13), and to present their renewed bodies/selves to God (Romans 12.1–2). In the process a new body, as it were, comes into view: the body of Christ (Romans 12.5 and 1 Corinthians 12.12–27).

To understand what this means in the context of our discussion about God's justice, we need to recall one of Paul's criticisms of the way the church at Corinth observed the Lord's Supper: they – or some of them – did not discern the body (1 Corinthians 11.27). By this Paul meant two things: they did not recognize that the bread and wine they shared represented the body and blood of the crucified Jesus – with all that that entailed – and, second, they did not see that all of them who shared in that sacrament were members of the body of Christ, and so members 'one of another' (Romans 12.5).

This image, in Paul's day, had a history. We might even say it had 'form'. Historians and philosophers in the world of Greece and Rome made use of it – but in a way very different from Paul (Chapter 2, section ii). For them, it tended to be an image which the upper classes used to put the lower classes in their place. ('We all have our part to play in society, but yours is down there.') Paul, as we saw, uses it very differently. In his version we hear from two different groups of limbs or organs; first, there are those which, like the foot (v. 15), wish they had a more exalted role, and so feel they don't really belong to the body at all. Then we hear the 'voice' of those members of the body only too aware of their exalted status, and who say to other members, 'I don't need you!'

But this isn't all that Paul says – with his eye, all the time, on the situation at Corinth. He goes on to say that there is a bias to the weak and lowly members in the body (vv. 22–24), and concludes by stating that the body simply can't be divided up, and the mutual care of its members for each other is a crucial mark of its health: 'God has so arranged the body, giving the greater honour to the inferior member, that there may be no dissension within the body, but the members may have the same care for one another. If one member suffers, all suffer together with it; if one member is honoured, all rejoice together with it' (1 Corinthians 12.24b–26). Churchgoers will be used to hearing sermons on this passage about everyone playing their part in their church. I am not denying that, but I argue now that this teaching of Paul about the body has a far wider application. We should expect that, not only because of the way authors contemporary with Paul used it, but, above all, because Paul was preaching a new creation – God's new creation – and the Church as the firstfruits of that creation (for example, Galatians 6.15, Romans 8.22–23). In Chapter 4, section i, I suggested that baptism, in the light of Paul's teaching about Jesus as 'the last Adam', means joining the human race as God intended it to be. So there are good theological reasons for widening the application of 'the body' beyond the Church to what we have called God's new world: a universal human society.

Towards a universal, human society

But now we must ask ourselves: *how* is all this relevant for the complex, globalized world we live in? People who – rightly, in my view – have rejected a fundamentalist approach to the Bible may go to the opposite extreme, and reduce the Bible to a marginal place in their approach to life. At the same time, we need to be wary of simplistic solutions to complex modern problems from well-meaning religious people – not least those writing books about Paul! The apostle lived in a world vastly different from ours – that is very clear. But, for Christians, his letters have scriptural status, and so, by that very fact, are relevant. And if this is still the world of the God Paul talked about, then we have a further reason for expecting the apostle to have a message for our time.

Two recurring phenomena in the world today often jar horribly with Paul's vision of a new creation. I refer to general election campaigns and news bulletins. In one recent election campaign, a candidate declared that his overriding priority was to make his country safe. Political leaders of most countries would say the same – at least, they would if they wanted to be elected. In a frightening world, that is understandable. Yet the question must be pressed: are nation-states, in their behaviour, to live by the principle of the survival of the fittest, or to live as if they really belong to the same body – that is, the human race?

We can pose the question in a more detailed way, in the light of Paul's teaching in 1 Corinthians. A powerful nation may so easily proceed, like 'the eye' or 'the head' (1 Corinthians 12.21), as if it did not need other members of the human family: 'I have no need of you'. A weaker or smaller nation easily feels, like the foot or the ear (vv. 15–16), 'I do not really belong to the body at all'.

The problem we are discussing here is familiar enough. Most of us live much of the time as if we were not members of 'a body' at all. Or else we pay grudging, half-hearted recognition to the fact that we can't live as if other people weren't there, or as if we had no wider obligations to society; paying tax is a regrettable necessity, and so on. A distinguished economist, Joseph Stiglitz, writes of how 'each group in society focuses on a part of reality that affects it the most'.[1] Stiglitz wrote out of his experience at the World Bank. If, as some allege, the IMF and the World Bank are simply the mouthpieces of the richest nations imposing their preferences on the poorer nations, such policies run contrary to Paul's vision of what we may call creation's blueprint.

'Isn't that natural?' we say. Yes, it is – and Paul would agree with us. But he would go on to say that this is life 'according to the flesh', and will it be enough to save us from self-destruction? We can hardly expect politicians to conduct an election campaign with their eye only on Paul's teaching, and not on what we tend to call 'political realities'. Yet would not Paul say that the deepest reality of all – of which we must all take account – is what he calls 'the righteousness of God'?

Similarly, the priorities reflected in our news bulletins (and most of our newspapers) seem natural, too. They suggest, for example, that people in my own country are much more concerned about higher prices for their electricity than about the deaths of a hundred people caused by a terrorist bomb on the other side of the world. Opening hours for doctors' surgeries are deemed to be more important than the misery created by an earthquake in, say, Indonesia. Certainly, if the news item which comes first, or which captures the front page headlines, is, by that very fact, thought to be the most important, or of the greatest interest to viewers and readers, then Paul's vision of belonging to a universal, human body is still a long way away.

We tend to say, 'It's only human', using the word 'human' in the lower sense of that word. Again, it's Paul's word 'the flesh'. But if we are to take the apostle seriously, we have to ask: will this 'all too human' way of living be sufficient to save us from self-destruction?

So Paul's image of the body, in which every organ and limb contributes to the whole, and therefore needs every other, applies not just to the Church, but to the world. It points us in the direction of what G. K. Chesterton once called 'a cosmic patriotism'. In more Pauline language, we might say that our first loyalty is to the God revealed in Christ, our second to the human race. We need to hear the two voices to which Paul gives expression: those who say – because that's how they feel – 'We don't really belong', and those who say – because their power or affluence has blinded them – 'We don't need you'.

God's economy

What are the economic implications today of Paul's vision of a universal human society? It is easy to use the Bible to score political points, and politicians of both right and left have occasionally done so in the past. An American Quaker once wrote a searching book called *The Peril of Modernizing Jesus* and, similarly, we need to be wary of the danger of modernizing Paul by making him a socialist or a conservative in our own image.

But it is one thing to try to prove a point by enlisting Paul in our support. It is a more demanding task to ask whether Paul, if we really listen to him, might have some searching questions to put to our society, and the way we conduct our affairs. Should not Paul's belief in God's righteousness and justice – the two terms, as we have seen, overlap – lead us to question aspects of contemporary capitalism? Is there not, as a friend of mine recently remarked, something self-destructive about capitalism, as we know it and practise it today? Thoughtful contemporary observers of capitalism are raising related questions. To quote Joseph Stiglitz again, 'the system of capitalism is at a crossroads, just as it was during the Great Depression of the 1930s'.[2] A Jewish religious leader makes a similar point: 'The paradox of competition is that it is benign only when counter-balanced by habits of co-operation.'[3]

It is relevant to point out that Paul's 'collection' was an economic project. The churches of Greece and Asia Minor contributed to the relief of poverty and famine among their fellow-Christians in Judaea. Some of Paul's churches, such as those in Macedonia (2 Corinthians 8.1–6), were less affluent than the others, but they still gave. Some, apparently Corinth, were less willing than others, and we don't know the outcome of Paul's lengthy cajoling (2 Corinthians 8 and 9). We don't even know whether the churches in Judaea received this offering from Gentiles; as we noted earlier (Chapter 1, section v), the Acts of the Apostles is strangely silent about it. But none of this – if we take seriously Paul's vision of God – affects the fundamental rightness of his project.

Paul may well have seen his collection as an expression of God's 'economy'. The word itself (Greek: *oikonomia*) occurs only in later letters (Colossians 1.25, Ephesians 3.2).[4] The background of the word is the Greek household (*oikia*, *oikos*, 'household' and 'home'), so the economy of God is how God administers, or wants to administer (with human co-operation), his household. So this collection between churches was 'the firstfruits', a cameo, of God's new world.

Paul's collection is hardly an economic blueprint for the immensely complicated world in which we live. But, again, if God, and God's economy, is the reality at the heart of our world, then perhaps Paul has something to say to us after all. His collection, for example, stands the axiom of the survival of the fittest on its head. But in this new world, where the richer help the poorer, it is not a question of the rich impoverishing themselves: 'I do not mean that there should be relief for others and pressure on you, but it is a question of a fair balance between your present abundance and their need ...' (2 Corinthians 8.13, 14a). On the other hand, political 'realism' in our day has tended to say that if the rich are given free rein to make money, the poor will benefit, too. In fact, recent statistics of many countries show that the gap between rich and poor is widening.

Of course, the economic life of both a country and the world has to be regulated, but we neglect Paul's vision at our peril. Paul is saying something fundamental about the way in which human beings will not only survive, but flourish, because God made us that way.

By normal standards, this seems impossibly idealistic. There are parallels in the Sermon on the Mount. How can a nation-state love its enemies? What is to be done if only a minority of people in the world seek to live by the teaching of Jesus? But the Church cannot simply forget, or allow the world to forget, Jesus' message of non-violence, or Paul's teaching about God's economy and justice. Otherwise – Paul spells out the 'otherwise' in Romans 1.18–32 – when the human race centres its life on what is not God (Paul calls this idolatry), this life-draining idolatry makes us less than human, and whole societies and communities begin to fragment.

There is an important postscript to add to this discussion. The Bible's message from beginning to end is 'partnership': partnership between the Creator and the created, between God and humanity. So to be baptized into Christ means to join God in his mission to the world. That is at least part of what Paul means when he says that Christ joined sinful humanity 'so that in him we might become the righteousness of God' (2 Corinthians 5.21). That must surely include becoming God's agents for social and economic justice.

ii Paul and climate change

A spiritual and ecological crisis

In an earlier discussion, I raised the question of whether Paul's words 'I can will what is right, but I cannot do it' (Romans 7.18) might soon become the epitaph of the human race. At the time of writing, the signs are not good. There is now an impressive political and scientific consensus that the Earth's climate is changing, and that the world is warming. There are still a few dissentients, but they are looking increasingly like ostriches with heads in the sand. There is also a growing consensus that this global warming is at least partly, if not largely, due to human activity. So there is much to be said for the view that climate change constitutes the greatest challenge to the human race in our history thus far. Certainly our response in the next decade or two is likely to have far-reaching effects on our children, and on their children.

Paul, at first sight, seems an improbable source for any guidance on this growing crisis before us. But this is also about justice – not least because those peoples of the world which have contributed least to global warming are likely to be the ones who suffer most from it. (Already sea levels are creeping up over low-lying islands in the Pacific.) Similarly, though the problem is worldwide, the richer nations have a greater responsibility in that they not only have done most to cause the problem, but also can do most to ameliorate it.

As we have seen, in the Bible, divine and human righteousness belong together; so, too, in God's economy, do spiritual and economic matters. Some of the wiser voices among us to-day are reminding us of this. Trust in each other, confidence in the future, a sense of fairness and justice, freedom from anxiety, violence and despair – these are spiritual matters, inseparable from the complexities of our social and economic life. So to live as if economics alone determined human life, for good or ill, is to deny our God-given humanity. Chief Rabbi Sacks has written, 'The only thing that makes social or economic trends inevitable is the belief that they are.'[5] Is there a spiritual dimension to the climate change crisis? Yes, there is, both in its causes – which I shall come to later on – and in humanity's response to it. For example, it would be easy to despair. The former vice-president of the USA, Al Gore, has written of the spiritual paralysis which can readily result from our plight: '... hope itself is threatened by the realization that we are now capable of destroying ourselves and the earth's environment'.[6]

Humans and nature stand or fall together

The danger of spiritual paralysis and despair in the present situation is real, and in its place, Christian faith does not offer a facile, cheap optimism. Paul preached a gospel of hope, and we shall return to this later. But, first, there is another connection which Paul, and the biblical tradition as a whole, makes which we easily overlook. It is the interrelatedness of our human world, and the world of nature.

An early myth (Genesis 2—3) linked human wrongdoing with a divine curse upon the earth (Genesis 3.17), and we must not make the Bible incredible by treating this ancient story as historical. But nor must we dismiss it as irrelevant because it is unhistorical. A comment by a great twentieth-century theologian, Paul Tillich, may help here. In a sermon which he called 'Nature, also, mourns for a lost good',[7] Tillich pointed out how biblical stories such as these symbolize both the forces of destruction and of salvation at work in the world. And he linked two 'tragedies': 'The tragedy of nature is bound to the tragedy of man [sic], as the salvation of nature is dependent on the salvation of man [sic].' This seems a plausible interpretation of Romans 8.19–22, one of the texts on which Tillich's sermon was based. These words, among the most mysterious the apostle Paul ever wrote, are worth quoting in full:

> For the creation waits with eager longing for the revealing of the children of God; for the creation was subjected to futility, not of its own will but by the will of the one who subjected it, in hope that the creation itself will be set free from its bondage to decay and will obtain the freedom of the glory of the children of God. We know that the whole creation has been groaning in labour pains until now ...

So Paul, in line with the mythical story of Genesis 3, connects the world of nature with our human world; and Paul and the writer of Genesis are not the only biblical writers to do so. One more example, from the Old Testament prophets, must suffice:

> Hear the word of the LORD, O people of Israel; for the LORD has an indictment against the inhabitants of the land. There is no faithfulness or loyalty, and no knowledge of God in the land. .... Therefore the land mourns, and all who live in it languish; together with the wild animals and the birds of the air, even the fish of the sea are perishing (Hosea 4.1, 3).

Many other passages in the Bible carry the same message, for example, Isaiah 24.4–7, and Revelation 19.2, with its reference to 'the great whore who corrupted the earth ...' – an indictment, as the preceding chapter shows, of the greed and economic oppression underpinning the Roman Empire.

So Paul is in good biblical company, however difficult his words in Romans 8 might seem to us today. It is tempting to dismiss the connection between our groans and longings and those of creation as fanciful poetic imagery, yet though we must honestly recognize that 'nature red in tooth and claw' preceded human beings upon the earth by many millions of years, contemporary experience suggests that our alienation from nature – and perhaps from God – has greatly added to the travails of the natural world. The ecological degradation of huge tracts of Russia and China is only one of many examples we could list.

So there are two important pairings which Paul and other biblical writers make: spiritual and economic issues are inseparable and, second, the destinies and well-being of our human world and the world of nature also belong together. With these in mind, we continue our inquiry into what Paul might have to say to us in this looming planetary crisis.

A gentle dominion

Paul wrote Romans 8.19–22 as part of a letter to a church in the capital city of an empire. He wrote in the years which followed the Augustan age, when imperial propaganda trumpeted the redemption of Mother Earth, thanks to the emperor's beneficent rule. In these verses, Paul seems to be turning this propaganda on its head: creation, he says, 'has been groaning in labour pains *until now* [my italics]' (v. 22) – so much for the golden age of Augustus and his successors!

'Labour pains', however, suggests that a future birth is imminent: the birth of God's new age. (The image was a familiar one in Jewish Messianic expectations.) But how, or when, will this happen? Paul writes how 'the creation waits with eager longing for the revealing of the children of God' (v. 19). It is difficult to be sure exactly what Paul is thinking of here. What *is* clear is the connection he makes between the transformation of nature and human transformation ('the revealing of the children of God'). When that happens, the devastation of nature, depicted in the prophets, lamented in the book of Revelation, will be reversed.

Thus Paul's vision in Romans 8 has relevance not just for human beings' relations with one another and with God, but also for our attitudes to what we rather self-centredly call 'the environment'. (Perhaps God has a less human-centred perspective on things than we do. The Psalms of the Old Testament suggest that the rest of creation was praising God long before we came along.) Paul's references to Adam (for example,

1 Corinthians 15.45) show that he knew the creation stories of Genesis, so in the religious tradition he inherited, humankind had a distinctive, even unique, role to play ('made in God's image', Genesis 1.27). In this tradition, the rest of creation is not so much our 'environment', as our responsibility. The 'dominion' entrusted to humans (Genesis 1.28, Psalm 8.6–8) is a dominion in God's image: gentle and compassionate.

The desire for more

So is there a word of hope from the apostle Paul? I believe there is, though it may not be what we are willing to hear. The letter to the Colossians makes an intriguing equation: Paul (if it is Paul here) defines greed as 'idolatry' (Colossians 3.5). 'Greed' here means far more than over-indulging oneself with chocolates and the like. My dictionary defines the original Greek word behind 'greed' (*pleonexia*) as 'a desire to have more'. More of anything? More money? More property, comfort, leisure amenities? Is wanting more of any of these things really idolatry?

Perhaps we should ask where the desire for all these things come from. Paul's answer – 'idolatry' – seems, in our complex world, censorious, far-fetched and simplistic. He might have been more convincing had he said, 'The desire to have more comes from insecurity, anxiety about the future, the pressure to keep up with everyone else, to do the best we can for our children.' But this may be to individualize the picture too much and, as I have suggested in the course of this book, that is one of our besetting sins in reading Paul in the 'developed' world today.

There are deeper, more far-reaching questions to ask about where the desire for more comes from. Why are governments of some developed countries still – yes, still – talking of higher levels of prosperity for their citizens? Why do rich people and rich countries fiercely resist the suggestion that incomes might be frozen, profits limited, lifestyles reined in – even when the suggestion is made for the sake of the poor? Perhaps the deepest question of all to be posed in the light of Paul's equation of desiring more with idolatry is this: what functions, in the lives of individual people and of entire nations, as their 'god'? In practice (whatever we may think our creed is), our god is whatever is ultimately important for us, and so the things around which we organize our life.

So the first, deeply unfashionable word from Paul in the face of the global warming crisis is a call to repent of our idolatry. This language, unfortunately, is associated with a fundamentalist Christianity which many today rightly find incredible. But the language has to be interpreted, rather than rejected.

A *change of direction*

Paul never uses the word 'repent', and hardly ever the word 'repentance' (only at Romans 2.4, 2 Corinthians 7.9 and 10), but as repentance in the Bible means a change of direction or a change of heart, we can safely say that the idea of repentance is there in Paul's teaching. Idolatry, as we have seen, consists of mistaken, life-draining choices: above all, the basic lie of opting for god-substitutes rather than God (Romans 1.18–23). These mistaken choices, illusions and lies darken our minds and hearts (for example, verse 21), so repentance involves the re-making of our minds so that they begin to conform to 'the mind of Christ' (Philippians 2.5).

This change of direction can be described with other language borrowed from Paul. It is to opt for God's wisdom, over against human wisdom (1 Corinthians 1.18–25). It is to join in God's own intercession for the healing of the world (Romans 8.26–27) and, not least, to recognize that sharing resources (Paul's collection again) is a defining characteristic of God's new world.

As the Bible keeps on insisting, we must hold spiritual and economic matters together. There can be no real repentance – that is, change of direction – which is not both spiritual and economic. In view of the growing urgency of sustainable development, there are two questions which Paul's vision of a universal human society presses upon us:

1 How can I justify what I have if the world's limited resources make it impossible for everyone else to have the same as me?

2 How do we realize, spiritually and economically, God's saving action and justice for everyone?

iii Paul and suffering

Modern communication, especially television, has enabled us
today to know about more human suffering – for example,
wars, famines and earthquakes on the other side of the world
– than any previous generation. So it is perhaps not surprising
that many people do not believe (or *no longer* believe) in God,
because of the suffering which they see in the world. What
does Paul have to say about this problem, which seems to have
become one of the main obstacles to belief in God today?

What Paul doesn't say

First, we need to look more closely at the 'problem' of suffering.
I put it like that – 'the problem' – not for one moment to imply
that we have imagined or exaggerated it. But is thinking of suffering as 'a problem' the only way to look at it? Suffering, of
course, is always unpleasant, and sometimes excruciating. Yet,
generally speaking, suffering seems to be more of a problem for
those of us living in more comfortable, affluent countries. And
it is a fact that many people have found God, or come closer to
God, through suffering. So are we missing something?

Paul never comes remotely near saying 'A bit of suffering
will do you all good', and he doesn't say either that God sends
suffering – the only possible exception being when he talks
about his 'thorn in the flesh' (2 Corinthians 12.7b–12). As we
saw in an earlier chapter (Chapter 2, section iii), Paul is here
using language reminiscent of the book of Job in the Old Testament. The 'thorn' was a messenger of Satan, even if God
allowed it (v. 7). Paul told the Corinthians that he had three
times asked God to remove the thorn. God did not do so, but,
in Paul's words, gave a different answer: 'My grace is sufficient
for you, for power is made perfect in weakness' (v. 9). What
difference did that answer make to Paul's suffering? It did not
remove the problem of the thorn (whatever it was), with all

the pain and frustration it must have caused. But, to judge from the words Paul uses here, God's answer meant that Paul received an experience of God's grace and power which otherwise he would not have had. There are people in our day who have had similar experiences. John Hull, onetime professor of education at Birmingham University, who lost his sight while still a young man, said in a television interview: 'I have seen things in my blindness that I never saw before.'

Despite this impressive testimony, I am not now arguing – nor, I think, does Paul – that suffering is justified by its outcomes, but I am suggesting that to discuss it as a 'problem' from a position of relative affluence and comfort may not enable us to get to the heart of the matter. Even so, it must be conceded that Paul does not discuss suffering in the way we do very much at all. It cannot possibly have been because there was less of it in his lifetime, nor because he was too preoccupied to notice. Life for the majority of people in Paul's day was much harsher, shorter and poorer than it is for most of us in the affluent areas of the world.

The most difficult aspect of suffering for many today is the suffering caused by natural disasters such as earthquakes and tsunamis, or by painful illnesses or diseases, particularly when they strike a child. Paul has little to say about such suffering, perhaps because of the very fact that life was so short and harsh for most people. Yet he was not entirely a stranger to such suffering himself. His catalogues of his own sufferings include not only those inflicted by other people, but also 'dangers from rivers', and 'danger at sea', including being shipwrecked three times (2 Corinthians 11.25–26). (How many 'unanswered' prayers lie behind this list?) His rhetorical question in Romans also includes both suffering at the hands of others, as well as 'famine' and 'nakedness' (8.35).

Is it worth it?

The closest Paul comes to what we regard as the problem of suffering is, in fact, earlier in this chapter in Romans: 'I consider that the sufferings of this present time are not worth comparing with the glory about to be revealed to us. For the creation waits with eager longing for the revealing of the children of God' (Romans 8.18–19). This is Paul at his most un-modern, but we must frankly acknowledge that what we perceive and experience as the problem of suffering is likely to be far greater if we believe that this life is all there is. Even so, Paul's message, as we have argued in the previous section of this chapter, cannot be reduced to 'pie in the sky when you die'. In the end, each of us has to make an existential decision about suffering. The Old Testament scholar Walter Brueggemann has suggested that how a person reacts to their suffering is the acid test of their faith. In fact, how we respond to suffering, to life and to God are all intimately connected. In weighing our response, we cannot avoid simple, yet profound questions such as, 'Is life, my life, worth living? And, if so, what is the best way to go about it?' Another important question in this context, in the light of our earlier discussion in Chapter 4, is this: 'Am I going to respond to life as a fully "paid-up" member of the human race?'

But perhaps there is a prior theological question. Some people find suffering an insuperable obstacle to belief in God because omnipotence, for them, is the first, and perhaps the defining, attribute of God. We should frankly acknowledge that there is a limit to the extent to which we can fulfil Milton's objective 'to justify the ways of God to man'. Instead, like Paul, we start somewhere else.

'The fellowship of Christ's sufferings'

Something had happened to Paul to make him not only see suffering differently, but also to experience it differently. However, in order to understand Paul properly, we need to clear out of the way a quite widespread misinterpretation about the death of Jesus, and the Christian faith in general – one that was briefly referred to in Chapter 3, section i.

Christians often think of the death of Jesus as 'substitutionary', and by that we mean he was the innocent one, and we, selfish, faithless creatures that we are, the guilty party. So if anyone had to die (so this line of reasoning goes), it should have been us, not Christ. But from the important image of Christ as the one who suffered in our place, we can, and sometimes do, draw the erroneous conclusion that Jesus suffered as he did *so that we won't have to*. This, though, is a travesty of the gospel. Such a view makes nonsense, not only of Jesus' call to his disciples to take up their cross, but also of Paul's teaching about being 'crucified with Christ' (Galatians 2.19), and being 'baptized into his death' (Romans 6.3). By that Paul did not mean a quick baptismal dip which, like the jab of an inoculating needle, is something we grin and bear for a moment, and then it's all over. Paul meant far more.

The great New Testament scholar Rudolph Bultmann rightly saw that this kind of language in Paul – and there is a lot of it – means: making the cross of Christ our own. Through our baptism 'into Christ' – however slowly or imperceptibly this happens – we begin to experience suffering in a different way, and to see it in a different light. In this context, Paul writes about the sufferings of Christ, which, it seems, are not finished yet. True, Christ died once for all – Paul shared that belief with other New Testament writers, notably the writer of the letter to the Hebrews. Yet he can also write of sharing Christ's sufferings (literally 'the fellowship' – *koinonia* – of Christ's sufferings), and even, if he wrote Colossians, of completing 'in my flesh ... what is lacking in Christ's afflictions for the sake of his body, that is, the church' (Colossians 1.24).

It is possible that Paul's understanding of suffering changed and deepened over the years. If it did, it was almost certainly due not to his advancing years alone, but to what happened to him. As we saw in the second chapter of this book, 2 Corinthians is the letter in which Paul talks about his suffering most – almost certainly because the Christians at Corinth were like those today who appear to believe that Christian faith brings happiness and success, not suffering; in other words, if you're ill, it must be because you haven't enough faith.

Paul preaches a very different gospel. (We may wonder whether those Corinthians had what could be called a 'gospel' anyway.) Once a crucified Messiah – even a crucified God

– became central to his faith, suffering could no longer be explained simply as the result of sin. That is sometimes tragically true, of course, but not the whole story. Paul's participation in the sufferings of Christ was, it seems, lifelong, and sometimes extremely severe: countless floggings and near-death experiences, including the synagogue penalty of the 39 lashes (five times), and the Roman punishment of a beating with rods (three times) form only part of the long catalogue which Paul lists in 2 Corinthians 11.23–29.

So what is going on? Do Christians, in becoming Christians, let themselves in for more suffering? It would seem so. Certainly, if we could be whisked by time-machine to Thessalonika or Philippi to put that question to Paul's converts there, they would have agreed. When Paul writes about the sufferings of Christians, he doesn't mean a toothache or a headache which they could equally well have had in their pre-Christian days. He means the kind of suffering which they experience because, and only because, they have adopted the Christian faith.

Yet Paul is extraordinarily positive about this suffering. He is positive about it because of the resurrection of Jesus. Baptism doesn't just let the Christian in for extra suffering; it is the gateway to life – God's new life – of which the resurrection is the most powerful symbol and proof. But though belief in an existence beyond death is a vital part of Paul's perspective on suffering, it is not the whole of it. For Paul, the painful suffering and the joyful victory, the dying and rising, belong inseparably together, and may be experienced now, as he told his young converts again and again (for example, 2 Corinthians 1.3–7).

This is a strange, uncongenial message for us in the comfortable West. The Christian writer John Stott has said, 'The place of suffering ... is hardly ever taught today.' Yet it would be misleading, even one-sided, to say that Christians suffer more as a result of becoming Christians. They may also suffer less, in some ways, than they used to. In time, they will lose the kind of suffering which goes with an egocentric approach to life. By this I do not mean for one moment that people who are not Christians are all egocentric; that is clearly not so. But to be faithful to Paul, we have to say that one of the hallmarks of *genuine Christian* living is selflessness ('I, yet not I', Galatians 2.20). So, for example, if before your baptism you had thought that life owed you something, or that the world owed you a living, or that people were there primarily for your benefit, you would have been inviting the kind of suffering which inevitably goes with resentment, bitterness and disillusionment. By contrast, there is real happiness in the Christian way, as Paul's frequent references to thanksgiving and joy show, not least in his letter to the Philippians: 'Rejoice in the Lord always; again I will say, Rejoice' (Philippians 4.4; cf. 3.1). So there is a profound paradox in Christian experience: the Christian takes on more suffering or, at least, suffering they otherwise would not have had – and they are much happier.

iv Paul and people of other faiths

This seems yet another strange subject to question Paul about. His world was so different from ours, but there is more to be learned from the apostle than first meets the eye. We begin by looking at two speeches by Paul in the Acts of the Apostles. In keeping with the conventions of Greek and Roman historical writing, the speeches may be largely the work of the author of Acts, rather than the words of Paul himself. But the differences between the way 'Paul' speaks in Acts and the way Paul writes in his letters have been exaggerated. There *are* some differences – for example 'Paul' in Acts 13.38–39 speaks about being justified in a different way from Paul of the letters – but the speeches to Gentile audiences in Acts 14.14–17 and 17.22–31 are in line with what Paul tells us was his evangelistic strategy: being 'all things to all people' (1 Corinthians 9.22). That did not mean telling people what they wanted to hear, but it *did* mean establishing as much common ground as possible with your hearers.

That is an important part of an inter-faith conversation, say, between a Moslem and a Christian. If both conversation partners simply use the occasion to accentuate their differences, the conversation probably won't last very long, or it may turn out to be the only conversation they have. It is likely to be a far more constructive occasion if they seek to discover how much they have in common, without minimizing their differences. So what can we learn from these speeches?

God everywhere

First, there are signs of God everywhere. You don't have to step inside a religious world in order to find God. Nor are God's presence and activity confined to our own religious tradition – in Paul's case, a Jewish-Christian tradition. God had, in one sense, left the Gentiles to themselves (Acts 14.16), but in another sense he had not, because creation itself testifies to his goodness (v. 17) – though that is not always obvious. In other words, God has withdrawn in order to give us space, but not withdrawn so completely as to leave us clueless about himself. Paul in his letters seems to be saying something similar in Romans: 'For what can be known about God is plain to them, because God has shown it to them. Ever since the creation of the world his eternal power and divine nature, invisible though they are, have been understood and seen through the things he has made' (Romans 1.19–20).

Paul goes on to express some difficult ideas about the consequences of human idolatry, which prevent us reading the book of creation in the way that God intended. That is a difficult idea, but it is arguable that if humankind were not so busy, preoccupied and, above all, oblivious to the mystery of our existence, we might be more thankful than we are. (Paul clearly sees thankfulness as one of the basic human responses to God (v. 21).)

But what of other religions? Before we turn to Paul's speech at Athens, we need to look at his attitude to idols. The apostle doesn't pull his punches. 'We know,' he says in effect, agreeing with the more confident Christians at Corinth, 'that idols don't really exist, and that there is only one God' (1 Corinthians 8.4). In fact, one of the most striking changes in Paul's Gentile converts was that they 'turned' from idols in order to worship the living God (1 Thessalonians 1.9, Galatians 4.8). Idolatry, according to Paul, damages, and ultimately destroys, those who practise it. Worshipping what is less than God makes us less than human (Romans 1.18–32).

For some Christians, this rules out all faiths except Christianity. But we cannot dismiss other faiths in this way. Islam and Judaism are as passionately opposed to idolatry as Christians are. Hinduism and Buddhism have statues of different deities, which some Western Christians wrongly call 'idols', when in fact they are more like the icons or images of eastern Christianity – windows through which we pass to the mystery of God. So Paul's strictures simply cannot be transferred to world faiths today. And, as we've already seen, Paul, according to both Romans and Acts, acknowledged the presence and activity of God everywhere.

So why couldn't the idols Paul criticized be regarded like, say, the statues of Hinduism, as icons of the one true God? The crucial test, I suggest, are the associations which any worship has and, above all, the effect the worship has on the worshippers. Gentile worship, accurately or inaccurately, tended to be associated in Jewish minds with immorality, and so stood self-condemned. Former Vice-President Al Gore, in a book from which I have already quoted, offers a present-day example of how a modern obsession can erode human life: 'We are monumentally distracted by a pervasive technological culture that appears to have a life of its own ... continually seducing us, and pulling us from the opportunity to experience directly the true meaning of our own lives.' Gore goes on to quote Psalm 115, noting how people came to resemble the idolatrous artefacts with which they were 'fatally enchanted'.[8]

So did Paul believe that people could find God through their own belief-systems? I avoid the emotive word 'paganism' here because the religions of the Mediterranean world in Paul's day were so varied. Although, as Paul observed, that world was a polytheistic one, with 'many gods and many lords' (1 Corinthians 8.5), some people believed, or dimly saw, that behind all the different faces of the gods and goddesses, there was one high God. This fundamental belief in one God was the common ground which Paul, according to Acts, sought to establish with his hearers at Athens. (The Greek text of Paul's sermon is engraved on a metal plaque in modern Athens at the foot of the Acropolis).

Vincent Donovan, in *Christianity Re-discovered*, adopted a strategy remarkably similar to Paul's in his first meeting with the Masai people in East Africa. He told them that he recognized they knew about God long before he had come along, and that they were a very devout people. Donovan didn't believe that God loved Christians more than he loved the Masai, or that God had forgotten about them until he had come along.[9]

So Paul at Athens begins by acknowledging the religious seriousness of his audience (Acts 17.22). Next, he finds an opportunity in an inscription he has seen – 'To an unknown God'. Archaeologists have found no such inscription, and even the Church Father Jerome thought Paul got it wrong: what, according to Jerome, he should have said was 'To the gods of Asia, Europe and Africa, gods unknown and foreign'.[10] But perhaps Jerome was engaging in a little saintly pernicketiness here. 'To an unknown God' certainly expresses an important dimension of ancient religion: make sure you don't leave any god out! So here is Paul's window of opportunity.

Establishing common ground

To win his audience, however, Paul must establish more common ground, and this he does in the verses which follow, even to the extent of quoting a Greek poet, and saying something with which many a Greek philosopher would have heartily agreed: 'In him [that is, God] we live and move and have our being' (Acts 17.28a). In modern terms, Paul hasn't quoted the Bible once yet – only a Greek poet and perhaps, for good measure, a philosopher as well. How many Christians can pay Moslems or Hindus the complement of quoting appreciatively from their scriptures? But at last we do arrive at what we might call the explicitly Christian bit of Paul's speech – though only two verses (vv. 30–31)! He doesn't even mention Jesus by name, but it is clear who he means from the reference to the resurrection.

Will this do? Some have thought that this Athens sermon is a pale reflection of what the real Paul would have said. Did Paul simply have an off-day, or had he left his sermon notes in Corinth? Maybe the real Paul would have mentioned the cross, however briefly. But this speech cannot be so far from the Paul who declared his readiness to adapt (*not* sell out) to his audience by 'being all things to all people'. As for it being a dud sermon, or a disastrous experiment never to be repeated, space on a papyrus roll was too precious to waste in this way. Ancient writers, including historians like Luke, included model speeches, not dud ones. And the response to the speech at Athens is what the response to the preaching of the gospel always is in Acts: some believed, and some did not (17.32–34).

So I am suggesting that Paul as portrayed in Acts, and especially at Athens, offers us some guidelines in interpreting the wider world in the light of the God whose presence and activity are everywhere. In particular, Paul shows that inter-faith conversations proceed by *both* an honest recognition of differences *and* an exploration of common ground.

We need now to return to the question I posed earlier: did Paul believe that people could find God through their own belief-systems? On the evidence of the Athens speech, it seems he believed that people had intimations of and clues about God, because that is how the Creator has made both the world and humankind, making possible a sincere and widespread human search for God (v. 27). But a fuller knowledge of God comes only through Christ, marked out by God through the resurrection to be the world's judge (vv. 30–31).

A good life without being a Christian?

But there is more to be said in the light of what Paul himself wrote. People outside the churches are sometimes heard to say, 'I can live a good life without going to church'. Christians, reluctantly or otherwise, acknowledge as much, perhaps suppressing the question, 'Then what is the point in going to church?' In Britain, where Christianity tends to be equated with morality, such questions are never far away. Paul, it seems, had no difficulty in acknowledging that there were good pagans around: 'When Gentiles, who do not possess the law, do instinctively what the law requires, these, though not having the law, are a law to themselves. They show that what the law requires is written on their hearts, to which their own conscience also bears witness ...' (Romans 2.14, 15a).

And this from the apostle who wrote that all have sinned! But Paul is not contradicting himself. The point here is that everyone has a conscience, a sense of right and wrong, and so no one can finally makes excuses before God. So here is another piece of the jigsaw. Paul doesn't say that these people don't need the gospel; the point for Paul was that, in the gospel, God had spoken a definitive, reconciling word. But he clearly saw that there were people outside his Judaeo-Christian tradition who, at least some of the time, observed the law. And by 'law' he meant, remarkable as it may sound, the law which included the two greatest commandments: to love God and our neighbour as ourselves.

One of the problems many of us have in discussing questions like this is our limited experience. This can be especially true of a religious 'professional' like myself; the Church easily becomes an all-absorbing activity. To coin a current phrase, some of us 'ought to get out a bit more'! So it can come as a surprise to discover that Paul got out and about a great deal. Even if his Jewish piety was originally exclusive and narrow, that need not mean his experience of life was. In any case, his extensive travels as an apostle deep into what, as a Pharisee, he would have thought of as Gentile territory gave him the chance to see God's presence and activity in unexpected places. Simon Peter's experience, of discovering that God had reached the home of a Roman centurion before he did, was the kind of experience Paul may well have had.

Jesus and an inherited faith

So far, we've built an argument based on God's omnipresence, but what of Paul's claims about Jesus? Belief in Jesus, after all, constitutes the heart of Christian faith, and the speech at Athens, despite the length devoted to establishing a real rapport with the audience, does not leave Jesus out. Some well-meaning people, in their praiseworthy concern to establish good relations with people of other faiths, downplay the significance of Jesus. But this simply will not do. A Christianity in which Jesus is marginal is, at best, a pale reflection of its true self; at worst, it is a contradiction in terms. Here Paul's attitude to Judaism can help us.

At first sight, however, this looks unpromising territory. The subject of Paul and Judaism is a minefield! But it may help to recall where Paul began, and where, in a sense, he ends. He grew up to be, in his early adult years, a devout Pharisee (Philippians 3.5–6). Did he ever leave Judaism? The answer, I think, has to be 'yes' and 'no'. Similar questions may be posed of other notable spiritual leaders who found that life-transforming experiences led them in radically new directions. Did Gandhi remain a Hindu? Was John Wesley still a practising Anglican at the end of his life? So Paul may be said to have left 'Judaism', a word, incidentally, which he uses only once (Galatians 1.14). But he remained in the faith of his fathers (and mothers). What he gave up, like a coat which no longer fitted, or like a perspective rendered out of date by new events, was a particular version of that faith. According to the Judaism he left behind, the Messianic Age had yet to dawn, for the Messiah was still awaited. So, in this Judaism, the law of Moses remained as the distinguishing mark of all who embraced the faith – and that included Gentiles who converted to Judaism. All this Paul left behind. I think we should also add, in the light of current Israeli–Palestinian conflicts, that Paul ceased to believe that the promised land and its boundaries were a vital part of Israel's identity. God's 'gifts and calling' to Israel are irrevocable (Romans 11.29) and, it seems, 'the promises' stand (Romans 9.4). Yet Paul never quotes God's promise of the land; like the letter of the law, it has been left behind. But Paul still counted himself a member of God's people, Israel. So there has to be a 'yes' and a 'no' in our answer to the question 'Did Paul leave Judaism behind?' Did he consider that fellow-

Jews who had rejected Jesus still belonged to Israel? The answer to this is not so straightforward. Paul categorically says, '... not all Israelites truly belong to Israel' (Romans 9.6), but earlier verses suggest he is far from giving up on them (9.1–5) and, much more importantly, God hasn't given up on them either (Romans 11.25–29).

It is important to recognize that long-standing members of the Church experience spiritual odysseys similar to Paul's. Where they end up is not where they began. They may still be in the Church, but where they are now is not where they were. Along the way, there may have been conflict with fellow-church-members with whom they previously saw eye to eye, but not so now. Yet they would be wise to be restrained in their pronouncements on the spiritual state of those people. Even so, Paul has some sharply critical things to say about the 'Judaism' he has left behind, and its people. They have a zeal for God, but a zeal uninformed by the revelation of Christ and, perhaps most crucial of all, they don't really know the foundation of their own faith, 'the righteousness of God' (Romans 10.2–3). They have replaced God's righteousness with a version of their own.

Those of us who claim to be, or aspire to be, Christians must see in these verses a reflection of ourselves. By our moral indignation and fulminations against the godless, we can only too readily exhibit a zeal for God uninformed by a knowledge of Christ. As for 'righteousness', a hard morality easily replaces that divine 'morality' whose predominant characteristic is putting right, bringing justice to, and healing a world gone wrong. (In the previous chapter, I quoted the moralistic creed of a popular newspaper which, sadly, is read by only too many churchgoers in Britain.) But Paul had other things to say about the Judaism he left behind. Astonishingly, he can now say: the law served a useful purpose in pointing the Jewish people to Christ (Galatians 3.23–25, Romans 10.4), but it can no longer be the defining characteristic of God's people. So, while some continued to avoid eating pork, or continued paying an annual temple tax and observing the Sabbath as a matter of conscience, those observances are no longer required of all. Paul, it seems, sat lightly to them (1 Corinthians 9.19–23).

Despite Luke's portrayal of Paul as a devout Jew, then, we have to say, on the basis of what he himself wrote, that there was a Judaism which he left behind or, at the very least, which he felt free to move in and out of – at considerable personal cost. But – and this is so important – Paul never abandoned his Jewish faith. Is this a contradiction in terms? That he left 'Judaism' behind, but retained his Jewish faith? In the way that I have tried to describe his journey, no, it is not a contradiction – but it is frequently an uncomfortable place in which to be.

Some conclusions

In what way is this relevant to our multi-faith situation today? In several ways, Paul himself can properly be described as a 'multi-faith' person or, to be as accurate as we can be, one who combined in his own faith both the old and the new. His life's work is also testimony to how the Holy Spirit can create new kinds of Christians which most of the 'old' kind of Christians would never have dreamed of! I refer, of course, to Gentile Christians. 'Surely', many of the Christians in Judaea would have said, 'a Gentile has to stop being a Gentile in order to be a Christian?' 'Yes,' Paul in effect replied, 'but not by becoming a Jewish Christian.' Is it not possible – even likely – that in the twenty-first century new kinds of Christians will emerge, some the products of long, costly and searching inter-faith conversations?

Should Christians today seek to convert people of other faiths? Can we surmise what Paul would do in our position? Clearly he never lost hope that he would bring his fellow-Jews to faith in Christ. Some Christians think it wrong to try to convert adherents of other faiths, and it has been compared to teaching people to address God in a language not their own. I am not so sure. However, using language such as 'trying to convert them' sounds all too much like a human-centred, church-centred activity. It quickly becomes an exercise in making them Christians like *us* – with the unfortunate implication that we, not they, are right after all. That is not evangelism as Paul knew it. Far better to tell the story of Jesus – including his cross and resurrection – and leave the rest to God. Simeon and Anna, according to Luke, were devout Jews who recognized the infant Christ and welcomed him with open arms. Maybe other devout people in our day will do that too – provided we Christians don't get in the way.

v Paul and modern fundamentalism

The Bible, like the Church, has been heavily criticized in recent years. Feminists have found it male-dominated, and its language and cultures 'patriarchal'. Peoples on the receiving end of European imperialism have noted how their conquerors and oppressors justified, or tried to justify, what they were doing from the Bible. And, as we noted in the Introduction, the writings of Paul have played their part in this oppressive use of the Bible.

But the Bible, reflecting the God revealed in Jesus, should not be experienced – still less used – in these oppressive ways. Its fundamental purpose is to liberate people, not oppress them; to enhance life, in the way God intended, not to diminish it. But it is more likely to be used oppressively if its authority is misunderstood, or if it is interpreted in an all too wooden, and literalist, way.

This section is concerned to show that Paul's own use of the Jewish Scriptures (our Old Testament) does not support the fundamentalist view of things. Nor does it support any use of Scripture which is oppressive or inhuman. But, first, I shall offer one or two general remarks about the nature of the Bible's authority.

The Bible's contradiction of fundamentalism

Christian fundamentalists seem not to realize that the Bible itself contradicts their view of it. It is not 'inerrant'; it contains inaccuracies and even contradictions (though not fundamental ones). Writers occasionally get their facts wrong, or the different perspectives of various writers appear to contradict each other. For example, did Paul see the risen Christ in the way the other apostles did? He seemed to think so (1 Corinthians 9.1 and 15.3–8), but Luke saw it differently. By the time of Paul's (Saul's) conversion, Jesus had ascended to heaven, and so Paul's experience, real and life-transforming as it was, was not the same as that of the disciples in the upper room on the first Easter Day.

In a similar way, Paul and Luke differ in their understanding of Paul's relationship to his Jewish faith, and to his Pharisaic past. Luke, as we have seen, portrays Paul consistently as a law-abiding Jew; perhaps he wished to accentuate one particular dimension of Paul's missionary strategy, that of 'becoming as a Jew to win Jews' (1 Corinthians 9.20). Paul's overall strategy of being 'all things to all people', and his conviction that no food was unclean in itself (Romans 14.14), meant that he cannot have always observed Jewish food laws. This may account for why Luke has Paul say (Acts 23.6) 'I am a Pharisee', whereas Paul himself as good as says 'I *was* a Pharisee – but not any more' (Philippians 3.5–7).

So the Bible itself does not support the often exaggerated claims made for it. Christians do their faith and the Bible a great disservice by claiming the wrong things for their Scriptures. Even the much-quoted verse in 2 Timothy (3.16) does not make the claim for Scripture which it is supposed to do: 'All scripture is inspired by God and is useful for teaching ...' Bearing in mind when this was written (whether by Paul or a disciple of Paul), it can hardly be a reference to the whole Bible. Second, though all Christians will believe in the inspiration of Scripture, inspiration need not mean – and, given the evidence I have just cited, *cannot* mean – inerrancy. In fact, 2 Timothy 3.16 claims too *little* for the Bible; to say it is 'useful for teaching' is an understatement, to put it mildly!

When we turn to Paul's use of his Scriptures, it is tempting to ask whether he was a literalist or a non-literalist. But this would be like asking whether he believed in the law of gravity. We must not try to fit him into one of our 'pigeon-holes'. What we can do is to observe the way he used *his* 'Scriptures' (that is, our 'Old Testament'), and ask whether he has anything to teach us today.

Paul's Bible, to judge from his many allusions to it and quotations from it, was the Septuagint, a translation of the Hebrew Scriptures into Greek, probably in the third century BC. It is highly unlikely, of course, that he would have carried his 'Bible' with him; that would have meant a veritable library of scrolls, one at least for each book. Not only would that have been physically impossible, but such scrolls were expensive and scarce. Instead, as many people in those days would have done, Paul carried his Scriptures in his head.

Christ, the Bible's meaning

So what can we learn from Paul's use of his Scriptures? Paul came to believe that the Hebrew Scriptures pointed forward to Christ, and it is no cliché to say that Jesus Christ is 'the fulfilment', the inner meaning, of the Hebrew Scriptures. This has practical consequences. To say that a *person* – in Christian belief, God incarnate – is the key means that the Bible cannot be a mere moral code or rule book. It becomes something else: the record of a transforming revelation. And that, of course, was Paul's discovery on the Damascus Road.

Once his Damascus Road experience had convinced him that Jesus was the promised Messiah, then this crucified and risen 'Son of God' was the key to interpreting his Bible. He says as much to the Corinthians: quoting a tradition which had been handed on to him, he says, '... Christ died for our sins in accordance with the scriptures, ... was buried, ... and ... was raised on the third day in accordance with the scriptures' (1 Corinthians 15.3–4). Our natural instinct is to ask, 'Which Scriptures?', but it is likely that Paul was thinking here of his Scriptures in their entirety: the whole of Scripture points to Christ crucified and risen. That is not immediately obvious, but if the death and resurrection of Jesus are the meaning and goal of God's age-long dealings with Israel and, at the same time, the meaning and goal of Israel's age-long pilgrimage, then we can say that Christ is the key to the Scriptures. Paul makes a similar point with reference to the law of Moses, the first five books of his Bible: 'For Christ is the end of the law ...' (Romans 10.4, 'end' here meaning 'goal'). This perspective affected how Paul read his Scriptures. For example, how should Paul now read the story in Exodus of how Moses' face 'shone' when he went in to speak with God (Exodus 34.29–35)? He had come to believe that the glory 'in the face of Jesus Christ' (2 Corinthians 4.6) far surpasses the glory of Moses. So, in Paul's view, that explains a puzzle in the Exodus story: why did Moses put a veil over his face? (It wasn't to stop the Israelites seeing the radiance of his face, as the story makes clear.) Paul's answer is: because the glory of Moses was a *transient* glory, destined to give way to the greater glory of Christ.

Much of Paul's writings consist of his re-interpreting of his Bible in the light of his new-found faith. To take another example, how and when he came to the conclusion that all the nations of the world, not just Israel, are included in God's new covenant is not clear. Perhaps it was the dawning realization that a crucified Messiah had abolished the ancient distinction between Jew and Gentile. But Gentiles don't get much of a 'look in' in the Old Testament, despite some notable exceptions, such as Ruth. Similarly, most references, though not all, to 'the nations' tend to be negative. But what Paul does, in the light of Christ, is to privilege God's promise to Abraham (or at least one reading of it) in Genesis 15.6: 'All the Gentiles shall be blessed in you' (Galatians 3.8, cf. Romans 4.17).

No one could have worked out from the 'Old Testament' alone that one day in Christ there would be 'neither Jew nor Greek' (Galatians 3.28), but now Paul can see the direction in which the Scriptures were pointing. There is a modern parallel to this. No one could easily deduce from the Bible that in Christ there is a fundamental equality of male and female (Galatians 3.28 again), but that is so. The relative invisibility of Gentiles in the Old Testament didn't mean that they were inferior to Jews. The relative invisibility of women in the Bible does not make them inferior to men, even though, tragically, biblical interpretation has 'form' in this area.

To grow a church

So what is the Bible for, according to Paul? It testifies to Jesus Christ, that is clear. But what other purposes does it serve? People might be forgiven for thinking that the Bible is there to provide ammunition, in the form of proof-texts, to lob in the direction of people we disapprove of. On the whole, Paul sees a more positive role for the scriptures: to shape the identity of the Church.

That is what he does in 1 Corinthians 10.1–13, where he encourages the headstrong church at Corinth to identify itself imaginatively with ancient Israel. That proud church might delude itself into thinking it had 'arrived'; its strong members were above and beyond temptation. Not so, says Paul, the Scriptures show that God's people are pilgrims in 'the wilderness', a place fraught with danger for the unsuspecting, or complacent, pilgrim. This is one of the challenges Paul presents to contemporary churches: will they read themselves into the biblical story, and understand themselves in the light of the biblical story?

A liberating or oppressive Bible?

But it remains true that the Bible can be, and has been, a very oppressive book. In the hands of the wrong people, it can damage people rather than give them life. Would Paul have understood that? I think he would, given his, admittedly cryptic, remark, 'the letter kills' (2 Corinthians 3.6). It's almost as if, for Paul, his Scriptures spoke with two voices.[11] Or, to put it more dramatically, he found there was a deep 'fault line' running through his Bible. There was the voice of the law, pronouncing a curse on all who failed to fulfil all its commandments (Galatians 3.10, where Paul quotes Leviticus), but there was another voice, the voice of the promise (Galatians 3.11), or what Paul calls in another letter 'the righteousness that comes from faith' (Romans 10.6 – contrast verse 5 where Paul again quotes Leviticus).

There is one simple, but vital, lesson for us to learn from all this. Does the way we use the Bible lead us to Christ, give us life, and help to liberate people? Or does it function as an oppressive authority which keeps people in their place? The contrast may be overstated, but I believe this is where Paul can help us. Many people today have, understandably, become suspicious of the Bible. It has been much misused by men – mainly men – in power. It will be important for the future well-being of the Church for us to start trusting, and even loving, the Bible again, but that can only be done if we read it, like Paul, in the light of Christ.

A conclusion

A chapter of this kind is bound to be tentative and partial as there are so many contemporary issues. Here, I have simply selected some which I feel passionately about, and to which I believe Paul to be especially relevant. What matters far more than agreeing with any conclusions reached here is the readiness of us all to continue these conversations. By that I mean the conversation between ourselves and Paul suggested at the end of Chapter 2. Here I simply want to add that such a conversation must include the biggest and most difficult questions of our time, such as those I have tried to address here. Above all, can Paul's vision of a universal, human society challenge us to realize it before it is too late?

Notes

1 J. Stiglitz, *Globalization and Its Discontents*, Penguin, Harmondsworth, 2002, p. 217.

2 Stiglitz, *Globalization and Its Discontents*, p. 217.

3 J. Sacks, *The Dignity of Difference*, Continuum, London, 2002, pp. 153–4.

4 Unfortunately, the Greek word *oikonomia* is translated in ways which obscure some of its meaning; the New Revised Standard Version and New International Version have 'God's commission'; the Good News Bible has 'God's task'; the Contemporary English Version has 'God's plan'.

5 Sacks, *The Dignity of Difference*, p. 86.

6 A. Gore, *Earth in the Balance: Ecology and the Human Spirit*, Penguin, Harmondsworth, 1993, p. 239.

7 P. Tillich, *The Shaking of the Foundations*, Pelican, London, 1962, p. 89.

8 Gore, *Earth in the Balance*, pp. 241 and 257–8.

9 V. Donovan, *Christianity Re-discovered*, SCM, London, 1982, p. 25.

10 C. K. Barrett, *Acts: A Shorter Commentary*, T. & T. Clark, Edinburgh, 2002, p. 268.

11 I owe the concept of 'two voices' in the law of Moses to F. Watson, *Paul and the Hermeneutics of Faith*, T. & T. Clark, Edinburgh, 2004.

Conclusion: Paul and the Question of God

Thinking about God

Many years ago I asked some people to discuss in small groups the question 'What do we mean by God?' It was a difficult question for anyone, and two people, I recall, looked thoroughly nonplussed, if not panic-stricken. I enquired what the problem was. They replied, 'We came tonight hoping that you would tell us the answer'!

If we think we know what we mean by the word 'God', perhaps we should pause, and ask ourselves whether we should. 'God' is one of the most mysterious words in our own language, or any other. It can be a troublesome, even dangerous word – as we have been reminded by what, rightly or wrongly, has been called 'religious terrorism'. In recent years, too, more than one distinguished scientist has argued that 'God' is now an outmoded concept. The most famous of these, Richard Dawkins, published a book which rapidly became a best-seller, *The God Delusion*.

So it is important to acknowledge that 'God' is not a straight-forward word, and it's not just a question of whether we believe in God or not. For one thing, we easily make God in our own image. Other people, especially those in authority over us in our early years – parents, teachers, church leaders – shape God for us. So many of us come to equate the voice of God with the voice of conscience: 'someone' whose main function is to make us feel guilty or uncomfortable.

What has all this to do with our discussion of Paul? In the

first place, what we understand by the word 'God' may not be what Paul meant. When we read 'God' in Paul's letters, we may invest that word with all the associations – good, bad and indifferent – which it has come to have for us. Our understanding of God may need to be purified and deepened.

But, second, we may not like all that we read about God in Paul, and decide that we simply can't accept today all that he believed about God. For example, was Paul's God a patriarchal god? Is the wrath of God a Christian concept? How far did Paul take over Old Testament understandings of God which we find hard to reconcile with a God of love? In Chapter 3, I suggested that Paul's understanding of God was refined and deepened by his encounter with the risen Christ. We now need to explore more fully just what this meant for him and, not least, what it meant – and means – in practice now.

Paul's crisis of faith

Many people come to faith in God through a crisis. A bereavement or a serious illness either brings them to faith, or deepens the faith in God they already had. (The opposite may happen, of course, as the sufferer asks 'Why has God allowed this to happen to me?') It is not that God 'sends' these experiences to teach people a lesson, or that suffering is good for us. But it remains a fact: some people come to belief, or a deeper belief, in God through a crisis.

Of course, it is not the only way people come to faith. (The birth of a child may re-awaken faith, for example.) But I mention it here because Paul hit a crisis. Even if that crisis – the Damascus Road experience – was different from what we used to think about it (Chapter 1, section iv), a crisis it still was. The revelation, in whatever form it came to him, of a crucified and risen Christ transformed and deepened his belief in God. Paul encountered God through a suffering human being called Jesus. What is more, Paul now saw God – or Jesus – in the very people on whom he was inflicting suffering: 'Saul, Saul, why are you persecuting me?'

Was all this simply the experience of one man long ago – and nothing more? No – what Paul teaches about God can do much to lead us out of the present morass into which we have strayed. Morass, I think, is the right word. Take, first, belief in God among religious people – and particularly people who go to church. It is possible to have too fixed a concept of God. G. K. Chesterton, in typical swashbuckling fashion, inveighed against those who 'keep a god like a top hat'. Such a god, even if it has a Christian name, and some Christian characteristics, is likely to be an idol, draining the life out of the church where that god is kept. There is likely to be, for example, a connection between a church's resistance to change, and that church's understanding of God – unless God doesn't come into the discussion at all (which sometimes happens). This is not to say that all change is good, but a church with a 'top hat' sort of God is unlikely to engage in more than cosmetic changes to its life and worship.

There is another church matter to consider here. The quality of some contemporary worship does not suggest that there is a lively awareness of God's presence among the participants. Many leave a church service wishing that they had experienced God's presence, and disappointed that they haven't. And if our worship is thin or shallow, that does nothing to help the churchgoer to live the rest of the week with a deeper awareness of God.

Beyond the Church, people hold a bewildering variety of beliefs about God, but many are, in practice, atheists; they live their lives with little or no reference to God. It is perhaps not surprising in secular societies – and such societies are likely to grow in number. But what is happening to all the citizens of those societies, including the Christians among them? Even where belief in God exists, it can be steadily eroded by over-exposure to contemporary culture and mass media which are by no means always sympathetic to the Christian Church.

Believing in God is not primarily a tradition we inherit ('my family have always believed in God'). Although it is a personal matter, it isn't, or shouldn't be, a private one. It is a life-long task and, above all, something to put into practice. Is it a choice we make? In a way, it is. George McLeod, the founder of the Iona Community in Scotland, once advised an agnostic enquirer, 'Live *as if* God exists'; such a person, in McLeod's view, would eventually come to believe that God does exist. Some will say that that is make-believe; it would be if God doesn't exist.

According to Paul, the truest form of belief in God is the result of an encounter with transforming grace. Paul, after the Damascus Road experience, saw the religious tradition he had inherited, the scriptures he knew, and the God he had believed in in a new light – the light of Christ. It is not easy to pinpoint how his beliefs changed, but in what follows I shall try to do that, with an eye on our contemporary world.

The boundary-crossing God

First, Paul came to believe that God crosses boundaries. He had always believed, as a devout Jew, in one God who had made the world, and who must, in a sense, be everywhere. But now he came to see that God specializes in bringing people together – especially people very different from one another. In fact, crossing boundaries is a defining activity of God.

Most obviously, Paul now saw that God had transcended, and in principle abolished, the boundary separating the Jew from the Gentile. The cross had been, to Paul's pre-Christian mind, God-forsaken Gentile territory where a man claiming to be God's Messiah had been publicly and humiliatingly executed. The resurrection changed all that, and now he saw that God's business was global. It always had been, of course, but earlier centuries had been building up to this climactic point: 'in the fullness of time' God sent his Son (Galatians 4.4).

But the Jew–Gentile boundary was not the only one which, in Paul's view, God had crossed. By sending his Son, God had crossed all the lines dividing humankind from himself. This is so fundamental to Paul's faith that it is worth spelling out in some detail. First, God crossed the boundary of enmity dividing humankind from himself, an enmity which lies on humanity's side, not God's (Romans 5.10). Above all, God in Christ had crossed the boundary of sin (Romans 8.3, 2 Corinthians 5.21).

'Sin', as I acknowledged in Chapter 1, is an extremely difficult word for many people today. We need to recall what was said in the earlier discussion: 'sin', for Paul, means falling out of relationship with God and failing to be the human beings God meant us to be. We tend to get preoccupied with 'sins' (plural), the symptoms, rather than the underlying ailment and failure. (Both these words are necessary: sin refers both to what spiritually ails us and to how we fail.) We often focus on the less important symptoms too, rather than, for example, the illusions, prejudices, idolatries and injustices which disfigure human life and God's world. Wherever 'sin' dominates human life (and Paul uses the language of domination), it is dehumanizing and destructive, morally culpable, and – not least – tragic.

God, according to Paul, crossed this boundary, and Paul's language is unmistakable, even shocking, especially in 2 Corinthians: 'For our sake he [God] made him [Christ] to be sin who knew no sin, so that in him we might become the righteousness of God' (5.21; compare Romans 8.3). The best commentary on this is a verse in Mark's Gospel, where the evangelist records that Jesus died feeling God-forsaken (Mark 15.34). It seems the very integrity of God is stretched to breaking-point. Someone has suggested that in this moment of Christ's death, the Father and the Son moved sufficiently far apart to accommodate the whole world in between.

The Church easily forgets that God has crossed this boundary or, to be more precise, we Christians often live as if God had not done so. When this happens, Christian communities tend to become simply gatherings of good, moral people who look askance at everyone who appears to be less spiritual and less moral than they are. When the Church remembers that God has crossed the boundary, then compassion is much more likely to inform its attitudes and shape its actions.

Paul also believed that God in Christ crossed the ultimate boundary – what he calls the 'last enemy' (1 Corinthians 15.26), namely, death itself. Whatever view we take of the nature of Christ's resurrection appearances, the conviction that God is defeating death (Paul uses the present tense in the verse just cited) lies at the heart of his faith. In those parts of the world where most people are living more comfortably, and therefore much longer, death is the subject we ignore as much as possible. To think about death, particularly our own death, is regarded as morbid and unhealthy. So the resurrection of Jesus is a neglected aspect of Christian faith. 'Aspect', in fact, is the wrong word to use here: the resurrection lay at the heart of Paul's faith, and constitutes the very foundation of Christianity. By crossing the final boundary of death, God in Christ has relativized all human-made boundaries – including some which Christians, misguidedly, continue to make. One example relevant to this discussion is what we say about God.

No longer 'our' God

I want to suggest that Paul's teaching shows that we are wrong in speaking of 'our God' (as some modern worship songs do), and even of 'the Christian God'. Paul, I am sure, would happily alter his rhetorical question in Romans, where he asked, 'Is God the God of the Jews only?' He answered his own question with 'no'; he is God of the Gentiles, too (Romans 3.29). Today, I believe, Paul would ask 'Is God of the Christians only?', answering 'No; he is God of Moslems too – and Hindus, and Buddhists ...' So when Christians (or anyone) refer to 'our God', as distinct from 'their' god (whoever 'they' might be), we have denied Paul's faith in a boundary-crossing God.

I should add that there is a place in Christian devotion for the word 'our' (but more particularly 'my') when applied to God. This is not to ignore 'Our Father ...', but in the Lord's Prayer there is no implied contrast between 'our Father' and some rival deity. The legitimate use of expressions such as 'my God' and 'our God' is best illustrated from a prayer in the Covenant Service of the Methodist Church: '... you are mine and I am yours ...' But this is the language of love and adoration, not of tribal religion, as in the too-frequently sung chorus 'Our God reigns'.

God is love

But what of the more difficult language which Paul uses about God? He writes of God's wrath (1 Thessalonians 1.10, Romans 1.18), of God's 'judgement seat' (Romans 14.10), and even of God's vengeance (Romans 12.19). Space precludes a long discussion about these difficult concepts, but in trying to understand what Paul teaches about God, we have to decide where we are going to start. That is to say, which fundamental conviction about God in Paul's letters is the key to all the rest? I suggest that we take as our interpretative key a verse which, admittedly, Paul did not write, but which several passages in his letters lead us to suppose he could easily have written. It is found in a later letter of the New Testament: 'God is love' (1 John 4.16).

Is this wishful thinking? I think not. Paul's teaching about God's wrath and judgement can be understood in the light of this fundamental conviction. But his teaching about God's grace, love and righteousness cannot be understood if we proceed in the opposite direction, starting with God's wrath and judgement. To put it another way: we allow the revelation of Christ – Paul's Damascus Road revelation – to be the starting point for our understanding of God.

This brings us back to some of our fundamental mistakes in the way we think and speak of God. If we suppose that God is 'a being' – a supernatural one, but still a being – we are likely to credit God with emotions all too like our own. God loves, God gets angry, God has standards to maintain – above all, standards of righteousness and justice. By thinking of God in this way we run the risk of diminishing God's love and, in the process, seriously distorting what Paul means by God's wrath. If this has been our Christian 'God', Paul can help us to see that our god has been 'too small'. This in no way reduces the seriousness of all that Paul has to say about wrath and judgement. Closing our hearts and minds to the light, the truth and the love of God is always tragic, diminishing and – in extreme instances, perhaps – self-destructive. However, we humans are poor judges of whether other people have closed their hearts to God, and we don't often err on the generous side. By contrast, God in his love does not give up easily, if ever:

... it is not by any afterthought that we can do justice to that boundless patience and holiness of God, which loves goodness everywhere, labours for it, and delights in it everywhere. We have often thought of God as though it were 'all or nothing' with him. But it is not true. In his mysterious humility he tends the last smouldering lamp in every rebellious heart ... It is he who defends the last strip of territory against the invasion of passion, when all the rest is gone, and raises mysterious defences about beleaguered virtues whose doom seemed sure. When he is denied or unrecognized in his own person, he still lingers ... dimly apprehended as a sense of duty, or some indestructible principle ...[1]

There are two passages in Paul's writings which take us to the heart of his understanding and experience of God. The first comes from 1 Corinthians, and a little background may help us to appreciate some familiar words afresh. The nineteenth-century Prime Minister Benjamin Disraeli famously charged his arch-rival Gladstone with being 'inebriated by his own verbosity'. The church at Corinth may have been inebriated by not only their verbosity, religious and otherwise, but even by their Christian experience. To such headstrong Christians, Paul had this to say:

If I speak in the tongues of mortals and of angels, but do not have love, I am a noisy gong or a clanging cymbal. And if I have prophetic powers, and understand all mysteries and all knowledge, and if I have all faith, so as to remove mountains, but do not have love, I am nothing. If I give away all my possessions, and if I hand over my body so that I may boast, but do not have love, I gain nothing. Love is patient; love is kind; love is not envious or boastful or arrogant or rude. It does not insist on its own way; it is not irritable or resentful; it does not rejoice in wrongdoing, but rejoices in the truth. It bears all things, believes all things, hopes all things, endures all things. Love never ends ... And now faith, hope and love abide, these three; and the greatest of these is love (1 Corinthians 13.1–8a, 13).

It is important to give love the primacy Paul gives it; love is not just another quality or virtue to coexist with others. Like faith and humility in Paul's writings, love embraces everything and everyone. It has no limits. It is utterly foundational to Christian faith and living. So where did the inspiration for these verses come from? It is fanciful, though not entirely out of the question, to suppose that Paul witnessed the crucifixion. Even if he did not, Acts tells us that he saw the lynching of Stephen who, according to Luke, died praying for the forgiveness of those stoning him to death (Acts 7.60).

Our second passage strengthens the view that we are right to derive Paul's understanding of God from the cross and resurrection of Jesus. It is one of three great climaxes in his letter to the Romans. (The others are 11.33–36 and 15.7–13.) Paul began to expound his new understanding of God's saving 'righteousness' from 1.16 onwards and, finally, he reaches a triumphant conclusion:

> What then are we to say about these things? If God is for us, who is against us? He who did not withhold his own Son, but gave him up for all of us, will he not with him also give us everything else? Who will bring any charge against God's elect? It is God who justifies. Who is to condemn? It is Christ Jesus, who died, yes, who was raised, who is at the right hand of God who indeed intercedes for us. Who will separate us from the love or Christ? ... No, in all these things we are more than conquerors through him who loved us. For I am convinced that neither death, nor life, nor angels, nor rulers, nor things present, nor things to come, nor powers, nor height, nor depth, nor anything else in all creation, will be able to separate us from the love of God in Christ Jesus our Lord (Romans 8.31–35a, 37–39).

This was Paul's life-transforming *credo*. But we should not forget his repeated emphasis: believing in God is a lifelong task, something the believer practises every day of their lives.

Note

1 W. R. Maltby, quoted in R. Newton Flew's *The Idea of Perfection in Christian Theology*, Oxford University Press, Oxford, 1934, p. 341.

Questions for Group Discussion

This book has been written in the hope that it might prove useful to church study groups, so some questions are offered here as a basis for group discussion. One difficulty which most groups will face will be the amount of material in the book – unless they have many weeks available to work through it. From my experience of church groups, and the busy lives people lead today, that is unlikely! So I have tried to anticipate how a group might divide up the material, and provided questions accordingly.

1 Introduction and Chapter 1, sections i to iii

- Do the similarities between Jesus and Paul seem to you greater than the differences between them? Or is the opposite true? Was Paul Jesus' most faithful interpreter (Introduction, section iv)?
- Which aspects of Paul's teaching do the group find most difficult? Choose one or two of the difficult passages discussed in Chapter 1 (sections i to iii), asking 'If that is how Christians *then* tackled *their* problems, how should we tackle ours now?' (section ii).

2 Chapter 1, sections iv to vi

- Did the arguments of section iv change your understanding of Paul's conversion? Try imagining what happened to Paul, and what it meant to him, from his point of view, by looking together at Galatians 1.13–17 and Philippians 1.4–11.
- Has the traditional picture of a guilt-ridden Saul of Tarsus

(and similar pictures of people like Luther and Wesley) had too big an influence on our understanding of Christian conversion and evangelism?

3 Chapter 2, sections i to iii

- Read parts of Paul's discussion of meat offered to idols in 1 Corinthians 8—10, and try to imagine the dilemmas of being a Christian in Corinth, and of *where to draw the line* in daily encounters with paganism. Allow your imagining of their dilemmas to suggest some modern parallels.
- Do Paul's experiences recounted or reflected in 2 Corinthians help us in our Christian lives? Look at specific examples, such as his despair (2 Corinthians 1.8), his painful humiliation at Corinth (2.1–11), his thorn in the flesh (12.7–10), or the Corinthians' problems with an apostle whose life was cruciform.

4 Chapter 2, sections iv to vi

- Imagine the revolution and the shock waves created by Paul's policy of bringing Gentiles to faith in God without requiring them to keep the laws of Moses (section iv on Galatians). Does this first-century controversy have relevance for us today? (If the group wishes to concentrate on this, they might like to read Chapter 4, section ii, as a development of the Galatians' section.)
- Imagine the conflicts at Rome between Christians with diametrically opposite views about the issues mentioned in Romans 14—15 (section v on Romans). Explore the modern significance of Paul's arguments here. (If the group wishes to concentrate on this question, they might read Chapter 4, section iv, as a development of the section on Romans.)

5 Chapter 3, sections i and ii

- Which aspects of traditional Christian teaching about the cross and resurrection does the group find most difficult?

Does Paul's teaching, as outlined in section i, help, or does it make matters worse?
- Read together Galatians 2.15–21 (not forgetting the background as outlined in Chapter 2), thinking of the faith of Jesus before their own (section ii, and the footnotes of the New Revised Standard Version). Do the group find this new approach helps their own faith?

6 Chapter 3, sections iii and vi

- Read Romans 12 together, with the discussion of section iii in mind, and concentrating on the verses which seem most challenging and important to the group.
- Consider the argument of section vi: does the gospel according to Paul have to be shocking to religious people?
  (Section v of this chapter might be usefully discussed with Chapter 5, section ii or section v.)

7 Chapter 4, sections i, iii and v

- Try 're-thinking church' in the light of Paul's teaching, as summarized in these sections.
- Might Paul's teaching be a catalyst for the renewal of the Church today? Review the arguments of section v in the light of this question.
  (For sections ii and iv of this chapter, see the suggestions under Chapter 2 above.)

8 Chapter 5, sections i and ii

- *Does* Paul have a relevance today far wider than the Church? Consider this question in the light of Paul's teaching, as summarized here, about God's righteousness or 'the body'.
- Are the questions at the end of section i questions we should be asking ourselves in the light of Paul's teaching?
- With reference to the crisis of global warming, does Paul challenge us to a change of direction – that is, repentance? Discuss with reference to Romans 8.19–22, and the sugges-

tion here that the Bible holds together spiritual and economic matters, the human world and the world of nature.

9 Chapter 5, section iii

- Are we surprised, or not surprised, that Paul says so little about what we call the 'problem' of suffering? Is there a limit, as suggested here, to the extent to which we can 'justify the ways of God'?
- Does Paul's experience, and his teaching, help us with our experience, both of our own suffering, and our experience and sharing of others' suffering?

10 Chapter 5, section iv

- Read together Paul's sermon at Athens (Acts 17.22–31) and think through the contemporary implications of his 'strategy' here. How might we act upon this in our own situation?
- 'Long-standing members of the Church experience spiritual odysseys similar to Paul's. Where they end up is not where they began.' In the light of this statement, and the arguments of this section, share experiences, and where they seem to beckon. (For section v of this chapter, see the earlier suggestion under Chapter 3.)

11 Conclusion

- Is the God to whom Paul bears witness a 'boundary-crossing' God? Can members of the group add their own testimony to Paul's? Should we be more careful in speaking (or singing) of 'our God'?
  (In view of the content of this, the final section of the book, only one question is suggested, as the session might be a more reflective one, culminating in an act of worship.)

Suggestions for Further Reading

The following books are quite short, and accessible to the non-specialist reader:

Morna D. Hooker, *Paul: A Short Introduction*, One World, Oxford, 2003.
David G. Horrell, *An Introduction to the Study of Paul*, Continuum, London, 2000.
N. T. Wright, *Paul: Fresh Perspectives*, SPCK, London, 2005.

In addition, the commentaries in the series published by Epworth are scholarly, yet readable and relatively short.